New Methods in RE Teaching

Oliver & Boyd

Acknowledgements

The authors and publishers thank the school pupils who gave permission for their artwork to be reproduced in this book. See page 229 for a list of contributing teachers.

Designed by Cauldron Design Studio
Illustrations on pages 25, 197, by Sarah Lenton,
and on pages 8, 9, 16, 19
23, 128 and 129 by Chris Richards

ISBN 0 05 004303 X

Oliver & Boyd
Longman House
Burnt Mill
Harlow
Essex CM20 2JE

An Imprint of Longman Group UK Limited

First published 1990
Eighth impression 1995

Set in 10/12pt and 11/14pt Times Roman
Produced by Longman Singapore Publishers Pte Ltd
Printed in Singapore

The Publisher's policy is to use paper manufactured from sustainable forests.

Contents

Foreword

This handbook for teachers resulted from the work of THE RELIGIOUS EXPERIENCE RESEARCH PROJECT (since re–named the RELIGIOUS EXPERIENCE AND EDUCATION PROJECT). The Project itself arose out of the work of the Alister Hardy Research Centre at Manchester College, Oxford. By the early 1980s the survey work of the Centre had made it clear that very large numbers of people in this country interpret some of their life experience in 'transcendent' or 'religious' terms.

These experiences are by no means confined to people who are formally religious, but they are of great importance in the study of religion. The problem for teachers is how to introduce this dimension of religion to pupils in a way that makes sense to them and is also educationally responsible.

My background is not in the field of Religious Education, but during a period of sabbatical leave in 1982, I had the opportunity to study with Garth Read, John Rudge and Roger Howarth at the RE Centre at Westhill College in Birmingham, and also to visit a number of centres in the United States specialising in experiential learning in religion. As a result, I prepared a research proposal on experiential learning which was supported by the following colleagues, to whom I am very grateful: Professor John Bowker, Dr Brian Gates, Professor John Heywood–Thomas, Professor Edward Hulmes, Dr Jonathan May, Jack Priestley, Edward Robinson, Geoffrey Robson, Professor Ninian Smart, Alan Webster and Dr Glyn Yeoman.

The proposal was given very generous financial support by the Dulverton Trust, the Sir Halley Stewart Trust, the Hibbert Trust and the John Paul Trust. This meant that the Project was able to employ Alison Jones (now Leech) as Research Fellow. Alison spent two years cooperating in the development of teacher training programmes and pupil activity materials in her work with the Project.

I am grateful to numerous teachers from different parts of the country who have assisted the development of the Project and I wish to acknowledge in particular the work of the group of primary and secondary teachers who met over a period of two years in Nottingham University and devised or tested many of the materials appearing in this book. They include: Jenny Abram, Dai Bevan, Julia Bigger, Phil Doughty, Nancy Driver, Ruth Harris, Tom Limb, Alan McKenzie, Brian Netto, Vivien Peters, Kathy Raban, Sister Margaret Mary Ryan, Charles Reilly, Roger Stevens, Mike Wallace, Alan Webster and Jonathan Yarnell.

When Alison was appointed as an Adviser with Cleveland LEA, a consortium of writers was formed to prepare this book. Their names appear on the cover. I owe a great debt of gratitude to each of these colleagues in different ways, both for their contributions to the book and for what they taught me about religious education. As a group we are collectively responsible for the contents of the book and any errors should be attributed to us and not to anyone else mentioned in the list of acknowledgements.

Finally, all members of the consortium are deeply indebted to Ginny Straugheir, for two terms Research Fellow in Nottingham University and, since then, sub–editor of the materials the rest of us have produced, and to May Orton, who throughout the life of the Project has been and continues to be its efficient secretary. Without Ginny and May this book would never have seen the light of day.

David Hay

Director
Religious Experience and Education Project
School of Education
Nottingham University

PART ONE

Introducing the new method

Religion and spirituality

The main part of this book is a set of exercises which we believe will be useful to teachers who want to help their pupils or students to understand something of the ways in which people with spiritual or religious belief experience the world. It is a response to the numerous requests in recent years in journal articles, DES documents and in more and more LEA syllabuses for attention to be given to the spiritual dimension of religion. (A list of these references is given in the bibliography.) The issues we address in Parts 1 and 2 are important for all teachers because they pose basic questions about our image of ourselves as human beings, about how we relate with our pupils, and about appropriate learning models.

In a society such as ours, in which there are ambiguous feelings about religion, spirituality is a contentious area. We therefore feel it is necessary to state at the outset that this book is *not* trying to get teachers to generate 'religious experience' in the classroom; even if that were possible, we would not encourage it. One of our main objectives is to help pupils to become aware that their own way of seeing the world is only one among many possible perspectives; thus assisting the development of the skills of empathy. Rather as a novel cannot be appreciated unless the reader enters into the story, although not thereby becoming a part of it, so religion also needs to be entered into in order to be appreciated properly.

For several decades, Religious Education teachers have found themselves working in a deeply secularised Britain which contains substantial communities belonging to several religious faiths. Quite rightly, teachers began to want to move beyond an approach which, at least implicitly, assumed that their role was to induct pupils into the Christian faith. Ever since the publication of *Schools Council Working Paper 36* more and more teachers have looked to what is called the 'phenomenological' approach and this has been encouraged by the pioneering work of Ninian Smart and the team who produced *Journeys into Religion*.

'Phenomenology' has come to mean, in the minds of many, a concentration on external, public 'phenomena' as part of an 'objective' study of religion. But it is not what was meant by the authors of Working Paper 36.

Phenomenology attempts to make a direct and simple investigation of people's experience, but experience understood as always and inevitably *subjective*. Phenomenologists talk about setting aside (or to use technical jargon, 'bracketing out') their preconceptions about reality in favour of an unbiased investigation, so far as that is possible. They also tell us to take people's inner intentions seriously; that means we have to enter our own and others' personal worlds, in the course of our investigation of reality. Applying this to the study of religion, it means that without an appreciation of the *intentions* of religious people, the publicly visible phenomena of their faith are likely to seem remote or meaningless to the pupil.

In our view, any area of education requires the ability to appreciate what the world looks and feels like to other people whose experience of life is not the same as our own. This entering into the world of another person is inevitably difficult or even painful, particularly if that person also belongs to another culture. It involves admitting to ourselves that our own perspective is only one among many. In turn, that implies that we need to become more sensitively aware of our own subjective experience if we are to be free to appreciate that of others.

The same level of self-awareness is required of teachers in relation to their understanding of their pupils. As in the case of all practical work, it is important that we should be familiar with the general approach to learning presented in this book, before using the exercises in class. If you intend to use an exercise, but are not familiar with the area of experience it introduces, it is advisable to try it out for yourself first.

Primarily, this is a book you 'do'. The exercises are

not meant simply to be read and thought about. The thinking should arise from the doing. Nevertheless, it is important to explain why we feel that the perspective we advocate is central to the concerns of teachers, and certainly those with responsibility for religious education. In the course of the chapter we will illustrate points we wish to make with two practical exercises. They will also serve as examples of procedures which have proved successful with pupils in school.

> To understand how somebody else experiences the world, we have to take their inner experience seriously, and that involves an awareness that we have an inner experience of our own.

A perspective on religion

It is very easy to think of teaching as nothing more than a process in which someone who 'knows' instructs someone who does not know. But there is another, perhaps more profound, aspect to our task as teachers which was originally pointed out by Plato. He saw the teacher primarily as someone who helps pupils to recognise what they already potentially know. This process of 'freeing the mind' is not easy and includes removing taboos or rigidities that may prevent children from having conscious access to what they know.[1]

This ancient and challenging interpretation of the teacher's role is one with which we have a lot of sympathy. As teachers of Religious Education we need to be able to identify what our pupils already 'potentially know' about religion. We also need to help them to overcome any barriers which prevent them from bringing what they already know to light. The simple exercise below has been used successfully with older pupils in secondary school and with teachers on in-service courses, to help clarify what the words 'Religion' and 'Spirituality' mean to them. You might like to try it now.

Constructivist

Brainstorming on religion and spirituality

A brainstorm can be used to generate a variety of ideas on almost any subject very quickly. If possible this exercise should be done along with three or four other people.

1. Take a large sheet of paper and write the word RELIGION in the middle. Appoint someone to write down ideas. For the next five minutes, the members of the group call out as many associations with the world 'Religion' as they can think of. Everything must be recorded. There should be no discussion or censorship of ideas. All ideas should be respected!

2. Repeat the exercise on another sheet of paper, this time with the word SPIRITUALITY.

3. Examine the similarities and differences between the associations triggered by the two words, and on a third sheet of paper express in some way (perhaps a picture, or diagram) the relationship between religion and spirituality as your group sees it.

Pages 8 and 9 show the responses of one group to this exercise.

Brainstorm on religion

Brainstorm on spirituality

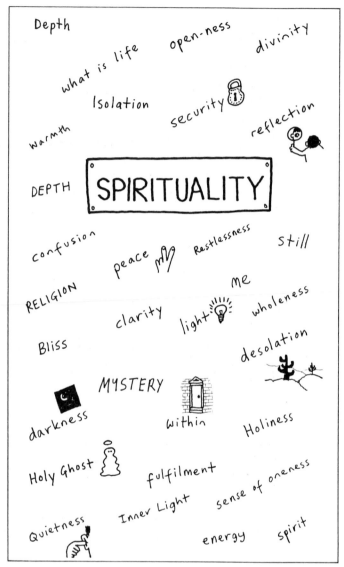

Relationship between religion and spirituality

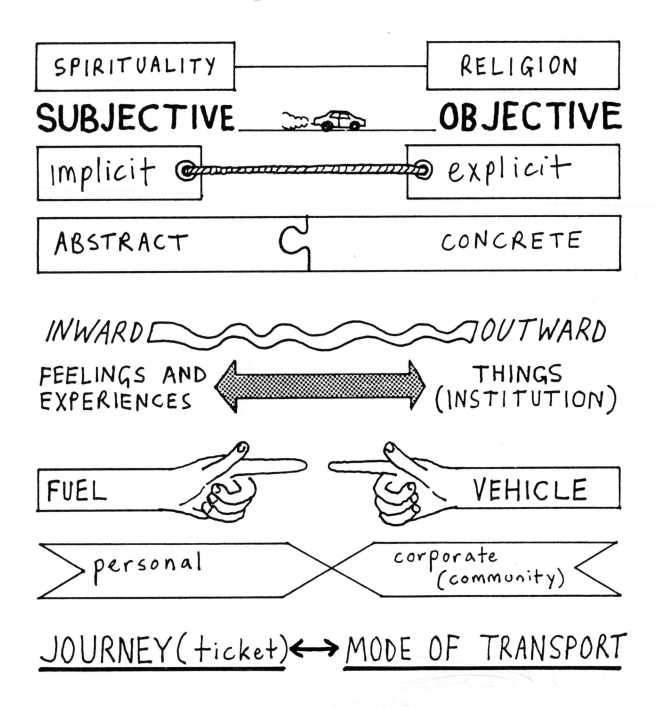

Some people see very little difference between the meanings of 'religion' and 'spirituality', but our experience of doing this exercise many times with different groups is that most people do see a difference. They tend to associate the word 'religion' with external things like buildings, religious officials and public rituals such as weddings or funerals. 'Spirituality' usually makes people think of more obviously personal matters like prayer, meditation and love. Often, it seems, religion is seen as cold and unattractive, caught up in the brutalities of history, whilst spirituality is perceived much more positively as something tender and warm. Yet everybody acknowledges that religion and spirituality are closely connected.

The subjective side of religion

The most obvious aspects of religion that students are potentially knowledgeable about are public phenomena — churches, temples, synagogues, festivals, gatherings for worship, doctrinal and credal statements, violent and bloodstained argument between people of different religious persuasion, debates about scriptural truth and almost every kind of symbol imaginable (crescents, crosses, stars, wheels, Yin and Yang *ad infinitum*).

But for the religiously committed, there is another dimension which is more important than these public phenomena. Believing members of religious communities are aware of a sacred realm of personal *experience* for which the public aspects of their faith provide the context and the interpretation. The historical religions, endlessly colourful, creative, tangled up with politics and every other dimension of life, are in all cases the public expression of an inner experience of the sacred.

And if the rituals and activities of religion, however vivid, politically significant or aesthetically moving are *not* an expression of, or response to, the human experience of the sacred, then they are not religious. At best, they are well-meaning make-believe, at worst, corrupt. The danger of hypocrisy, that is, concentrating on outer phenomenology to the point where it excludes the inner dimension, is something the great religious teachers are constantly pointing out. In the teaching of Jesus, people who do this are labelled 'whitewashed tombs that look handsome on the outside, but inside are full of dead men's bones and every kind of corruption.'[2]

It is the personal experience, the inner *intention*, that matters to the religious believer, and without some grasp of that intention, students will have no real understanding of religion. They will be rather like Victorian anthropologists, perhaps observing with real curiosity the habits, beliefs and artefacts of strange tribes, but separated by an experiential *apartheid* from genuine understanding. Publicly available phenomena are not enough.

For exactly the same reason, it is important to add that those approaches to religious education which regard it as moral education or personal and social education are equally inadequate. To avoid the intention is to avoid the heart of the matter.

It is very easy to take an interest in religions because of their colourful customs, the beauty of their architecture, ceremonies or art forms, because of their doctrinal and ethical beliefs, or even because of the political power they exert. But if we fail to grasp that all of these things have grown up as a response to the experience of a sacred dimension to reality, we can have no understanding of the religious believer.

References

1. The implications of this idea for contemporary understanding of Western religion are discussed in, Northrop Frye, *The Great Code: the Bible and Literature*, Routledge and Kegan Paul, 1982

2. St Matthew's Gospel, Ch. 23, v. 27

Chapter 2

Seeing through another's eyes

Teaching about the intention

Religious education must perform two tasks if it is to face the question of the religious believer's intention squarely. First, it must honestly present religion for what it claims to be — the response of human beings to what they experience as the sacred. Secondly, religious educators must help pupils to open their personal awareness to those aspects of ordinary human experience which religious people take particularly seriously. It is important to note at this stage that both tasks, whilst they point directly at the sources of religious motivation for the believer, still leave open questions of the ultimate truth of religion. They are therefore educational rather than indoctrinatory in intention.

To illustrate the centrality of the experience of the sacred, here are some examples of those kinds of experiences which people in contemporary Britain often interpret religiously.[1]

Permanent awareness

Very few people (approximately 2 per cent of the British adult population) claim to be permanently aware of a sacred dimension to their experience. Amongst members of the theistic religions, this is usually felt to be an awareness of the presence of God. Sometimes, as in Buddhist *vipassana*, meditative practice is directed to the development of a continuous awareness of true rather than illusory reality. (There is an exercise on *vipassana* on page 85.)

Spontaneous religious experience

A much larger number of Britons believe that from time to time during their lives they have experienced some sort of direct religious awareness.[2] Typically for a person living in a theistic culture, this falls into a category called 'numinous experience' by scholars.[3] Usually people report themselves to be surprised by an unexpected awareness of God or some other sacred presence such as an angel or a saint. Although the awareness is rather like a perception, they don't usually perceive anything through the normal sense organs. We now know that experiences of this type probably occur from time to time in the lives of around half the adult population of Britain and possibly more.[4]

These people are by no means always orthodox members of religious faiths; nearly half of them never attend a place of worship and quite often they are unwilling or unable to name the 'presence' because they do not wish to have it associated with any religious institution. Nevertheless, they tend to use traditional religious vocabulary when they describe their experience, because they live in communities whose language has been shaped by religious beliefs.

People who experience this awareness are usually better educated and in a better psychological state than people who say they have no such experience.[5] There is thus a striking paradox running through our society, since the popular stereotype of people reporting such experience is that they are most probably stupid or slightly mentally unbalanced.

There are certain circumstances in the lives of religious people where they particularly feel they are laying themselves open to religious awareness. These are associated with practices and beliefs about reality which do not correspond with the interests and metaphors of secular interpreters of the world. Here are some examples:

Ritual

Religions contain many rituals which enable the believer to relive important moments in the history of that religion, moments in which there is an especially powerful manifestation of the sacred.[6] Thus, amongst traditional Jews, not only is daily life suffused with a network of rituals concerned with maintaining an awareness of the divine presence, but also during the year there are special high points at which there is an entry into the sacred history of Israel. The best known of these, to non-Jews, is Passover. Within Christianity, the central ritual is the Mass or Communion Service, at which there is a re-creation of the scene at the Last Supper when Christ shared himself, giving his body and blood to his disciples in the form of bread and wine.

Contained in both Passover and the Mass lies a multitude of sub-rituals, which in some cases can include the smallest details of gesture and clothing. The total intended effect is first of all to remind each believer of the presence of God, and in many cases that is followed by a direct awareness of that presence.[7]

Reading sacred literature

From an early age, children brought up within a believing community come to experience the sacred books of their religion in a particular way. Believers interpret them as more than records from the past; the words also speak to them in the here-and-now. This is especially true in Islam, where the divine presence is in the words of the Koran themselves. For Sikhs, the sacred text *is* the living guru. In Judaism, the hearing of the reading of the Law in the synagogue is similarly to hear, literally, the word of God.

This is the basis for an almost universal method of scriptural meditation in which the reader takes a short passage and reflects at length on its content. At times it appears empty and the reader might as well be gazing at a newspaper. On other occasions the words grip the reader who sees them as speaking directly to him or her.

A dramatic example of the directness of such an experience in a Christian context was portrayed in the film *Chariots of Fire*. The Scottish athlete Eric Liddell, a member of the British team competing in the 1924 Olympics in France, has refused to run on a Sunday because of his religious convictions. Having thus let down the nation and his team mates, he is invited on that day to read from the Bible in the Scottish Church in Paris. Clearly torn, because his mind is constantly flitting away from the service to the international gathering, he finds himself reading the sentence, 'Before Him, all nations are as dust'. To Liddell, God has spoken, things are put into a larger perspective and his mental agony is removed.

Life as the language of God

Believers frequently come across the experience of reality, in a sense, 'speaking' to them. Sometimes this is through the noting of odd or extraordinary patternings of experience.[8] Or people may experience their dreams as religiously meaningful.

More frequently, however, it is the total, untidy experience of everyday life that believers interpret as God's dialogue with them. It is here, in religious groups that concern themselves with social change, that believers sometimes claim to experience God in the voice of conscience or discontent. In this case their experience is more to them than simply making an ethical decision or feeling a sense of outrage at injustice; it is felt as a direct encounter, a request from God.

Meditation, prayer, contemplation

For committed religious people, this is the heartland, the school in which they enter most deeply into the reality of their religion. Often devotion to God is central, as in Christianity or in the Bhakti tradition in Hinduism. Through such prayer, believers transcend a restricted notion of where God is to be found and for them, religious maturity comes with an increasing direct experience of the presence of God in all people and all places. Out of such experience of loving and being loved by God in prayer, may arise the motivation for people to enter into the social and political issues of the day, to struggle in desperate causes and if necessary sacrifice their lives.

In other Hindu traditions and in Buddhism, meditation is concerned with the dispelling of ignorance. Now that communities following the great Eastern religions have become part of the British scene, prayer and meditation tend to be seen in the wider society more as a means of 'waking up' or 'opening the spiritual eyes'. Contemporary developments in spirituality in Britain are extremely rich and varied, drawing not only upon cross-fertilisation between Europe and Asia, but also on a sophisticated use of the techniques of psycho-analysis, an understanding of humanistic psychology and a recovery of the arts of spiritual direction, or the following of a guide or guru.[9]

Learning to empathise

From our perspective, religious education which avoids the experience of the believer, from fear of the charge of indoctrination or because the teacher feels ill-equipped, is indeed a failure. To concentrate on externals such as discussions of doctrine, moral stances, pilgrimages, rituals and so on, is to ignore the most central issue in religion — its spirituality. Even debates about the 'truth' of religion can be irrelevant. For example, the problem of suffering, often seen as counting against the existence of God, is not seen that way by the believer. For the religious person it is more likely to generate an angry question directed at God, "Why do you permit such agony; don't you care about your creation?" It is important to note again that we are not saying here that devout people are necessarily correct, but to ignore their perspective is to fail to take them seriously as fellow human beings, grappling with the universal problems of existence. The difficulty is that in the highly secular world of late twentieth-century Britain, many pupils are for most of the time radically divorced from either the ways of perceiving or the areas of ordinary human experience that are of central interest to religious people.

> There is an extraordinarily rich variety of religious experience to be found within the religious traditions represented in this country. To have a real understanding of those traditions, we need to learn to empathise with that realm of human experience.

A widespread set of metaphors for reality dominates the way we interpret life. Secular metaphors suggest to us that we should see the world *as if* it were simply particles and space. Because matter is so basic, we are inclined to see consciousness *as if* it were a product of matter. Hence the contents of consciousness, including religious belief, can be seen *as if* they are 'produced' by material circumstances. Modern sceptical theories of religion usually have this as a basic assumption.

Acquiescence to these metaphors often tends to make us look 'outward' for explanation; to avoid or downgrade 'inner' experience. The world is seen as something to be used as an instrument to make a living, to protect one's self, to provide goods and entertainment. This may or may not be a reasonable choice, but if it is seen as the basic commonsense way

to deal with reality, it makes it very difficult to enter the world of the religious believer with any real empathy. The exercise below illustrates how adherence to a single perspective can block our awareness of alternatives.

An exercise on ways of seeing (with acknowledgements to Don Ihde[10])

When you look at the diagram below, what do you see?

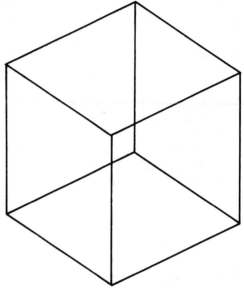

You probably saw a cube.

If you looked at it for any length of time you will have noted that something happens to it. It 'moves'. Take some time to watch in what way it moves. How fast does it move? Can you slow it down or speed it up? Can you stop it from moving?

Probably you found the last request quite difficult. So here's a 'story' to tell yourself that will help you to slow down the movement, or even stop it for a short time: Imagine that you are standing underneath the cube, looking up at it. When you do that, the bottom surface provides a focus for your attention, and the cube stabilises, at least for a short time.

If you tell yourself that you are standing above the cube looking down on it, you see it in a different way. Try to see both at the same time. Impossible, isn't it! By choosing to look at the cube in a particular way, you cut out other ways of looking at it. Telling a particular story about the cube is what helps us to stabilise it in one position.

This may seem a strange use of the word 'story', but as the exercise develops, you'll see that it isn't so strange.

If we wanted to be dogmatic, we could say that as a matter of physical fact the diagram is an arrangement of lines on a flat piece of paper. It is two-dimensional. It is obvious this is the case, but as a matter of experience the first thing nearly everybody sees is a three-dimensional diagram of a cube.

But now, here is a story that Don Ihde tells which will help you to see it differently. Imagine you are a member of a tribe of Indians living deep in the tropical rain-forest of the Amazonian jungle. You've never seen a cube in your life, because they don't exist in the forest. But the tribe honours a special insect as its totem and all members of the tribe wear an insect badge from the moment of birth. The badge is a stylised picture of a six legged insect, with its legs stretched out to touch the sides of the hexagonal-shaped badge.

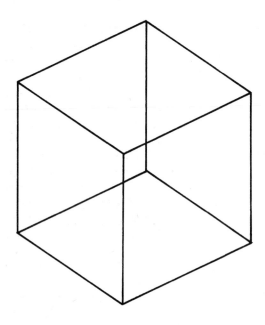

When you look at the diagram and see it 'as' an insect badge, you will probably find that it is quite easy to see it as flat.

You may say that the story does help you to see the diagram as flat, but after all it is still much easier to see it as a cube. But if you had not been brought up in a culture which surrounds you with cubical shapes from the day you were born, would that be so? If you told the imaginary Amazonian that the diagram could be seen as a cube, she might admit that you could see it that way, but for her it might be much more obviously an insect badge.

In the exercise we have just done, the diagram can be seen in a number of different ways. The way we tend to see it is heavily, but not entirely, determined by our life history and the stories we tell ourselves about it. It is not totally fixed, because we can be told, or make up for ourselves, other stories which change our perspective. What cultures seem to do is to select a story or a set of metaphors from which it is possible to interpret or cope with the world coherently. There is nothing wrong with this; it is not necessarily a matter of right and wrong; but as in the case of the cube we often concentrate on one perspective to the exclusion of other possibilities.

References

1. The examples presented are drawn somewhat more frequently from the Christian tradition than others because it is still the most familiar to the majority of British people. But it would run counter to our contention that religion is a universal human phenomenon, if that practical decision was taken as a denial of the rich variety of religious cultures coexisting in contemporary Britain.

2. Data drawn from national surveys conducted for the Alister Hardy Research Centre in Oxford by National Opinion Polls Ltd. in 1976 and Gallup Poll in 1985 and 1986.

3. Rudolf Otto, *The Idea of the Holy*, (Tr. John W. Harvey) Oxford University Press (2nd Edn.), 1950.

4. For a review of the data see, David Hay, *Exploring Inner Space* (2nd Edn.), Mowbrays, 1987.

5. *Ibid.*

6. Mircea Eliade, *Myths, Dreams and Mysteries*, Harper Brothers, 1960.

7. Religious awareness which is awakened through ritual is probably more common in faiths other than Protestant Christianity. The suspicion of ritual and the emphasis on the need for conversion within Protestantism seems to be associated with a much greater frequency of 'spontaneous' religious experience.

8. C.G. Jung, *Synchronicity*, (Tr. R.F.C. Hull), Bollingen Series, Princeton University Press, 1973.

9. For some examples, see the annotated bibliography at the end of this workbook.

10. Don Ihde, *Experimental Phenomenology*, Paragon Books, 1979.

Chapter 3

Widening horizons

The religious education teacher as deindoctrinator

The metaphor system of a dominant culture can be sufficiently powerful to act as unintentional indoctrination. The pictures of reality that we carry round in our heads are often taken to be absolute statements, indeed, 'true' doctrine. A consequence of this is that when someone's experience appears to contradict 'official' reality, a kind of cultural brainwashing tends to make them suppress and keep secret that experience, for fear they will be thought 'out of step', stupid, or even mad.

Research conducted over the past few years suggests that in the case of religious experience, fears of this type, though widespread, are unnecessary. The work of the Alister Hardy Research Centre has made us much more aware of the frequency of reports of religious experience in this country. (See Part 4 page 206 for further information.) As we mentioned earlier, it is probable that half or more of the adult population of this country believe that they have had such experience, though not by any means always associated with religious orthodoxy. People who are well educated and in a good state of psychological wellbeing are more likely than others to report it.

We know that experiences of this type tend to turn up during adolescence, corresponding approximately with the age of puberty. Statistically, it is very likely that a proportion of the members of every class from about the third year upwards in the secondary school will believe that they have had such experiences. In a survey of reports of religious experience amongst British and Irish teenagers, conducted by Edward Robinson and Michael Jackson, over 50 per cent of the six and a half thousand people questioned felt they had had a numinous experience or something like it.[1]

The figures for mystical or 'peak' experience were just below 80 per cent.

Secondly, we know from a study of large numbers of contemporary written accounts that quite a number of people recall religious experience occurring for the first time in childhood, sometimes at a very early age. On the basis of this, Edward Robinson, in his book *The Original Vision*, discusses the idea that young children may have an awareness of transcendence which is lost during the educational process, as they grow older.[2] The implication is that it is particularly important for teachers in primary schools to be aware of this area of experience.

The fact that pupils believe that they have had such experiences does not of course mean that religious interpretations are correct. But it does mean that at least some members of almost every school class have the potential to understand what is meant by the 'inside' of religious faith, as experienced by adherents.

Social pressure is something of importance for all members of a class, whether they believe they have had religious experiences or not. Social pressure makes it very difficult for someone deeply immersed in the dominant culture (we might call such a person a dogmatist) from taking seriously the perspectives of those from different communities of belief. As one member of our writing consortium put it, 'the *status quo* is noisy'. We do not easily take up alternative ways of seeing, especially in matters of personal importance. Another way of expressing this is to suggest that what is denied by a culture is often what unsettles it. We might add that this applies to all aspects of life, not just religion or irreligion.

Religious educators are sometimes accused of attempting to indoctrinate their pupils. But when religious education is correctly understood, it becomes clear that it is the reverse of indoctrination. What it does is to demonstrate that there is more than one perspective on reality. It enlarges, rather than diminishes, freedom.

Religious education therefore has a unique and important role which also presents special problems for the teacher:

1 It is difficult to help pupils from a secular environment to take seriously an interpretation of reality which differs from their own because:

i) different areas of human experience are taken to be important;

ii) a different array of metaphors is used to describe the world.

2 It is difficult to help pupils to have a genuine appreciation of faiths other than their own, in a multi–faith environment where differences of culture involve wide differences in the language and metaphors used to refer to the world of the sacred.

SOME RESEARCH FINDINGS

religion

experience

MORE LIKELY TO BE PRACTISING MEMBERS OF A RELIGION **BUT** 46% OF THOSE REPORTING EXPERIENCE _NEVER_ ATTEND A PLACE OF WORSHIP

MORE LIKELY THAN OTHERS TO BE CONCERNED WITH ISSUES OF SOCIAL JUSTICE

MORE LIKELY THAN OTHERS TO BE HIGH SCORERS IN MEASURES OF PSYCHOLOGICAL WELL-BEING

PEOPLE REPORTING RELIGIOUS EXPERIENCE ARE

LESS LIKELY THAN OTHERS TO BE STATUS-CONSCIOUS

SLIGHTLY MORE LIKELY THAN OTHERS TO BE FEMALE THAN MALE, THOUGH ONE AMERICAN SURVEY FOUND THE REVERSE

MORE LIKELY THAN OTHERS TO FIND MEANING IN THEIR LIVES

LESS LIKELY THAN OTHERS TO BE MATERIALISTIC

LESS LIKELY THAN OTHERS TO BE RACIALLY PREJUDICED

MORE LIKELY THAN OTHERS TO HAVE HAD A GOOD EDUCATION

For this reason, our proposals for the central tasks of the RE teacher are also twofold:

1 **To help pupils to learn to be aware of and to take seriously their own inner experience and their potential to be aware. Hence, learning to respect the inner experience of other people.** During the two years in which teachers were developing the materials for this project, it became clear how little most pupils are aware of their own inwardness or potential for awareness. They are fascinated and greatly surprised by being shown what it is to use a systematic method to relax, to be aware of their breathing, to become still, to be aware of the body, to observe the meanderings of the imagination and to attend to the here–and–now of their own experience.

Such areas are of crucial importance in the inner life of the religious person and are developed to very high levels of sophistication in many of the religions of the world. Until recently, these very ordinary, not specifically religious aspects of human experience, were unfamiliar in secular culture.[3] They therefore need to be formally introduced, if the pupil is to have any grasp at all of the ways in which religious people view life.

2 **The second thing which needs to be taken seriously is the role of metaphor in focusing and interpreting our experience of life** (as indicated by the exercise 'Life is like . . .' on page 126). Religious people do not simply enter ritual, or meditation, or the reading of sacred writings, without any intention. They do so carrying expectations within themselves which are denoted by use of words like, 'wait', 'listen', 'be mindful', 'place yourself in the presence of God', 'remain in the here-and-now' and so on.

So we need to help pupils to be aware of the power of language and intention to structure our experience, but not by entering into religious practice in a 'confessional' sense, because that would be contrary to the educational objectives we have already accepted.

There are also a number of 'directions in which religious people look' which can be examined more directly, because they impinge on everyone's life. We are thinking here about the experience of awe and wonder.[4] Do we on careful inspection find some sort of pattern or meaning emerging in life? What about the question of identity — "Who is this body which by an apparent accident of history has a name, a sex, a nationality?". What is it to consider oneself as situated in the vastness of the universe?

The relation between religious education and personal and social education

The implication of what we are saying is that if religious education is to do its job it cannot be conducted at arm's length. The subject matter of religious education, unlike much of traditional education, is deeply connected with the inner experience of the pupils themselves. None of us can expect to understand the subjectivity of another person without attempting first to become aware of and to understand our own inwardness.[5] That implies an entry into personal and social education.

Some teachers of religious education see the current interest in PSE as a threat to their subject, but from our point of view, it is an excellent opportunity. Though the model of the person in PSE often seems to be drawn implicitly from a secular perspective, it does respect the inward functions of the mind. From the religious believer's point of view, to take that aspect of personal experience seriously is to take an interest in familiar territory. But there are some qualifications we would like to make.

At the beginning of Chapter 1, we drew attention to the recent concern shown at governmental level about the fields of spiritual, moral and social education. In part this has stemmed from a widespread anxiety about the evident growth in the experience of meaninglessness and despair in society, with an associated increase in violence and the breakdown of a sense of community.

We believe that there are social and political reasons for this state of affairs. But there may also be an important spiritual dimension to be considered. The issue is a complex one and not at all easy to understand. Nevertheless, research evidence gathered in Britain and the United States over the past few years, appears to show that people reporting religious experience very often associate it with the discovery of meaning and a sense of moral responsibility in their lives.[6] If that proves to be the case, then it would seem that religious awareness does have important social implications.

It would in our view be an error of the greatest magnitude to attempt to use religious (or for that matter moral or social) education with the intention of exerting social or political control. It was just such an attempt which corrupted and discredited religion for large sections of the population in nineteenth–century Europe.[7]

It is important to say again that we are not advocating an attempt to 'give children religious experiences'. Even if that were possible, and we doubt if it is, such a procedure would come close to indoctrination. Nor are we advocating that teachers should require pupils to talk publicly about personal experience; in many cases such a procedure could become a kind of violence against a pupil. Nor are we trying to 'dilute' religious education by surreptitiously replacing it with social or moral education. The true intentions of the kind of religious education we are proposing are:

- To show that the implicit (and in our culture usually heavily secularised) 'model of the person' that we have in our heads radically affects the way we experience and relate to the world.

- To help pupils to increase their awareness and appreciation of the variety of religious responses of human beings to reality.

- To show that these alternative ways of being human are also personal possibilities for ourselves.

To succeed in such objectives is to cooperate with students in increasing their personal freedom and their understanding of others. In the next chapter we will explain in more practical detail how to use the learning model we are adopting to achieve these objectives.

> One of the major purposes of religious education is to enlarge the perspectives of pupils and to increase personal freedom by releasing them from 'single vision'.

References

1. Edward Robinson and Michael Jackson, *Religion and Values at Sixteen Plus*, AHRC/CEM, 1987.

2. See, Edward Robinson, *The Original Vision*, Seabury Press, New York, 1983.

3. The remark is of course too sweeping; see for example the highly sensitive writing of secular commentators like Marghanita Laski in *Ecstasy*, The Cresset Press, 1961.

4. A number of authors have written very helpfully on awe and wonder, e.g. Robin Minney and Maureen Potter, *Awe and Wonder in the Classroom*, Durham University School of Education, 1984.

5. See for example, Thomas R. Blakeslee, *The Right Brain: a new understanding of the unconscious mind and its creative powers*, Papermac, 1980.

6. David Hay, *Exploring Inner Space*, Mowbrays, 1987.

7. See for example, Jennifer Hart, 'Religion and Social Control in the Mid-Nineteenth Century', in A.P. Donajgrodski, *Social Control in Nineteenth Century Britain*, Croom Helm, 1977.

The learning model

A spirit of exploration

'It is not down in any map; true places never are.'

(Herman Melville, *Moby Dick*)

Let's begin with a story to discover and explore the model of learning. The following tale of the explorers opens up discussion about the aims and approaches in religious education.

Consider what the story says about:
- the nature of learning;
- the nature of religion;
- the nature of RE.

This is best done as a group exercise; your first reflections can then be shared and refined with others. The points listed after the story may help when you are working through the story on your own.

'The journey of a thousand miles starts with a single step.'

(Chinese proverb)

THE LIMITS OF MAPS

Some explorers found a beautiful undiscovered land. When they returned to their home, they told their friends about this country, describing the valleys, the hills, the rivers, the trees, animals and plants. They told them "You must go there for yourselves, our words can not do justice to that land." Their friends were excited and keen to hear about the land for themselves. They asked the explorers to draw them a map to guide their journey and to show them exactly where the land was. They refused, saying "No, you must set out and find the way for yourselves. There are many different routes and we only know one of them."

However, they insisted, and after a time the explorers relented and drew a map for them. Their friends were excited by the map and spent days planning for the journey, discussing which route they would take, and what the land would look like. But they delayed, deciding that they had first better prepare thoroughly for the trip.

Perhaps too, they needed to know more about maps, how to read them, and how to understand what picture the map showed. Years passed, the map was studied, then copied and passed on to others. Schools were set up in map reading. The explorers were sad and went away. No one visited the land.

What does it all mean for me?

While reflecting on the story we came up with the following points:

1 If a map is to be any use you have to recognise that it *is* a map. It is not just a picture or diagram but outlines a territory which is a more complete reality. You also need to know that the symbols on the map represent the features of that land. The map alone cannot reveal the true nature of the country. Real learning can only take place if the map helps you to find that land and experience it for yourself.

2 In the same way that the symbols on maps give a very limited account of the reality to which they refer, so the real power of religious symbols is evident only to those who glimpse a deeper reference.

3 Maps are important. Without them you may get lost, or else stay at home, not wholly aware that other places exist. In this respect, religious traditions are rather like maps, since they can alert us to the possible existence of a deeper reality and offer paths through difficult terrain.

4 Maps are public or communal in the sense that they convey a general, consensus, view rather than a personal impression. Spiritual traditions are public in that they are shared, but they are always perceived in an interior and personal way.

5 The explorers were *right* to draw the map in response to the demands of their friends. It was a way of helping them get to the land. By analogy, a religious tradition could be seen as a way of assisting or guiding people towards truth, enlightenment, fulfilment, understanding, God.

6 The explorers were also *mistaken* to make the map. Although it was requested, and made, with good intentions, the map became an insuperable obstacle when placed in their friends' hands. Now they will never go because they think that the reality of the map is sufficient. This happens in RE when the externals of the religious landscape are not penetrated and the spiritual realities to which they point are never discerned.

7 Like the explorers, the teacher of religious education is caught in a similar dilemma. RE requires both attention to maps (the religious traditions) and, somehow or other, access to the lands they describe. Without some understanding of the religious person's perspective and experience these traditions are only finely drawn pictures and not maps at all. RE is not about religion unless it engages the spiritual.

Types of explorer

The claim that only adherents can understand a faith, implies that RE should be nothing but nurture into the beliefs and practices of a particular religious tradition. Unlike the explorers' friends, confessionalist RE teachers would eagerly set out with their pupils for the land of experience, expecting to find corroboration for the accuracy of their own map. On their return they would be eager for pupils to use that map and criticise any version with differing contours.

The established alternative to confessional RE has been an objective and descriptive approach to a number of world religions; a 'Cook's Tour' which often, mistakenly, went under the banner of 'phenomenology'. In the context of this story, such an approach would be represented by the enthusiasts who eagerly collect the work of different map-makers. Their interest lies in cataloguing the technical details of the maps and noting their similarities and points of disagreement. They would never set out for the land or even entertain the possibility that it might exist.

Another group (who have limited interest and knowledge about religion) nevertheless think that it can be a useful way of instilling a certain mode of behaviour in the young. Wasting no time on details of cartography, this group would merely roll up the map tightly and use it to clip the ears of the wayward.

Setting aside this last group, let's consider further the strengths and weaknesses of the first two groups of would-be explorer-teachers.

The confessionalists

Their priority is essentially Christian nurture; seeing the school as an extension of church and family. Although in state schools this is seldom linked to a specific denomination, there are teachers whose general aim is to encourage children to adopt Christian beliefs and values.

Their strength lies in the ability to take belief and commitment seriously. Convinced of the power of the spiritual domain, they recognise that belief can affect life-style and decision-making.

Their weakness lies in their reluctance to represent seriously the experience of other faiths. There may be a tendency to ignore or denounce anything that is not sanctioned by their own beliefs. Consequently all reality may be reduced to their own perspective and the convictions of others dismissed.

The world religions school

By embracing world religions the content of RE was massively expanded and teachers could choose to describe the dimensions of religion in a detached way. This approach seemed to meet the needs of a society in which people are of many faiths and none.

Their strength is in their efforts not to distort what believers say and do. They attempt to prevent any misrepresentation by being constantly aware that each perspective is only one of many possibilities. By according respect to both the familiar and the foreign, they point out the richness and variety of religious expression and so widen religious horizons.

The weakness of their approach is that it neglects experience. While talking about experience they consider active involvement to be improper. Consequently they offer no methods or tools to gain access to the believer's experience. Unable to convey the fascination of a faith and what inspired the energy of its saints or the endurance of its martyrs, their approach can be clinical or sterile. The *affective* dimension is wholly ignored as the passion of belief is dispassionately presented.

Which way?

In religious education it seems that both these methods of exploration are essential and yet at the same time untenable. The confessional is anchored in, and offers access to, experience. It is therefore strong on the actual but limits alternatives. Conversely, the approach of the world religions school is strong on alternatives. It can offer a range of religious perspectives, as long as these are merely described. But it can give nothing of the actuality of the experience which lies at the heart of faith. RE ought to offer both the variety and openness of the descriptive approach and also some real sense of the spiritual experience which lies behind the wide spectrum of belief and practice. Recent documents which refer to the spiritual dimension of the curriculum imply that it is this sense of experience which is essential if the real nature of religion is to be grasped.

How do I get there?

In state schools, one problem has been that the spiritual is generally considered inappropriate for traditional didactic methods. Most people would say that the area of the spiritual is not understood, is too vague a concept and cannot be defined. Yet when asked to brainstorm on the words 'religion' and 'spirituality', everyone has a response and can express their understanding to the point of producing a consensus of opinion.

The great religious traditions have sophisticated ways for developing spiritual insight and growth in their followers. These methods are used within a context of devout adherence to certain conventions and systems of belief and are therefore thought to be unsuitable for use in the state education system. This creates difficulties when teaching about this area of human experience in schools where assumptions about a common belief system and culture cannot be made.

A further problem is that a teacher–controlled, 'one–way–system' of imparting knowledge does not promote understanding and appreciation of inner experience.

Words and symbols are inadequate and cannot reveal directly the reality which religions attempt to describe and lead their followers towards. All the major religious traditions are clear about the limitations of human reason and logical thought. They concentrate on the necessity of action, of doing and of being. The learning model presented in this book follows this view, stressing practical experience, the value of intuition as well as logical thought, and direct engagement with our own learning. This applies to teachers as well as pupils.

The itinerary

There is no list of contents here such as might be found in a book on world religions. Instead some areas of experience are presented which seem to be essential for an educated understanding of the spiritual dimension. The exercises outlined in this book provide a vehicle or route for increasing awareness of this world of the spiritual. Although teacher–initiated they acknowledge and build on the learning experiences of the pupils and encourage them to develop respect for their own inwardness as well as that of others. The metaphors for learning are based on exploration and not inculcation.

With this in mind, the areas of experience to· be explored in a religious education which is concerned with the spiritual would include:

Acclimatising so that learning can take place. This requires consideration of the quality of all the relationships within the classroom; those of pupil with pupil and of teacher with pupil, so that there can be freedom for the open and honest exchange of views.

Raising awareness aids the development of skills of inward focusing and of receptivity. It pays attention to feelings and to inner states of mind and emotion which are the prelude to effective listening and increased understanding.

Embodying awareness recognises that the nature of experience is subjective and therefore differs from person to person. Everyone's experience has its own validity dependent on their personal history, motivation and intention. Attention is drawn to the unrealised potential of self and others.

Framing awareness continues developing the skills of empathy through the recognition of different perspectives, being able to see the world through the eyes of others.

Extending awareness reflects on meaning. Stepping over the boundaries of rational language and thought, it looks at personal and collective images. It raises the ultimate questions of creation, collective myths of meaning, life and death, and the connection of the individual to the universe.

While this approach offers a vehicle in which pupils can approach the spiritual world it does not alter the underlying tension between two of the aims of religious education. These are: helping pupils to understand the perspective of the religious person without suggesting or implying that they should personally adopt a particular perspective, and helping pupils to develop their own individual responses to the spiritual dimension.

These are justifiable educational aims. It is not enough to carry on reading and studying the maps. The lands must be visited — the area of the spiritual cannot be understood without some degree of engagement.

> **Experience and intuition are higher than all human reason . . . We do not understand the world when we are pondering over its problems, but when we are doing the world's work.**
>
> (P. Vaihinger *The Philosophy of As If*)

The plan of action

Now let's get back to our starting point and see how this can be put into practice in the classroom.

Suppose the explorers have persuaded you to follow in their footsteps and you are starting to plan your own journey of exploration. What advice can they offer?

When travelling in new lands explorers, whether teachers or pupils, often have to rely on intuition. Concentrating on the here–and–now of experience, they also reflect on and learn from that experience. Ever cautious and always well prepared, they are no longer surprised that danger may loom when least expected nor that anxious moments can lead to exciting discoveries.

Exploring the spiritual dimension in school is largely uncharted territory for many teachers as well as their pupils. They may do well to follow the explorers' example by adopting a learning model which expects students to focus on their own experience as well as looking at the maps. Then thoughts, actions, senses and feelings are all brought into play and reflected upon as the whole person becomes involved in the journey of exploration and discovery. Help and support can be given and received through the sharing of those experiences with others, though sometimes thoughts and experiences may not be expressed and the pupil may choose to travel alone.

The approach to learning

Concerns and support

The approach to learning adopted in this book falls naturally within the realms of religious education and personal, social, and moral education. Although their intention may be somewhat different, these subject areas share common emphases on self, relationships and values which, of necessity, use distinctive methods of learning. The teacher of religious education has to consider particular core concerns. Those which benefit from this approach include:

- Raising and deepening personal awareness of the spiritual.
- Appreciating how symbols, images and metaphors are used to express or convey the meaning of difficult and otherwise inexpressible thoughts and feelings, especially the religious and spiritual.
- Sharing and recognising very different, and sometimes contrary, religious perspectives on reality.

Implicit within each of these three core concerns is the continuing need to create a sense of respect and value for our own experience as well as that of others, so that pupils can gain some personal understanding of the nature of religion and the way religious people see the world.

Raising and deepening awareness

Sharing and recognising different perceptions

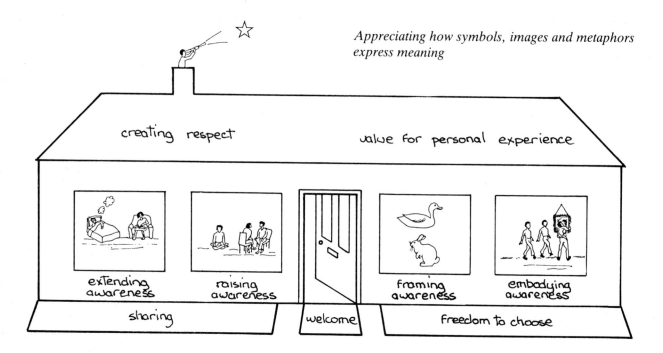

Appreciating how symbols, images and metaphors express meaning

These core concerns relate to the areas of experience described earlier and which form the basis for the activities — the 'what you do' — outlined in the next section. They also reflect the most appropriate principles of method — the 'how you do it'.

This may require a reappraisal of traditional teaching methods so that pupils can take responsibility for their own learning. There is always a tension in this kind of teaching between positive direction and guidance, on the one hand, and accepting open outcomes which the pupils determine and control on the other. This in turn affects the teacher's role and approach. You may find that the central teaching virtues needed most frequently are those of compassion and a real sense of care and concern for the pupils.

In teaching RE your responsibility lies in providing a variety of activities and experiences that reflect a 'whole person' approach to learning. Not just talking, writing or drawing but providing an integrated and balanced programme using active involvement, meditative reflection, physical exploration and sensual experience (meaning here 'of, or relating to, any of the senses'). Your leadership is based on knowing the territory for yourself, and planning the pupils' starting point. It is up to you to open up the opportunity for their exploration and be responsible for their safe return. This approach to teaching and learning requires deeper awareness on the part of the teacher as well as the pupils. You should therefore endeavour to remove all sources of threat from the learning situation — including your own anxieties. Your worries about getting it wrong or of unexpected outcomes can be a source of unease in any learning situation you lead.

Initially you may have to start in a very directive way, telling pupils what to do and giving support as they do it for themselves. As far as possible, begin with the experience of the pupils. Plan the lesson so that you provide them with space to choose. This creates a sense of freedom in their learning and shows that you respect and value their experience as well as your own. This is difficult to achieve all the time, but at the very least can be used as a basis for critical evaluation of what you do and what you plan. The methods and activities you decide to introduce should be chosen to promote the learning of the pupils rather than the learning you think the pupils need.

Your role is to support pupils in sharing their experiences and in making clear what they have learned. It does not include specifying what is explored, seen, felt or understood. Try not to tell them what they think or what they will learn; let them decide that for themselves.

You also need to recognise that exercising freedom to learn involves choosing how and when to learn and this includes the option to withdraw. Pupils who are reluctant to enter into particular learning experiences will need your support. You can give them a sense of freedom to choose but provide them with other opportunities by renewing the challenge later. If someone does choose to opt out, you can encourage them to join in again, when they wish, without creating too much attention or fuss. While showing that you believe opting out can be reasonable, you can also help the others to recognise that withdrawing from an activity or the group can be difficult to do. Don't forget that opting out may also have consequences for the whole group that they might need to consider.

By presenting learning possibilities in a variety of ways, you can reopen options for learning which may have been missed, avoided or refused because of inappropriate timing or structure. This approach contains built-in 'permission' for both teacher and pupils to fail. As with the explorer who reaches some kind of danger or dead-end, you too can retrace your steps, think again and try a new route.

However surprised you may be, you can still support the unpredicted learning or insight which pupils express in the group. By providing a supportive climate it is possible to minimise the risk entailed in sharing and self-revelation. You can help the group to take time to listen carefully and check their understanding of what each person says before they make any judgements. Obviously, there needs to be particular sensitivity towards any negative or destructive personal comments.

Conditions where everyone respects the learning experience are important if different perceptions are to be shared and acknowledged. People need as much space as possible to express themselves clearly, without feeling that they are being hurried. If you openly accept a wide variety of different perceptions yourself then others may be encouraged to offer their views. This will also help those who want to offer or deny different experiences to see that everyone can have a valid perception which should be respected.

While the learning may be planned to be open and explanatory it never means that just any kind of behaviour is acceptable. As leader, it is your job to establish accepted boundaries and limits in the particular lesson or scheme of work. The structures described in the following chapter indicate some of the boundaries and any departure from these needs to be controlled. This helps the rest of the group by giving them a greater sense of security. If the group is unsure about what is required you can give the lead by sharing your own examples and/or aspects of yourself.

In each learning session you should be prepared to be flexible, responding rapidly to cues and changes of mood within the group. This flexibility is held in tension with the prescribed limits of a planned scheme and form of learning you had determined, as you ask yourself whether it is time to move on. This means planning so that some time will be available, when required, to consider the concerns of individual pupils. Occasionally it might even be necessary to postpone the next part of the planned session to allow for this additional reflection and discussion.

You will also need to find ways of discovering the readiness of individuals and the group to move on. This may mean helping them recognise what they know already and can be one of the more exciting aspects of this work. The central activity of your role lies in your ability to help the learners articulate, at least to themselves, what has been learned. This can be done by suggesting language and images you know the group can use to express and communicate their own experience.

It is not always possible for people to express what has been learned. Nor do you always need to know about it. It is enough that pupils have a sense of achievement and have had the opportunity to decide whether or not to share their learning — sometimes it may be simply none of your business!

In all this you will need to recognise that it is frequently important to take the pace of work from the pupils themselves and to avoid being rushed along by pre-set content and specific timings. It can be a very slow process, but the quality rather than the quantity of the work seems to matter most in the end.

> Leaders are best
> when people barely know they exist,
> not so good when people obey and acclaim them,
> worst when they despise them.
> But of good leaders, who talk little,
> When their work is done, their aim fulfilled
> The people will say, "We did it ourselves".
>
> (Lao Tse)

Classroom management

It's your turn now

> We cannot discover
> new oceans
> unless we have courage
> to lose sight
> of the shore.
>
> (Andre Gide)

Chapter 4 used the tale of the explorers to draw out the model of learning which is most appropriate to 'experiential RE'. Like all stories it has a beginning, a middle and now it needs an ending. You know where you want to go, you've taken advice and you're almost ready to set off. Ever–cautious and perhaps a little nervous, you decide to have one last look to check that you are fully prepared.

It is important to make sure that you have packed your bag carefully — you, the teacher, must pay detailed attention to how you plan, lead and review each lesson. Remember that for this kind of learning to be effective (affective), the *how* of what is done is as important as the *why*.

Each lesson you lead is like a story, it too needs a beginning, a middle and an ending. Your first task is to decide why you are telling that particular story.

> "Young people who are often perceived as being objects of our teaching can actually teach us a great deal. They have layers of inner depth which we as teachers should maybe spend more time trying to empathise with."
>
> (Alan McKenzie, Becket Comprehensive)

First choose an exercise

Purpose (objectives)

You need to be clear about why you have chosen to use a particular structure. The choice, which might be your own judgement or achieved through negotiation with the group, will be made according to the needs of that group, the context in which you are teaching, the demands of a syllabus or scheme of work, the ethos of the school and so on.

The purpose can be translated into definite objectives. Ideally, this means that you have decided that by the end of the lesson you will have covered certain predetermined areas. When planning a lesson your first thoughts may centre around either: clear objectives which then lead to the choice of an appropriate structure, or an intuition that a particular structure is appropriate. Reflection should disclose the underlying objectives.

Once you have an idea of the *why* of the proposed lesson then you can determine the *how*. Again there are two options which reflect a general tension. You may choose between an open learning experience, involving exploration and discovery, with pupils learning what they want to learn, or detailed programming of sessions, involving clear goals which are easily evaluated, definite development and predictable outcomes.

A third consideration is how this session will fit the overall scheme of work you intend following with that group.

Conditions (preparation and planning)

The group — ask yourself how the pupils are likely to react to what you are planning. Are they ready for it? Are you ready for what they may make of it? Have you any plan for dealing with unexpected outcomes? How will you help the group recognise what they have learnt?

Group size — how predictable are the numbers of pupils in the group and how will this affect what goes on in the activity? What strategies can you use to group or pair everybody in the class when required without causing unnecessary disruption?

Time — how much do you need and how much is available? It is important to be realistic and, where possible, flexible about the amount of time given to each structure. You can't squash them into brief parts of a lesson. The length of time it takes to complete an exercise can vary considerably from group to group. It is often important to take the pace from the pupils to allow them time to develop points of interest and concern or to move on to the next stage sooner than you had expected.

Changing the classroom layout may help

Space — how much space is available and how can it best be used? Altering the arrangement of furniture can change the climate of the classroom, and help you to use the area in the way you wish.

Materials — is everything you require to hand and organised so that the distribution of materials does not interfere with the activity?

Planning the lesson

THE BEGINNING
(Introduction to the lesson/activity)

At this stage your aim is to create the right atmosphere which will prepare the group for the experience you have planned. When setting the scene you need to be aware of whether you want the group to be sedentary or active, in small groups, pairs or on their own. Will the session require an energetic response, or a receptive and reflective mood which needs encouragement and support?

As leader, your own manner of direction and response indicated by the tone of your voice, actions and demeanour are important. Your instructions must be clear, direct and audible and your tone supportive. Everyone should feel comfortable and at ease, so don't spring surprises. You can reduce any worries by explaining to the class that you want them to try something new, ask for their cooperation and invite them to share the responsibility for what happens:
"I'm not sure how this will work out, but let's try it and see — O.K.?"
Or:
"I'd really like your help on this today. It's something I haven't done before. Let's give it a go and we can all have our say about it afterwards — all right?"
It is important for pupils to know that there are no right or wrong answers. Accept that some pupils may have problems or find an activity difficult. You can provide for this by telling them you don't expect everyone to find it easy to do what you suggest. Anyone who feels really uncomfortable can sit quietly or perhaps leave the room if that is appropriate. Afterwards you can have a quiet word and sympathise with anyone who found it hard.

A short introductory activity may be needed to set the right climate. It also gives you the opportunity to judge the mood of the pupils and you can then decide whether your lesson plan is likely to succeed. In case you suspect it will not work, you should have an alternative plan, or some way of making the necessary changes.

Don't be disappointed if things don't go exactly to

plan. When trying out something for the first time the class may be anxious and unsure. Changing the established routine and pattern of a lesson may unsettle the class but you can alleviate some of their worries by being yourself and introducing changes gradually. Pupils are bound to be uneasy if the teacher's behaviour and approach are suddenly and radically altered. Insecurity and anxiety may be shown by fits of giggling, loud comments or questioning, "Why aren't we doing proper work?"

There are several things you can do if pupils disrupt or refuse to cooperate with what you are trying to do.

You may decide to carry on regardless, hoping that the disturbance will die down. Showing that you have confidence in your material may reassure those who are nervous.

You may choose to stop the activity and then talk over the problems with the class. You can ask, "What's the problem? What can we do to help?" Allowing people to voice their worries can encourage them to try again, now that they know you are taking them seriously.

You may choose to abandon the exercise as inappropriate for this particular group at this particular time. You could then try something different.

You may decide that the material is unsuitable and plan other activities which will help the pupils build up their confidence.

Be prepared to make mistakes (and to learn from them) but also be prepared for success. It's easy to think of reasons why it won't work but most teachers find that their classes respond very positively.

THE MIDDLE
(The main learning experience)

You have chosen the structure to lead the pupils into an experience; but that experience is *theirs*. This has implications for how you lead and means being ready to accept and be sensitive to the unexpected reactions of individuals or the group. You must also be aware of how the pupils respond to the unexpected. However surprised you may be, support the unpredicted learning or insight expressed in the group.

You can show your respect for the pupils' experience by using their words or images and getting them to clarify what they mean rather than interpreting for them. Taking your cue from their comments and reactions you can develop the session in their terms:

"How can you describe that feeling?"

"Could you state that another way?"

"Can you draw a shape or use colours to say what it is?"

Don't impose your own constructions on their reality. Never tell anyone what their experience was like. Instead of saying things like, "I noticed you were all working well together", or, "I see you don't feel very happy about that", use open, non-directive questions such as: "What happened then?" and "How do you feel about that?"

Consider the provision you can make for individuals to think about and digest their individual experience in their own way. You can build in pauses for private reflection and review or you can respond to cues from within the group and ask: "Shall we stop here and spend some time thinking about that?"

THE ENDING
(Drawing out the learning)

This is a vital part of the lesson and must not be left out (it often is!). Time must be allocated to draw out the learning. A good rule of thumb is to give about the same time for processing the learning experience as for the experience itself. 'Processing' does not mean simply 'reporting back' or describing what happened. The time is used for pupils to *reflect* in a variety of different ways on what they have felt, discovered, thought about or concluded.

You will have to decide whether the processing is best done alone and privately, with a partner, in friendship groups, with the whole group, or a combination of these. One question to bear in mind is: Do I need to know what has happened or what has been learned? The answer may quite often be NO.

Those who learn something unexpected will need extra support and encouragement; others find they simply cannot use words to express what has happened. These pupils may need much more time than you had intended making available in that session. Learning does not always have to be expressed in speech. A wide use of different media such as drawing, modelling, body sculpture, role–play, poetry, dance, movement and recorded observation, as well as writing, can all help to absorb an experience and promote reflection on something which would otherwise be difficult or impossible to describe.

A variety of questions can be used to help pupils reflect on their experience. Initially it is possible to open up discussion by asking a simple question such as, "Did you all enjoy that?". A consensus "Yes" or "No", or divided opinion, helps to reveal the mood and reaction of the group and may encourage pupils to respond to more searching questions later. Asking questions which invite a "Yes" or "No" response will help you to gauge the direction to take when developing the discussion.

When drawing out the learning experiences of individuals and the group, you will need to use more open–ended questions, for example, "How do you feel about that?", "What happened that interested you?'' or "What have you discovered?''. These 'What' and 'How' questions are usually much easier to answer than the question 'Why?'. It is often difficult to recognise and express the motives underlying an action or response. Even when we are aware of our motives they may be too private to reveal.

It is important to use the words of the group when responding to and promoting their reflection on what has occurred. This will help them to clarify for themselves rather than accepting your, probably inaccurate, interpretation. It is their experience they are being asked to consider, not yours.

Reflecting on an experience can be done in three stages.

Stage I Reflection on the event itself.
"What happened?"
"How did you find that?"
"How did or do you feel about it?"
"At what point did you feel most comfortable or uncomfortable?"
"What did you notice others doing?"

Stage II Recognition of what has been learned.
"What do you remember most in this?"
"What was important for you?"
"What have you learned about yourself? About others?"
"Can you give your reasons for . . .?"
"Can this be interpreted in another way?"

Stage III Application of the learning (if appropriate at that time).
"How does this affect you?"
"What will you do differently now?"
"What has changed for you?"
"What have you discovered?"

The third stage may be more appropriate for a review of several sessions or a specific topic or scheme of work rather than after one particular session.

Closure

You will already use a variety of little rituals to signify the ending of a lesson. These will be in the form of both words and actions. "Begin to put your things away" or "start to tidy up" or "finish what you are doing" are all signs of the beginning of the end. You can allow time for this, and for questions, or a summary at the end of a lesson. The ending may also be the time to discuss the theme of the next lesson, and to prepare the class for any follow up work.

Often the reflection and processing time will round off a lesson very well although sometimes it will be helpful to find another way of ending or closing a session with a final exercise. Closure is especially important when the class has shared an experience which might leave them 'high' or 'low'. 'Grounding' or 'coming back to earth' are evocative metaphors which describe what may be needed.

Next time around

VARIATIONS

Using the open–ended learning experience does not mean you can expect the structures to work by themselves. To get the best out of the exercises you will have to adapt and repeat them to suit your specific needs. Re-presenting an activity at a different stage of the group's development, can create a new, but familiar, learning opportunity.

EVALUATION (the post–mortem)

You will want to assess the effectiveness of the lesson in the terms of the objectives with which you started. The pupils may use other criteria to judge the effects and effectiveness of the lesson and these may not always be the same. Third year pupils of The Becket School, a Catholic comprehensive in Nottingham, offered the following advice to teachers:

'Understand what you are doing before telling the pupils what to do.'

'Let the children find out about themselves before finding out about God.'

'Explore inner feelings and ideas, which are felt but never truly thought about. Ask others about their feelings too.'

'Don't underestimate the truth and faith the children will present to you.'

'Be open. You can't expect other people to be truthful if you aren't yourself.'

and they commented:

"My ideas of religious experience have changed because before I thought religious experience was when God appeared to the chosen few but now I see it's an everyday occurance. It's not for the chosen few but for everyone."

"I liked the way we were allowed to use symbols instead of putting down exactly what was special to us. We are the only ones who really know what they mean."

"I learned I could tell a teacher things I would never dream of telling even my best friends."

"You can only learn by your own mistakes and also, you can only learn by experience, even though I have only experienced fourteen years of life."

The evaluation of lessons by you and your pupils can form the basis of future planning and action. Two uses of evaluation which are of particular concern are:

1. A review of how the learning objectives have been met or whether they are still relevant, and
2. A review of the choice and organisation of the learning experience.

▶ 1 The learning objectives can be assessed either in drawing out the learning or develop out of it. If the pupils take part in this type of evaluation it can be important as another aspect of learning in itself. It may be appropriate at the end of a particular session or after several sessions on the same topic. Typical questions you might ask are:

Did you reach the objectives of the session?
Has the session been any value or use, if so, what?
What has been learned and how do you know?
What has been discovered that will help to plan where to go next?
Has it been worthwhile?

▶ 2 The second use of evaluation reviews the choice and organisation of the learning experience. It focuses on the leadership of the group and the method or way of learning. It can assess how well you and the group are using the learning experiences and activities which are presented. Raising awareness of how we learn and what is needed to help this process is a way of promoting reflection on the nature of learning itself. Here some responsibility for the way the pupils learn is shared with the leader. Typical questions you might ask are:

How well did it go?
How was the timing?
What difficulties did you have?
How can we avoid problems in the future?

Evaluation of this kind is best used either after the first few sessions or at the end of a complete scheme of work or a topic. It will tell you how your approach to this kind of teaching is being received and you can discover what improvements you will need to make next time.

This is what some teachers have said:

"Teachers must be able to cross the traditional barrier between 'teacher' and 'pupil'. They must be able to reach out to their students, to become part of the group."

(Maureen Harrison, Teesdale Comprehensive, Co Durham)

"I'm on an equal footing with the children, as opposed to being a dictator at the front. I use the blackboard for information but I don't stand there and dictate hour after hour. There is hardly a lesson where I'm not an equal with them, talking with them rather than at them."

(Jonathon Yarnell, Quarrydale Comprehensive, Nottingham)

"My discipline has become lighter with the group as the year has progressed. I trust them more and they also seem to trust me. I do not need to be heavy-handed and strict as they don't 'try it on' with me. Absentees always check up on an exercise they have missed and I have often been asked, "Do it again please, Miss". This is not normal behaviour. They value doing the exercises and regret missing them."

(Ruth Harris, Harry Carlton Comprehensive, Nottingham)

"Take a risk, if you have a chaotic lesson take it very calmly and remember it's not the children's fault — it's just the natural learning together. Most families have chaos and disasters from time to time and I think an occasional disastrous lesson is very good — for me anyway. It stops me becoming complacent."

(Charles Reilly, Christ the King Comprehensive, Nottingham)

PART TWO

Classroom activities

Guide to the structure of the activities

The description of each exercise appears within a regular structure or format. The following guide offers brief comments on the layout used for all the structures.

As you would expect, the title of each exercise attempts to suggest something of its flavour, so in this case it is:

Layout tryout

Purpose

Each structure begins with an explanation of its intention which provides a rationale for the exercise and relates it to a specific area of experience.

Time needed: any estimate of time is just that. Many teachers find that they often underestimate the time required so some guidance is given. However, experience shows that a structure used with one group may only last for ten minutes while a different group may need more than sixty minutes to explore the potential of the same exercise.

Materials needed: some structures do not need any additional materials. However, it is generally a good idea to have plenty of large sheets of plain paper, writing paper, crayons and pencils available. The opportunity for drawing and writing may arise unexpectedly. (See 'Comments' below.)

Conditions

There are some things you need to know or to do before using the structure. These prerequisites may range from the physical conditions, like the lighting in the room, to the emotional climate and the mood of the group.

You may need to be aware of particular problems such as potential embarrassment or awkwardness. Certain questions may be noted, for example, 'Do you feel comfortable with what you plan to do?' 'Are the pupils ready for this experience?'.

Procedure

This section tells you how to carry out the structure. On the right–hand side of the page are the step–by–step instructions for the class. Practical advice to the teacher is given in the left–hand column. This is rather like stage directions which are set aside from the main action but are essential to it.

In this column, and in line with the transcript opposite, you will find notes to assist the smooth running of the activity. You may want to add your own notes and comments here too.

1. The principal instructions are set out **in bold type** within a sample script.

2. This suggests how the teacher could **present the exercise** to the class.

3. The instructions are simply a guide. You will have to **modify the script** to suit your own style and situation.

Drawing out the learning

Each structure includes a section which is designed to guide you, the teacher, in drawing out the learning. This is a very important part of any lesson. It is the time for reflection and for discussion when pupils can think about what they have learned and, when appropriate, listen to what others have discovered. The aim is to review the experience in a manner which is helpful for the pupils and this will vary according to the age and skill of the group. Drawing out the learning can involve talking in pairs or in small groups, as well as responding to direct questions from the teacher. Writing a poem, sitting in silence, drawing a picture or symbol, going for a walk, are all ways which can help pupils to reflect.

Closure

Sometimes it may be important to find a way to end or close an experience, therefore some structures include suggestions for rounding off the activity.

Variations

Many structures have been used in a variety of ways, and are open to further adaptation. In this section one or two variations on the theme are described. Specific examples of pupils' work and teachers' comments are given to show how that exercise has been used in religious education lessons. Examples may be from work with several age groups.

Comments

This section appears when and where necessary to provide any supplementary information. In this instance extra points are made about the information given in each structure to help you select and prepare for that activity.

Materials needed: Where materials are required they are often simple. Paper should be of differing sizes and in plentiful supply. Cheap, white lining paper can be bought in quantity with better quality paper available when required. The opportunity to make large drawings can be exciting. For example when a shy child drew a plant on a small sheet of paper the teacher asked him to draw it again on a bigger sheet, and then again on an even bigger sheet. As the drawing increased in size the colouring became bolder and stronger, and the boy's pride and joy in his accomplishment was more apparent.

Although many children will have their own crayons these are often felt tip pens or coloured pencils which either make too much colour or not enough. It is worthwhile, even for secondary schools, to provide plenty of good quality wax or chalk crayons.

Group size: is not specified since most of the structures can be used with any number of participants. You can exercise your own judgement in deciding how large a group you want to work with. Sometimes the size of the group will alter the dynamics and the nature of the experience.

Age range: of groups is not suggested either. Age categories tend to be restrictive, for example a book designed and advertised for eight to eleven-year-olds will be scorned by the fourteen-year-old. Yet concepts and themes normally introduced to sixth form students can fascinate six-year-olds, and sixth formers can gain fresh insights from activities previously regarded as childish games.

By modifying the language, pace and approach as necessary, many of the structures can be adapted to suit people of any age. Try a structure which interests you and don't be surprised if it works as well with seventeen-year-olds as it does with seven-year-olds.

Chapter 7

Getting started

INTRODUCTION

These introductory activities do not fall within the bounds of explicit RE (in the sense of studying the beliefs and practices of the world's religions), but they are an important preliminary to processes encountered later in experiential religious education. Part one gives a detailed rationale for the approach to learning which is adopted here and throughout this book. The teacher or group leader should be familiar with those chapters before going on to try out the exercises.

When preparing for any journey into unfamiliar territory, the explorers must equip themselves for the new conditions they will encounter. It is in the process of actually moving into different areas and learning to adapt to new conditions that they train themselves to become effective explorers. This process of acclimatisation is both a preparation and a beginning of the journey itself. During the exploration they will have to pause now and again, to take stock of how they are managing in their new and changing circumstances. They may need to adopt different ways of working as the climate and terrain make additional demands on them. (Changing Perspectives of a Classroom, page 207, shows how altering the geography of the classroom can induce a new and beneficial environment.)

Experiential RE asks pupils to explore inner aspects of themselves and they need the right kind of climate in which they can share personal views. They will need to recognise their own strengths and weaknesses and to value the distinctive contribution offered by each member of the group. They may have to rely on the experience and help of others to bridge gaps in their knowledge and understanding, building confidence so that individuals and the group can move into new and uncharted territory.

New ways of learning can seem like a waste of time, making pupils anxious or confused. To prevent this happening, some groundwork needs to be done which helps the pupils to accept what is going on. They can then involve themselves in activities which could otherwise be considered strange and puzzling. The introductory exercises indicate that particular forms of reaction or response are appropriate and that traditional methods of teaching are not being used. The structures can be a source of motivation and fun, making learning more enjoyable. Pupils begin to experience the process of learning through their own personal awareness and participation, gradually building a climate of cooperation within the group.

At times individuals or the group may need additional support if they find things a little demanding or when new experiences begin to challenge their assumptions. Then, and on other occasions, it will be necessary to do something to help the group to change its mood; to become more reflective or to take more initiative in what they are doing. The introduction of a light–hearted activity or a stilling exercise is helpful in **changing the climate** of learning.

Some pupils will have met similar procedures elsewhere; by taking them through a few of these activities you will discover how familiar they are with this kind of learning.

Acclimatisation should be considered in both long and short term planning of classroom activities. In the long term, the task of preparing a group to work together throughout the school year (or for a term or a series of sessions based around particular aims or themes) may justify a number of early sessions being directed towards acclimatising activities. (See page 49 for an outline of an induction course which uses these and other similar exercises.) A single lesson may also need a short introductory exercise to establish a setting for learning.

> **Religion and spirituality do not spring up as answers to abstract questions — they are our responses to what we experience.**
>
> (Carol Ochs, *Women and Spirituality*)

Beginnings

Much of the work in introductory sessions is about doing simple things in a slightly different way. Expectations are gently challenged and new possibilities opened up, preparing pupils for the work ahead.

Building effective working relationships within the group is a priority when beginning experiential learning. Initially this means getting to know everyone else in the group, exchanging names with people who are strangers and chatting informally with acquaintances. The following structures provide a lively method of meeting people, learning each other's names and then reflecting on the experience of being with others. By taking part in these exercises pupils begin to be aware of the ground rules that are needed when learning through direct experience. Working with others in a cooperative enterprise can lead to the recognition that other people are an important source of learning. These structures are examples of many kinds of ice–breaking activities which help pupils focus attention on other people in a more deliberate way. (The bibliography lists a number of books which outline other activities.)

> **Religion is insight into the common experiences of mankind.**
>
> (John S. Dunne)

Do you know what intelligence is?
It is the capacity, surely, to think freely, without fear, without a formula, so that you begin to discover for yourself what is real, what is true; but if you are frightened you will never be intelligent.

(Krishnamurti)

Saying hello

Purpose

This activity encourages contact with a large number of people within the group. It can help to reduce initial nervousness and take a step towards developing a sense of group identity.

Time needed: Thirty minutes

Materials needed: none

Conditions

Pupils who have not worked in this way before may find the activity somewhat strange and need added reassurance. The exercise requires sufficient space for everyone to walk around, therefore it may be necessary to move furniture out of the way. This could be done by the pupils or before they come into the room.

Procedure

When giving instructions you may need to modify your tone of voice. A quiet tone will promote a more reflective approach. Talk slowly and quietly and, if necessary, repeat yourself. The exercise needs an energetic and directed introduction to motivate and involve pupils from the start. Questions can be introduced during each stage of the activity to encourage reflection in preparation for drawing out the learning.

1. Imagine you are in a busy railway station. You don't know anybody and no one knows you, so you deliberately **avoid looking at other people**.
In a moment I'll ask you to **walk around the room** as if it's that railway station. You're in a rush to catch the train and you want

Pause for a minute or two.

to get through the crowds as quickly as possible. Keep well away from everyone else and make sure you don't bump into anyone. Does everybody understand? Start walking around the room, ignoring everyone else.

Pause briefly.

2. Stop. Now **think about what that experience felt like for you**. How did it feel to keep moving away from others as they approached you?
Keeping those questions in your mind **start moving around again, still avoiding any contact with other people.**

You may prefer to spend a few minutes following up their comments before continuing.

3. Stop where you are and stand still. **Think about that experience** for a second or two. You can **walk around the room again** in a moment but **this time make sure you look at other people as you pass them**. Try to catch their eyes. Don't stare at them, just use your eyes to acknowledge that they are there. **Notice your thoughts and feelings** while you do this. Ready? Off you go.

Allow a minute or two.

4. Stand still again and **think about that experience**. Remember what it was like when you moved around, ignoring everyone. How did that compare with what you've just been doing?

A short exchange of ideas is useful at this point.

5. We'll take that a stage further now. This time **as you pass someone, do something positive to acknowledge their presence.** For example, you could say hello, or smile, or nod, or even shake hands. You decide how you want to do it. Move around the room trying to make contact with as many people as possible.

Timing can be varied to suit the size of group.

6. Stop for a second. Now it's time to introduce yourself. **As you reach somebody, stop and tell them your name and a short sentence about yourself.** You could say something like, "Hello, my name is . . . and I . . ."

Give them long enough to meet at least half a dozen people.

7. Stop what you are doing and **stay with the last person you met**. Find somewhere to sit together so that you can talk to your partner without being disturbed.
Spend a few minutes talking about your feelings and thoughts during that exercise.

Allow five or ten minutes.

Drawing out the learning

After considering the experience with a partner, each pair could join another couple to compare ideas before the whole group talks about their reactions.

How did it feel when you ignored everyone?

What was it like to be ignored?

In what ways was it different when you made eye contact . . . and when you contacted them in your own way . . . and when you spoke to them?

Which was easiest for you?

What was the most difficult part about it for you?

What made it easy or difficult?

How far do you think your experience was the same as your partner's . . . or perhaps different?

Variations

First impressions: Moving around the room in silence, pupils look at each person in turn and consider in what ways they are alike. It could be something similar they are wearing, their height, age, or any other criteria they might choose. After considering a number of people in this way, they should select a partner they feel to be most like themselves. Sitting down together they can explain what led to that choice.

After exchanging ideas, they can walk around the room again, this time looking for someone least like themselves.

An alternative to this variation is to stop at each person in turn, look at them for ten seconds and then say something about that person. For example, "I see you are wearing a red tie". Do this for two or three minutes and then ask them to add a statement based on their impressions of that person. For example, "I see that you are smiling and I imagine you are enjoying what we are doing . . ." (The group needs to be sensitive about the possibility that a thoughtless comment can hurt someone's feelings.) The partner should acknowledge each comment by saying, "thank you". They can briefly check out the accuracy of their impressions as well as how they felt during the activity.

Asking questions: Groups which know each other well can still benefit from taking part in these, and similar, milling activities. This variation is also useful to change the mood of the group.

Give everyone a few minutes to think about a question they would like others in the group to answer. It can be about anything at all, from what they had for breakfast to something they are burning to know more about. After writing down the question on a card, they walk around asking as many people as possible to answer their question. Warn pupils to avoid questions which begin with the word "why". These questions ask for reasons and motives which can be very hard to answer. Anyone can "pass" on answering a question if they wish and every answer should be jotted down. After five minutes or so the group can reconvene to consider the questions they have asked and the answers received. How wide was the variety of responses? Were they the answers they expected? What surprised them? Did they ask the right question, or would they change their question if the exercise was repeated?

ACTIVITIES

Line-up

Purpose

To help people to introduce themselves and get to know each other by concentrating on the use of names. This activity encourages cooperation and begins group interaction. It also provides an appropriate warm-up to exercises in the **Myself, Me and You** and **Changing Perspectives** families.

Time needed: varies — allow at least ten-fifteen minutes

Materials needed: none

Conditions

This can be done with a new group or one that has been together for a while. New groups will need more time. The room needs to be arranged so that there is sufficient space to line up and sit in a circle. Some classes will find this approach to learning unusual and there may be initial embarrassment and reluctance to make the first move. Pupils may know only others by their nicknames, or be confused by spelling etc.

Procedure

You may wish to ask the group to move some of the furniture to make enough space for them to move into and form a line.

Pupils who do not know the alphabet can line up according to other criteria, such as height, or shades of hair or eyes from light to dark, distance from home to school and so on. Another possibility is for the teacher to arrange everyone in an alphabetical circle. Then each child can recite in turn, "My name is . . . ."

1. Let's see if we can find out/remind ourselves about each other's names. We'll do it by moving about a bit. Will you all stand up please?

Indicate where you want pupils to stand. The line may be straight or curved, depending on the area which is available. You may wish to demonstrate by putting several pupils into an alphabetical line–up, or by drawing a plan on the board.

You may need to offer help and encouragement to those who need it. Allow enough time for everyone to find their place.

You could start with A or Z.

Those who are in the wrong place can move.

With large groups it may be helpful to have two or three volunteers, especially if most of the group are strangers.

Tell the volunteer(s):

2. Listen carefully. I want you to **form a line, in alphabetical order**, from here . . . to here . . . Those of you whose first names start with letters at the beginning of the alphabet will stand at this end of the line . . . Those of you whose first names begin with letters towards the end of the alphabet will stand at the other end of the line, over here . . . You may need to check your name with the names of the others who are standing near you in the line to make sure you are in the right place.
Are there any questions?
Are you ready? **Go.**

3. Is everyone sorted out?
Now check with the person on each side of you to **see if you are in the right position**. Starting with this end of the line, **everyone in turn say your name out loud so that we can all hear**. We'll go along the line so **listen and see if everyone is in the right place.**

4. Now **mix yourselves up again**. Everyone move about for a few seconds in any direction.

5. Okay. Who thinks they can put people back into the alphabetical line?
The rest of us can help if the volunteer gets stuck. **Would someone volunteer to rebuild the line please?**

6. Everyone wait until you are shown where to go. It's (*name of volunteer*)'s job to try and put you in the right place. Let's see how quickly you can do it.

7. Don't worry about it but try to **say the person's name as you show him or her where to go**. When you are ready you can **begin.**

Comments

Don't hesitate to support or help but make sure you give them time to correct any mistakes themselves before you intervene. Try to prevent any unhelpful banter but allow the group to offer appropriate suggestions. Volunteers may encounter problems caused by shortened names, nicknames, mispronunciation or ignorance of spelling of names. This is not a test of the volunteer's ability but a simple way of encouraging a group to get to know and mix with each other in a friendly and cooperative manner. If the group enjoys doing this activity it can be continued with different volunteers trying to form the line.

Drawing out the learning

When the line–up has been completed ask the group to sit down either in small groups or as a class, sitting in a circle or semi–circle so that they can see everybody else. When everyone is settled ask them to think about that experience and consider these questions in discussion:

How difficult did you find that activity?
How many names were you uncertain about?
Was there anything in particular which caused you problems?
What was it like being a volunteer?
How does it feel when someone gets your name wrong?
How important are our names to us? What do you think makes them important?

Closure

You could ask them to follow a set formula such as: 'My name is . . .' or 'I am . . . and this is . . .'

8. Have another look around the group and make a mental note of those people whose names you forgot or found difficult. To help you do this we'll **go around the group slowly so that each person says their own name out loud and introduces the person sitting on their left.**

This exercise could be repeated at the start of the next session as a reminder of everybody's name.

Variations

Name game: Groups which already know each other's names should complete the line–up very quickly. They can take Stage 8 a step further by adding some information about themselves. For example, "I am Ann Foster and I enjoy singing". It is important that this additional information should be positive, revealing something they are interested in, feel they are good at or would like to do. This process can be extended by going round the circle again. The first person introduces herself, "I am Ann Foster, I enjoy singing". Then the person sitting next to her right (or left) gives his name and says something about himself, such as, "I am Muhammad Sajid the cross–country runner and this is Ann Foster who enjoys singing". This process continues around the circle until the last person has identified everyone.

Where do I stand? Another perspective of the alphabetical line–up can be created by doing it in reverse, starting with Z, Y, X, W, or people can line up according to surnames. Again, using several different line–ups according to various criteria in the same session can lead to comparison of different positions. Pupils can arrange themselves according to their length of name, height, shades of hair or eyes (from light to dark), distance from home to school etc. Drawing out the learning could include how feelings can vary, with some positions being regarded as 'better' than others. Some categories, such as, 'the most talkative person this lesson' can produce disagreement over some people's positions and stimulate discussion about our self–image compared to how others see us.

Acrostics

At the end of their first term at a comprehensive school, first year pupils were asked to form an alphabetical line–up as a way of introducing themselves to a new teacher. Supremely confident that this would be simple, the class of eleven- and twelve-year-olds milled around the room querying people's names and arguing over who should stand where. It wasn't as easy as they'd thought! It took several attempts before they sorted themselves out and a number of pupils expressed surprise that they were still unable to match names to faces. Discussion centred around their lack of knowledge of their classmates, how they disliked being called by the wrong name and the importance of names for our personal identity. They talked about the power they possess in knowing someone's name and being able to summon their attention.

For homework they were asked to discover the origin and meaning of their names and why they were given them. They had to think about their own names and create an acrostic taking each letter of their forename as the initial letter of words which aptly described their personal attributes.

Next lesson they arranged themselves in an alphabetical circle and took turns to read out their acrostics and talk about their names. This created a great deal of interest as the class learnt about each other's pastimes and ideals. Some pupils said they disliked their names and were pleased when others suggested suitable and sometimes amusing alternatives. Others were fascinated by the appropriate descriptions created by the acrostics and they went on to compare their views of classmates with the self-images revealed when discussing their homework.

After two hour–long lessons the group had discovered more about each other than in the previous twelve weeks in school. They demonstrated concern and sensitivity for each other's feelings and created a climate in which explicitly religious, or ultimate, questions were broached. Their interest in this work prompted a change to the syllabus to allow them to explore questions of identity by looking at rites of passage. In turn this proved an excellent introduction to multi–faith RE and suggested a new approach to religious education in the future.

Acrostics

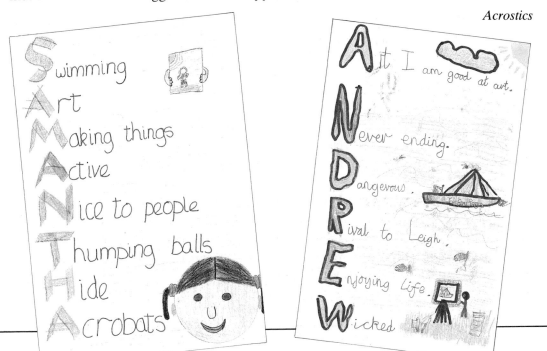

Who's here?

Purpose

This activity helps pupils to get to know one another and discover interests and experiences they share. It also encourages personal reflection by listening to, and responding to, the revelations of others, and provides opportunities to think in an intuitive way. The activity can be sub–divided and Stage 1 used to regroup pupils for another exercise or to encourage pupils to become more active following a period of quiet reflection.

Time needed: 45 minutes (Stage 1 only ten minutes)

Materials needed: Two pieces of paper or two large index cards for each person.
Coloured pens or pencils.
Ideas sheet. Have ready photocopies of "**Guess who?**", page 48.

Conditions

This exercise is intended to be positive, focusing on pupils' strengths rather than their failings. Teachers need to exercise sensitivity towards the feelings and experiences of individuals within the group and offer the necessary support. If pupils are unused to talking about themselves, some may be reluctant to participate. They should be encouraged and allowed to opt out of parts or all the activity if it is embarrassing for them. As they see others prepared to talk about themselves they may gradually become more involved in the activity.

There needs to be space to move around during Stage 1, while groups should have enough room to work without disturbance during Stage 2.

Procedure

Stage 1: 'Colour Me'
Give everyone a blank card.
Pause briefly.

Pause briefly.

Pause briefly.
If coloured pens and pencils are not available, they can write the name of the colour instead of their own name.

1. What's your favourite colour? Just spend a moment or two thinking about the colours you like.
Now think about the colour that best represents how you are feeling now. It could be your favourite colour or another one.

If you were to turn into a colour, what colour would you like to be?
Using a pen or pencil as near to your colour as possible, write your name down. Keep it to yourself and don't look at other people's cards just yet.

Some pupils may need extra persuasion to become involved in finding others with the same colour.

Once everyone is in a group, it may be necessary to sub–divide larger groups or combine small groups into manageable sizes, e.g. five or six pupils per group. If someone is alone in their choice, they may need further encouragement to see that choice as unique and special to them.

2. Has everyone finished? Now it's time to see if anyone else has the same or similar colour on their cards. Walk around the room and **find everyone who has chosen the same colour as you.** When you find them, stay together as a group.

3. Staying in your colour group, take it in turns to **say why you chose the colour you did**. For example, "I chose green because I think it's quiet and relaxed and that's how I feel today". Everyone should have a go and you can say as much or as little as you like about it. OK? Off you go.

Drawing out the learning

What did you think about that activity?
What was easy or difficult for you?
How far did the colours you chose reflect feelings, or experiences, or interests?
What surprised or interested you?

Stage 2: 'Guess Who?'
Pupils should work in groups of no less than five.

Give out new cards and photo-copied 'Ideas' sheet (see p. 48).

A checklist of points to remember should be displayed prominently or handed out with the 'Ideas' sheet.

You'll need to move about to get an idea of how well they are managing. As a rough guide,

4. Don't write your name on this new card. I want you to **write down** on one side of the card, between five and eight **statements about yourself.** Do not write on the 'Ideas' sheet.
Choose something special to you, things the others are not likely to know. Make sure you choose things you don't mind talking about.
Try not to make it obvious that those statements were written by a boy or a girl, if you can, but that's not too important.
Think about things that you are pleased and proud about; something you have achieved, or a skill you have, or something you know a lot about. There are a lot of ideas to get you started on the 'Ideas' sheet.
When you've finished, don't tell anyone what you've written or show them your card. **Keep your statements to yourself** for the moment, covering over what you've written, or turning your card over, and just wait quietly until everyone is ready.

allow ten minutes for this stage. Some pupils may not be able to think of five statements.

Pause briefly.

Pause briefly.

Pause, allowing approximately two minutes per person but keep an eye on the progress of each group.
Once they've worked through the activity, and understood what is going on, some groups may appreciate the chance to form new groups and repeat the exercise.

They could do a quick drawing of their chosen statement and explain it to the group.

Pause, allowing two or three minutes per person.

5. Right, now will you all **place your cards with the written side face down in a pile in the middle of the group.**
One person in the group pick up the pile and **shuffle them**, mix them up well, keeping the blank side uppermost so no one can see what is written on them.
Now the shuffler can **deal out the cards so everyone gets one.**

6. When you get the card, don't show it to anyone. Just look at it briefly. It doesn't matter if you've got your own card back.
Take it **in turns to read out to** everyone **what the card says.**
Once a card has been read out, **the group tries to guess whose card it is before going on to hear what the next card says.** If you do get your own card back, don't say anything, but pretend it's someone else's and do the same as everybody else.
When you have found out who wrote the card, return it to its owner. Any questions?
Off you go.

7. Has everyone got their card back? Look at your card again and **choose one thing that you'd like to tell the whole group about.** It might be a skill, or a memory, or something that happened to you. **Tell the group what it is and talk a little about it.**

Drawing out the learning

What do you remember most about doing this activity?
How did you feel while you were taking part?
What surprised you?
What did you notice or appreciate about the things others said?
What have you learned about others in the group?
What have you learned about yourself?

This could be done by discussion in small groups with the teacher moving around to assist each group as necessary. Or it may be preferable to bring everyone into a circle for a class discussion.

The one thing people have chosen could be written down on the blank side of their card and pinned up for all the group to see as their personal contribution to the group.

Variations

Who are you?
This exercise is designed as a lighthearted warm–up to this profound question. An important part of who you are is your name.

1. Stand in a space where you are free to move without impeding others. Begin to write your name in the space in front of you with the index finger of your writing hand.

2. Gradually make the movements bigger so that the writing of your name fills up all the available space.

3. Extend again so that you write your name, above, behind and to the side of you.

4. Repeat with your other hand.

5. Now experiment by writing your name with other parts of your body. You might like to try your head, elbow, hip, knee and so on.

6. Use your feet to write your name by stepping it out on the floor.

7. Finally make a 'signature' dance by adding body movements to the stepping pattern of your feet.

"Guess who?" (Ideas Sheet)

Don't write your name down, but do write five to eight statements about yourself, saying something that:

- is special to me that others don't know.

- I am prepared to talk about.

- is not obviously about being a boy or a girl.

- I am pleased about or proud of.

You may find it is difficult at first to think of anything to say about yourself. So here is a list of examples to give you some ideas. They are only examples and suggestions and if you think of other things *please* use them instead.

A time when I was brave was . . .
When I was younger I really enjoyed . . .
I value . . .
I am proud that I . . .
One of my strengths is . . .
I taught someone how to . . .
I have accomplished . . .
I received praise when I . . .
A new skill I have learned is . . .
I enjoy . . .
Something I would like others to know about me is . . .
An exciting thing I did was . . .
I helped someone else to . . .

IN PRACTICE

'The senses:' an induction course for RE

Teesdale Comprehensive is a rural secondary school attracting pupils from a wide area in south–west Durham. While the school tries to ensure that at least two children from the same feeder school go into each form, many first year pupils are inevitably strangers. To help pupils get to know one another and create the climate necessary for affective RE, Maureen Harrison developed this half–term induction course. Mixed ability classes of eleven and twelve year olds spend two thirty–five minute periods each week taking part in Acclimatising and Raising Awareness activities before starting a study of the Christian faith.

Lesson one

AIMS: Introductions, breaking the ice, relaxing the tensions of the new situation.

a) **Alphabetical line–up** by first names. This helps the students to find out each other's names, introduces the idea of a specific arrangement and reinforces the need to get to know each other.

b) **To the ship.** The group forms a single line down the centre of the room, running to the right when told 'To the Starboard', going left to the command 'To the Port' and back to the centre in response to 'To the Ship'. Commands are issued rapidly and the last person to get in line is out. This breaks the ice and releases inhibitions introducing the idea that RE lessons can be fun.

c) **Saying Hello.** Reinforces introductions in what should now be a much more relaxed atmosphere. Appropriate music can be used for this, and the following, exercise.

d) **Mill and grab** develops rapid group formation but it is sometimes necessary to instruct students to avoid their best friends. Groups are formed as quickly as possible in response to the teacher calling out numbers, apparently at random.

e) **Name game.** The required group size is achieved by Mill and Grab and each group sits in a circle. The first student introduces self, the second student introduces self and then the first student, the third student introduces self then the first and second students and so on.

If time permits there can be a second round, giving an interest as well as an introduction.

Some classes may not get this far in thirty–five minutes. They take longer to lose their inhibitions and they try to stay close to their friends.

Lesson two

AIMS: Reinforcement of interest and feelings of group identity generated in lesson one.

a) **Alphabetical line–up** should be much quicker this time.
b) **Line-up by height.** Discuss positions. Is anyone in the same position? Different arrangement, but same group.
c) **Alternative group arrangements** by any choice of the teacher; favourite animals, hobbies, hair colour, and so on. Discuss group arrangements, sizes, how many groups each person belonged to.
d) **Favourite pastimes.** In one large group each person mimes their pastime. The rest of the group must guess what it is (this is usually very easy). Discuss any unusual hobbies which may crop up, then discuss the reasons for choosing the favourite — is it what you are best at, is it a challenge? Introduce the idea of using talents to best advantage, relate to the parable of the talents and St Paul's teaching on the gifts of the spirit.
e) **End with Alphabetical line–up.** A volunteer puts people into place — surprisingly difficult for students.

Lesson three

AIMS: Development of group identity and achievement.

a) **Alphabetical line–up.** Volunteers should be much quicker by now.
b) **Human noughts and crosses.** This exercise demands quick thinking and quickly develops a strong sense of group identity. With one class I had to play Noughts and Crosses on the blackboard before they had any success with the human variety.

Lesson four: observation

AIMS: Development and awareness of sensory observations.

Instruction given, "Observe the room and write down what you observe." If any explanation of the word 'observe' is requested, take care to avoid naming any of the senses. Allow five minutes.
Volunteers read out their notes; discuss style (are they lists or descriptive passages?), the senses used (most will have relied on sight). Discuss their interpretation of the instruction 'observe'.
Discuss the way in which we experience the world through our senses, which sense is most valued, compensatory development when one sense is lost, etc. Students have a great deal to say and ask many questions, the teacher's role is simply to keep the discussion flowing.

Lesson five: sight

Students sit with eyes closed or heads on desks, whichever is most comfortable. A flower is placed on each desk. After five minutes they open their eyes, examine the object on the desk, then write a description of:
a) how they felt when they opened their eyes;
b) the object they found.
Several volunteers read out their descriptions. I then read a passage from 'Emma and I' by Sheila Hocken, in which the author described the moment when she received her sight after many years of blindness. We discuss her appreciation of colour in particular, then repeat the exercise.

Lesson six: listening

AIMS: Development of listening skills, learning more about each other.

a) **Hammer and Nail.** A fun way of finding a partner and avoiding best friends.
b) **Just a Minute.** In the time available, we only manage part of this exercise. This could be an advantage because students are keen to continue and look forward to the next lesson.

Lesson seven

Continue **Just a Minute**. Working in groups of six (three pairs) students discuss how they can tell if their partners are listening or interested. Students change groups to try to extend and share ideas. Finally, in a large group we discuss their findings. Each group produces work for a classroom display.

Lessons eight and nine

AIMS: Improvement in listening skills, identification of sounds, development of imagination.

For maximum cooperation the students choose their own groups of four. They listen to a soundtrack from a short piece of film and identify various sounds. The groups then make up and illustrate a story to fit the sounds, the tape remaining available for use whenever they wish. I am very much a background figure at this time, each group being in control of a task which is carried out responsibly and sensibly in most cases. Work is displayed when finished.

Lesson ten: taste and smell

Working in the same groups of four, each person in turn is blind–folded, given something to smell and something else to taste. Returning to the group they say what they think the two items are. All identifications are recorded, then checked for accuracy.

Lesson eleven: touch

The first person from each group had to identify one of four objects inside a 'feely' bag. With one item already identified, the second person repeated the exercise, rejecting the first person's object if they felt it. The fourth person in each group had the hardest task, having no choice about which article to identify.

Lesson twelve

AIMS: To promote a greater awareness and appreciation of human senses.

Recalling the experience of lessons 5–11, the class discuss the senses they have explored. Why only five? Is it possible to have more? How do human senses differ from those of other creatures? Again, the teacher is a background figure, prompting now and again to keep the discussion moving. Some students point out that since some people seem to have a 'sixth' sense then perhaps humans have more than five, but that an input from five senses is as much as most people can cope with.

Lesson thirteen

AIMS: An understanding of the Creation story in Genesis, an awareness of people's role/responsibility in the world.

We read the Creation story and discuss the theory of Creation 'versus' the theory of evolution; the idea of the senses as 'God–given'; humans' responsibility in the world. Most students wish to ask questions and to contribute their thoughts.

Lesson fourteen: communication and cooperation

Students have worked in groups and begun to develop a sense of group identity. We discuss their use of their senses in cooperating and working together to produce the best result for the group. We read Paul's teaching on the Body of Christ in 1 Corinthians 12 and discuss the idea of the group as a body with each member playing a part. We then discuss self–assessment, being honest with ourselves, reflecting on whether each member has played a part, or if some people see group work as an opportunity to sit back and let others do the work?

Each student writes a brief summary of the contribution of each member of their group — was it ideas, artwork, organisation, presentation skill, fluency in story-telling, etc? The groups discuss this exercise before writing it up for homework. The final paragraph is a personal assessment.

My reflections on these lessons

I have no reservations about the value of this work. I feel that I have a good relationship with my students which developed more quickly, and perhaps more closely than usual.

However, many students have asked, on behalf of their parents as well as themselves, "What has this got to do with Jesus?" Through discussion, I have tried to form a link with the Christian message but my main hope is that as they move on through the school, the heightened awareness of themselves and the world in which they live, their cooperation and attitude to others, developed through experiential RE will help in their understanding of why people believe, why people worship.

Parents are also in favour of the work we are doing. For example, one mother told me: "This new style of RE is much more interesting than the old–fashioned 'Scripture' we did at school. It involves the children more personally and concentrates more on their own experiences. If they learn to understand themselves first, it will help their understanding of religion later."

No doubt there will be those parents who think RE should consist entirely of facts gleaned from the Bible, but that comment is only one of many from interested, supportive parents. They show interest and visit the department on Parents' and Open Evenings. They accept that there is little to be seen in exercise books, since the work is experiential and most of the work which was written up was for display purposes.

(Maureen Harrison)

Raising awareness

INTRODUCTION TO AWARENESS

'The real voyage of discovery consists not in seeking new Landscapes but in having new eyes.'

(Marcel Proust)

Throughout the following groups of exercises, pupils and teachers are asked to concentrate on awareness. The instruction, 'Be aware', raises the question, 'Aware of *what*?' This exercise offers an answer to that question. Try it for yourself now; you'll need a piece of paper and a pen or pencil. It is also helpful if you do this exercise again with a few other people to see if, and how, people's perceptions differ from each other. You may also wish to use it with pupils to show there are many perspectives on reality.

Be aware!

1. For the next five minutes **be aware** and write down everything that you are aware of. If you are doing this with other people, don't discuss the instructions or communicate with anyone else during the next five minutes, and don't look at anyone else's paper.
2. Look at what you have written and consider your observations. Ask yourself why you chose to write down those particular responses?
    Was there anything you decided not to write down?
    How did you make these choices?
3. Compare your responses with the rest of your group.
    Has everyone made the same or similar observations?
    Are any of the choices wrong?
    What was understood by the instruction 'Be aware'?
(adapted from an idea of the philosopher of science, Karl Popper.)

Our experiences fall within three zones of awareness which John Stevens[1] defines as:

1. Awareness of the outside world

We rely on our senses to assess objects and events in terms of what we actually see, hear, touch, taste, or smell. I can *see* that the sun is shining as I *listen* to a lawn-mower in action, and *smell* the newly cut grass. In this way we derive some understanding of the world outside our bodies.

2. Awareness of the inside world

At times we are also conscious of what is going on under our skin. At this moment I am aware that I *feel* rather warm and have an itchy nose.

Together these zones of awareness present to me aspects of the reality of my existence at this moment.

3. Awareness of fantasy activity

In contrast the third zone focuses on my personal images of things and events which do not exist in present reality, although they do centre around the here and now. This includes all those thoughts which go beyond the present moment — reflections of the past encourage images which may explain, interpret, and compare. Our minds may be occupied with plans for the future, imagining what may, or may not, occur. Recalling the misery of hay fever in the past, I consider disturbing my work to close the window. Yet reality also lies within these fantasies which can help me become more aware of feelings, perceptions and actions.

> **'All that we are is the result of what we have thought.'**
>
> (*The Dhammapada*)

Awareness is like a spotlight, allowing details to emerge, sharpening and clarifying the image so that I can perceive more clearly. It is selective, directing attention to what I regard as relevant to me and excluding information which appears to be of no interest or value. My concentration span varies and so awareness is usually transient. Flitting from object to object, image to image, it moves quite rapidly at times, blurring the detail. There can be a tendency to generalise, to stray from the here and now — I may think I am aware of what is going on around me when really my mind is focused elsewhere.

Here and now: Attending to the here and now is not easy as my mind mulls over the past and contemplates the future, so often distracting me from what is actually going on in the present. We speak with some sadness of people who 'live in the past' or 'live for the future', recognising in these words that living in the present is more realistic. Whatever I do I do it now, not in the past, nor in the future, but NOW.

> Look to this day
> for it is life
> the very life of life
> In its brief course lie all
> the realities and truths of existence
> the joy of growth
> the splendour of action
> the glory of power
> For yesterday is but a memory
> And tomorrow is only a vision
> But today well lived
> Makes every yesterday a memory of happiness
> and every tomorrow a vision of hope
> Look well therefore to this day!
>
> (*Ancient Sanskrit poem*)

This realisation that the present moment is all that I have lies at the heart of religion. The concept of mindfulness in Buddhism can be seen in the light of consciousness of the moment. The mind is total awareness, just listening when listening, just seeing when seeing and so on. Jesus told his followers to be watchful, not merely staying awake but being alert and observant. The Jesus Prayer of the Eastern Orthodox Church is used as a mantra[2], repeated over and over again to concentrate the mind, still the thoughts and ultimately set the soul "face to face with God".[3]

Pupils can discover the value of the here and now for themselves. After experiencing one of the raising awareness exercises for the first time, a fourteen–year–old responded: "I felt very peaceful and alone. I felt as if I had no feelings or movement in my body except my eyes. I was imagining and putting my thought to what I was thinking. I felt very light and as if I was floating on air."

Without any prompting or direction from the teacher, she realised: "I am like this because I have put my troubles and thoughts behind me and thought of just one thing."[4]

Have another look at your responses to the 'Be Aware' exercise. If you have done it with others, you will probably have discovered a range of experiences in response to the same instructions carried out in the same place and at the same time. Experiences revolve around who you are and how you experience your existence so that even similar events can produce quite different responses.

Using this same exercise with older children it is possible for them to begin to understand that there are other ways of seeing the world. Thus to take a religious stance is not necessarily any different or more biased than other points of view; it is another perspective.

Having explored some of the problems inherent to awareness, pupils should also be able to see why it may be desirable to practise focusing awareness. Raising awareness in this way can help to increase the potential for self–discovery. By becoming aware of our experiences and sharing them with others we can begin to understand each other. It is to fulfil the aim of raising awareness that the next family of exercises is directed.

These structures are tools to help participants enter into a variety of experiences. They do not provide answers. Nor do they intend to induce change in the pupils. They simply provide opportunities to become more aware and perhaps to absorb that experience. Change may, and has to our knowledge, taken place but that is not part of the teacher's intention or effort, rather it is a consequence of the individual or the group's perceptions.

References

1. Stevens, John O., *Awareness: exploring, experimenting, experiencing*, Real People Press, 1971.

2. 'The Method' of using the Jesus Prayer is attributed to St Simeon the New Theologian.
   "Sit down alone and in silence. Lower your head, shut your eyes, breathe out gently and imagine yourself looking into your own heart. Carry your mind [i.e., your thoughts,] from your head to your heart. As you breathe out, say 'Lord Jesus Christ, have mercy on me'. Say it moving your lips gently, or simply say it in your mind. Try to put all other thoughts aside. Be calm, be patient, and repeat the process very frequently."

3. French, R. M., *The Way of a Pilgrim* (trans) S.P.C.K., 1972.

4. Seaham Comprehensive School, Co Durham.

LISTENING AND STILLING

Most of the time we are not really aware of the bustle of sights, sounds and sensations that are crowding into our awareness both from outside and inside our bodies. Usually we are on 'automatic pilot', because we are caught up in an endless round of remembering past events or wondering about what we have to do next. From the religious person's point of view, this low level of awareness is a kind of blindness, which gets in the way of important exercises like prayer, meditation or the attentive performance of ritual. To be done properly, these activities require participants to be sensitively aware of the here–and–now of their experience, so that they can be receptive to the possibility of insight or revelation. In certain kinds of Buddhism, awareness meditation is the central religious practice, whilst in Western religion, the Bible teaches believers to 'be still and know that I am God'.

The exercises in this family are designed to give pupils some direct experience of raising awareness of the here–and–now. Usually, it is an experience which they will enjoy, and with regular practice they may be able to gain an insight into the importance of the skill for religious people.

There are two sub–groups, **listening** and **stilling**, which are interdependent. In order to listen, we must first be able to still ourselves so that we can direct our awareness towards listening. Yet it is difficult to become still without having a focus for our attention; listening can provide such a focus.

LISTENING

'I can never tell you what you said, but only what I heard'.

(John Powell; *The Secret of Staying in Love*)

"Are you listening?" How often do we demand that pupils should "Pay attention" without giving them any practical help to do so? Listening effectively is an essential skill in our everyday lives; yet our hearing frequently resembles a radio receiving several stations at the same time. There are lots of noises and distractions buzzing around us which distort and obscure the messages we receive. This constant bombardment of messages from our bodies, our minds and our emotions must first be acknowledged before we can listen effectively. In doing this we become aware of body language, feelings and fantasies which influence our ability to interpret accurately the messages transmitted to us.

The ability to relate to other people in a positive way depends, in part, on our ability to listen to them. True listening involves deducing the meaning that is intended, not just by interpreting the words of another person but by being aware of the intention of the whole person and attempting to unwrap their own unique message.

Being able to listen is an important aspect of spirituality. Religious traditions teach many ways of learning to listen, for example, meditation can create a channel which allows the 'inner voice' to be heard. Listening in terms of religion involves both paying attention to oneself and being receptive to the transcendent. The paths of prayer and meditation lead the religious person to listen in the hope that spiritual awareness and insight will increase.

The following exercises help pupils to listen more effectively to themselves and to those around them. Their receptivity can be further improved by practising relaxation and stilling to clear the channels from bodily and environmental distractions which impair listening. Only then does it become possible to encounter feelings and imaginings without distortion and so discover "how we really are" at this present moment. These structures may also create opportunities for a deeper understanding of what religious people mean when they speak of listening to the Divine.

> **Listen to the rain — only listen.**
> **Listen to the wind — only listen.**
> **Listen to the sea — only listen.**
>
> (Laura Huxley: *You are not the Target*)

ACTIVITIES

Radio Gaga

Purpose

When in conversation we are often more concerned with what we are about to say than with listening. Our own thoughts get in the way of good communications. The message we receive is filtered through our selective listening and we may not grasp the full meaning of what has been said. This exercise compares the mind to a radio to demonstrate the constant distractions which divide attention and hinder effective listening. It also shows how it is possible to tune awareness to receive more clearly.

Time needed: Thirty minutes.

Materials needed: Radio (See *Variations* if a radio is not available).
Drawing and writing materials.

Conditions

Since this exercise uses sound, the location of the room could be important. Too many distractions created by external noises may cause problems. Conversely too few sounds may not provide sufficient stimulus. It can be helpful to encourage pupils to pair up with someone they do not know very well.

Procedure

Use the radio to demonstrate how difficult it is to tune in to one station when there is a lot of interference. For example, find a waveband where two stations are transmitting simultaneously or move from one station to another through a wave of interference.

As you do this explain what is happening.

Continue twiddling the tuner. Finally tune in to one station.

Turn the radio off.

It may take some time for the class to settle. Speak in a quiet, relaxed tone of voice. You could use any stilling exercise (see pages 72–86). It is helpful if the pupils close their eyes.

You may wish to draw attention to sounds such as voices, doors opening and closing, footsteps, air and street noises, birds, weather sounds, etc. as they occur.

You could draw attention to other noises, coughing, shuffling, the ticking of a clock, as appropriate.

Pause for a few moments.

1. Listen . . . As you **listen to the radio be aware of your thoughts** and reactions.

2. What makes it difficult to understand what is being transmitted?

3. Spend a minute or two talking about this experience with the person nearest to you.

4. Get yourself into a comfortable position and **be still** . . . Sometimes our minds are like the radio we have just been listening to. This time we are going to try to discover how to tune our minds in to the sounds around us. If you **close your eyes** you can tune out one station . . . the things that you can see. Now just listen. . . . First **listen to the sounds outside this room** . . . Perhaps you are aware of noises coming from another room.

5. Now change the channel and **listen to the sounds inside the room.** You may be aware of the sound of my voice . . . of someone breathing . . .

6. Now change again and **listen to the sounds inside your body** . . . You may hear your own breathing . . . a humming in your ears . . . you may hear your own stomach rumbling . . . you may be aware of the beat of your heart.

7. Now just **focus on one sound** and be aware of that sound for a moment . . . Keep listening to this sound . . .

8. OK. Now allow yourself to **tune in again to the sound of my voice** . . . to the sounds within this room . . . **be aware of** the presence of other people in this room . . . now slowly open your eyes and look at **your surroundings.**

Drawing out the learning

Encourage pupils to talk to a partner about their experience of being silent:

Think about the sound you heard most clearly. What was it like?
Try to picture it in your mind and then draw or write something to represent that sound.
You might like to show it to your partner and talk about your experience.
What have you learned about listening?
What are your comments on what you have been doing?

Ensure each pupil has writing and drawing materials, and that they have partners to work with if they wish.

Variations

It is possible to do this exercise without a radio. You may wish to omit stages 1–3 altogether or you could try:

Piggy in the middle

1. Arrange the pupils in threes. Whoever sits in the middle should be silent while trying to listen to what is being said by both partners who are talking at the same time.

2. Give them the choice of a number of topics and ensure that each person in a trio chooses a different subject, e.g. Something I enjoy doing; what I would like for my birthday; my favourite food; the best holiday I ever had.

3. Time a minute or two and then ask the person sitting in the middle to swop places with a partner and repeat the exercise. Make sure that everyone has a chance to be "piggy in the middle".

4. Ask them to consider what that experience was like for them when they were speaking and when they were expected to listen.

Just a minute

Purpose

Active listening involves giving your full attention to the other person rather than thinking about what you might say next.

This exercise, which is in three parts, allows pupils to experiment with the ways they ignore people and then to examine their use of body language as both conscious and unconscious means of communication. As skills increase, the listener tries to uncover the real meaning of what is being expressed by reflecting back the content and feeling of what has been said.

Time needed: Sixty minutes.

Materials needed: None until Stages 9 and 15 when writing and/or drawing materials may be required.

Conditions

This exercise can generate a lot of noise. You should watch for any pupils who may misinterpret the experience of being ignored even when they know that is the purpose of the activity. Some children may be tempted to use physical means of grabbing attention and it may be necessary to establish a few ground rules at the start, for example, "Do not touch anyone."

It is very important that everyone experiences 'the cold–shoulder'. If time is short you can divide this exercise into two or three sessions, ending and starting again at Stage 9 or after Stage 17.

Preliminary procedure

For each part of the structure:
1. Consider carefully how you wish to organise the class in small groups. You may think it more appropriate for them to work alongside the people with whom they feel most comfortable, or those they do not know very well, or else people chosen at random. Groups of three or four are ideal.
2. Devise some means of identifying each person in the group, e.g., numbers 1–4, colours, objects, which you could substitute for the letters of the alphabet used here.
3. Provide a selection of suitable topics about which pupils can choose to talk for one or two minutes, for example, What I did in the holidays; my favourite sport; how I would spend a million pounds; the best story in the world and so on.

Comments

Before beginning this series of activities it may be necessary to discuss different methods used to seek attention. In school, for example, pupils use bodily signals like putting up their hands to attract attention. Other, perhaps less acceptable, strategies include calling out, shouting or swearing, hitting or holding on to someone, or adopting a threatening attitude. Teachers assume somewhat different ways of gaining attention, using a position of dominance at the front of the classroom, speaking in a loud voice, varying inflection, using gestures or saying something which is unexpected.

Part 1: Take no notice

Procedure

If there is time and you think it is appropriate you could allow two minutes.

It may be necessary to explore different ways of ignoring, such as yawning, coughing, turning away. **Time one minute.**

At this stage it may be useful to suggest using more subtle or demonstrative methods of ignoring.

Repeat Stages 6 and 8 until everyone has been ignored.

4. Choose a topic you can talk about for a minute or two. Once everybody has chosen, **each person in turn will be asked to talk** for one minute. While that person is talking **everyone else should show that they are NOT listening.**

5. Are you ready? **"A" can begin now.**

6. Stop talking.

7. Before the next person speaks, take a few seconds to **think about what has been happening** and how you feel. Consider the ways used to show that people weren't paying attention.

8. Now it is "B's" turn to talk while everyone else ignores. Are you ready? **"B" start now.**

Drawing out the learning

It is important that this experience is discussed before going any further. This can be done in groups or as a class. You may wish to suggest that they record their findings in some way, e.g. by drawing a picture or symbol to represent their feelings when being ignored.

Continue with the activity.

9. Before we go any further let's spend a short time considering what has been happening.
How did we ignore each other?
What did it feel like to be ignored?
What did we do to try to get attention and to make ourselves heard?
What are the ways of showing that we ARE listening?

Variations

I don't see. Different aspects of listening can be demonstrated in a number of settings, such as working in pairs but sitting back to back, or sitting facing each other but with eyes closed.

Part 2: **Pay attention**

The emphasis now changes to the methods of indicating that we *are* giving attention. It may be necessary to demonstrate appropriate body language, e.g. leaning forward, eye contact, nodding the head, saying "mmmm", etc.

Procedure

Time one minute. If you allow longer than one minute make sure you alter the time given in the instructions to class.

With older pupils you could suggest that this time the listener gives verbal encouragement by asking questions and making comments. **Time one minute.**

Either discuss in small groups or with the whole class.

10. Find a partner from your group and **sit so that you can look at each other. Choose a topic to talk about**. It can be the same subject as last time or something different. Then decide who is going to talk first.

11. It is the listener's task to listen, not to ask questions or to speak. **When it is your turn to listen make sure that you give your full attention.**

12. Are you ready? The **first person can start to talk on their chosen topic for one minute, starting now.**

13. Stop talking and take a few moments to **think about what was done** to gain the listener's attention and how attention was being given.

14. Now it is the listener's turn to talk. Whoever was speaking last time must now concentrate on giving their total attention to what is being said. You have one minute to talk about your chosen topic starting now.

15. Stop talking. OK, let's discuss what has been happening and how you felt during the talking and listening.

Drawing out the learning

A natural follow–up to this discussion might be to compile a list of things we can do to show we are listening. A brainstorm, displayed as a wallchart or poster, would provide a more permanent reminder of actions and responses which assist listening. Or pupils could produce their own personal checklists of listening hints in the following way:

16. Think about what you have been doing and make a list of the things that showed your partner was really listening to you.

When you are ready **show your list to your partner and note any differences** you may have.

17. Now **leave that partner and form new groups of four**, making sure you are with people who are all from different groups.

Share your lists and notice the similarities and differences. Talk about them.

A final stage could be to negotiate a short list of listening priorities.

Variations

Mirror, Mirror. You could give secret written instructions to one person in each pair to mirror her or his partner's gestures and expressions. By using this technique pupils have the opportunity to explore some of their own body language which they may use, consciously or unconsciously, when talking and listening. (A video camera could also be used.)

Part 3: That's what I said

As listening skills improve, pupils could go on to demonstrate their understanding of what they have heard by reflecting back the content and feeling of what has been said. This can be done in a number of ways:

Procedure

Give a choice of topics, such as, 'If I ruled the world' or 'What I did at the weekend'. Allow a fixed time of two or three minutes for each person to speak and then a similar time to hear the reporting back.

Time should now be given to DRAWING OUT THE LEARNING so far.

18. In pairs, 'A' will talk to 'B' for two minutes. 'B' listens carefully and then has the same time to repeat accurately what you have heard.

19. Stop. 'B' will now repeat what 'A' has just said.

20. Spend a few moments thinking about how you found that experience.

'A': What was it like to hear someone else restating what you had just said?

How did it feel?

How accurate was their reflection of what you'd said?

Had you been misunderstood at all?

Did anything surprise you?

'B': How easy was it to remember everything you'd been told?

What did you find most difficult or easy?

How did you feel about repeating another person's views?

Repeat Stages 18–20.
Ensure that there is plenty of time to draw out the learning.

21. Now reverse roles so that 'A' listens while 'B' talks. When 'B' stops speaking 'A' will report back on what has been said.

Variations

Let me introduce you. After listening carefully to what has been said by their partners, they could take it in turns to introduce each other to another pair by explaining what their partner has been saying.

Check it out. Another variation involves noticing the mood and feelings which lie behind the words. These are then taken into account when rephrasing the content of what is said. The listeners can make comments or ask questions to check their understanding of what has been expressed. The content and feelings of their partner's words can then be reflected back by paraphrasing what has been expressed. For example, "So what you are saying is . . ." or "The feeling I am getting from you is that you . . .".

That's what I mean. Pupils could work in threes with the third person acting as observer. Taking it in turns, each person speaks to a partner who must then rephrase what has been said to the satisfaction of the original speaker. The observer's task is to ensure this is done; not allowing anyone else to talk until the speaker is happy that she or he is fully understood.

Moods. It is also possible to 'listen' to someone who is not talking, by becoming aware of their moods and feelings. Partners should sit opposite each other and clasp hands, A does not speak but recalls a past experience. By observing A carefully, B tries to enter into A's experience. For example, without saying which is which, A remembers, in turn, a time of anger and a second event of great happiness. B then has to decide whether the first memory was happy or angry. Pupils do not have to describe the events they remembered unless they wish to do so. After swopping roles and then talking about that activity with their partners there could be general group discussion on how feelings are communicated.

Closure

As listening skills improve, some pupils may enjoy ending a session by giving and receiving compliments. Any positive statement can be made in reply. The idea is that the compliment is accepted and acknowledged without embarrassment. You could add a stage 22, which might be: **22. You may like to compliment each other** on something you have shared while you were talking together, for example, "I liked . . ." You should reply to these comments with a smile, a 'thankyou' or a longer sentence such as "I'm glad I told you about that".

Let me see!

Purpose

Have you ever gazed at something for so long that it seems to merge within you? Perhaps the flames of a fire or something of great beauty appears drawn towards you, as though it is entering your mind — for a moment you and it are one.

This exercise is offered as a reminder that we use a number of senses to decipher the messages we constantly receive. Likewise several paths towards the spiritual or mystical use other senses apart from listening. For example, some Buddhists practise visualising the Buddha as a way to enlightenment, other religious people use icons, statues and mandalas (a mandala is a sacred symbol said to contain cosmic significance) to focus their meditation.

Time needed: Twenty–thirty minutes

Materials needed: Enough pictures or objects so that each pupil has something to look at, such as a selection of postcards or flowers. Writing and drawing materials.

Conditions

It is important that pupils should feel comfortable with their eyes closed. As little disturbance as possible will help them to settle and not feel the need to open their eyes. Once they have got the idea of what is required, they could do this at home.

Procedure

Either arrange a display of objects from which each person can choose an item at the start of the lesson or conceal the objects so that they can be placed unseen in front of each pupil once their eyes are closed. You may wish to organise the class so that everyone has a partner.

In a quiet, relaxed voice give the following instructions.

What I am about to ask you to do is not easy although the instructions sound quite simple. In a moment I am going to ask you to **sit quietly and keep your eyes closed for a few minutes**. When your eyes are closed you should find that you are more aware of your other senses. You may find it helpful to put your hands over your eyes.

Wait until everyone has settled. You could use any stilling exercise to help them to relax, such as:

1. Before you close your eyes **make sure you are sitting in a comfortable position**.
Now **close your eyes** and relax. Try to keep your eyes closed until I ask you to open them.

2. Now **take three deep breaths. Breathe in . . . hold your breath . . . and blow the air out through your mouth**. Do it again. Breathe in . . . hold your breath . . . and let the air out through your mouth again. Good. Now breathe like that once more . . . Breathing in . . . hold it . . . and breathe out.

If this is the first time the group has closed their eyes for any length of time you may suggest that they should:

Pause until you think the group is ready to move on to the next stage.

Try to keep your eyes shut for a little longer. Just use the time to **think about what is happening, how you, and perhaps others, are feeling**. We'll talk about this later.

Make sure everyone has something to look at. Whenever possible you should substitute the name of the item which is being observed for the word *object* in the following instructions:

3. **Now open your eyes and look at the** object **in front of you**. Look at it very carefully for a minute. Examine it closely and pay attention to anything you particularly notice. Then I will ask you to close your eyes again.

Time one minute.

4. O.K. Now you can shut your eyes again and keep them tightly closed. In your mind's eye **imagine the** object **you have just been looking at**. Try to see that object in your mind.

It may help if the object is put out of sight but can be quickly restored to full view.

5. Let's see how well you can **describe the** object **without looking at it again**.

EITHER: working in pairs:

You may prefer to omit the writing or drawing.

Take it in turns to describe your object in as much detail as possible to your partner who can write down, or draw, your description for you. When you have finished describing it you can open your eyes again.

OR: if they are working alone:

Allow sufficient time to do this before bringing the object back into view.

Making sure you don't look at it again, open your eyes and either write about, or draw, your object, giving as much detail as you can.

Short pause.

6. Have another look at your object. Do you see anything new? Perhaps there is something you didn't notice when you first saw it.

Now **compare your** object **with your description.**

Did you recall everything about it? What was most memorable — what did you forget?

Discussion can be in pairs, small groups or the entire class.

7. Spend a minute or two talking about this experience with the person nearest to you. As you do so you might want to **consider these questions**:

Drawing out the learning

Unless there has already been class discussion, you may wish to raise these questions again at the end of the session to gain feedback from a larger number of pupils.

What was it like for you when you had your eyes closed?
What did you like or not like about it?
Did you find it hard or easy to do?
How did you feel when you looked at the object **for the first time?**
What were your thoughts?
How simple was it to see the object **in your mind's eye?**
How accurately were you able to describe the object?
What is your reaction to this exercise?
How are you feeling right now?

Variations

Snapshots. You could ask the class to imagine their eyes are cameras and, if there is enough space, they can walk slowly around the room taking mental photographs with their eyes. After returning to their seats, they should close their eyes and visualise the room, trying to remember the details so they can describe the room verbally or by drawing or writing. Finally they should open their eyes and look around once more, deciding how much of the room they were able to remember, what were the easiest and hardest things to recall and whether there was anything in particular which made this easy or hard to do.

Well us talk and talk 'bout God, but I'm still adrift, trying to chase that old white man out of my head. I been so busy thinking 'bout him I never truly notice nothing God makes. Not a blade of corn (how it do that?) not the color purple (where it come from?). Not the wild flowers. Nothing.

(Alice Walker, *The Color Purple*)

IN PRACTICE

The value for RE teaching

Listening exercises are often associated with Personal and Social Education or Study Skills and it may come as a surprise to see these activities feature in RE lessons. Effective listening skills are essential if we are to develop an understanding of and empathise with other people, whether they are classmates or believers of another faith. Here three secondary teachers reply to the question, 'Why should I do these exercises in RE?'

Alan McKenzie used listening activities with third year pupils at The Becket School, Nottingham.

"Experiential learning starts with the secular in order to ease the approach to the sacred. There is always a risk that these methods will remain remote to RE unless the teacher helps pupils to see that religion is more than something that is passively done to them in a classroom or place of worship. To do this the teacher needs to establish and safeguard a relationship of trust and sensitivity within the group. It can sometimes be a tortuous experience to try to encourage a class to listen to each other. Accustomed to facing the blackboard and listening to the teacher, they may have had little opportunity to see the rest of the group, never mind listen to them. Pupils need to be more aware of, and sensitive towards, each other — a sensitivity which is achieved through knowing and understanding what is being said and which in turn leads to a feeling of empathy."

Maureen Harrison added listening exercises to the RE induction course for first years at Teesdale Comprehensive.

"Many pupils have asked 'What has this got to do with RE?'. No doubt there will always be people who think RE should consist entirely of facts gleaned from the Bible; but I was encouraged by the support of parents attending an open evening. 'This new style RE is much more interesting. It involves the children personally and concentrates on their own experiences. If they learn to understand themselves first, it will help their understanding of religion later,' was a typical comment. My main hope is that pupils will gain heightened awareness of themselves and the world in which they live, gradually coming to understand why people believe and how they worship. Somebody expressed it very well when they said you can't make a garment until someone has made the fabric; and that's what we're doing at the moment — we are making the fabric."

Janet English tried 'Take no notice' and 'Pay attention' with a group of over twenty slow–learning eleven and twelve–year–olds at The Avenue Comprehensive, County Durham. She was delighted with the results and commented afterwards:

"I was surprised at how well they worked on this, even bearing in mind the novelty of the exercise! There was no quibbling about finding another partner and they appeared genuinely interested in the exercise. There seemed little difficulty in speaking! They had quickly grasped that not only facial expressions but also other bodily movements help us to communicate and understand other people. I would previously have under-estimated how much they realised about their own and their partner's attitudes. Afterwards I asked how they had felt about doing this and the whole class said they enjoyed it."

Perhaps the real value of these listening exercises only emerges as the group continues working together, exploring sensitive and personal issues. Alan McKenzie's fourteen–year–olds were able to contribute their own ideas, confident that:

"You can be honest without people laughing at you."

"I can be more open and trust all my other friends. I don't bottle things up inside me any more."

"We could get to grips with ideas or questions which we've had but never fully explored."

"I always listen to what other people have to say. I feel whatever they say is just as important as something I say. The part I played in today's lesson was to be a listener."

Seeing is believing

Picture the scene — it is a glorious spring morning. Outside the daffodils are glowing in the brilliant sunshine whilst indoors, pupils enjoy their assembly on the wonders of nature. Keeping an eye open for the gardener, a teacher disappears into the school garden to purloin her visual aids, twenty–eight daffodils which she hides in her classroom. Today must be the day to live up to the demands of the RE syllabus and consider that most difficult of concepts, awe and wonder.

Assembly over, the first years enter the room to learn the weather has brought an added bonus — the planned lesson is to be abandoned. Instead of the usual work they find themselves chatting about the lovely day, their interesting assembly and the wonders of nature. Then the teacher asks them to close their eyes for ten minutes, putting their hands over their faces to make it easier to resist the temptation to peep.

As they sit in darkness the teacher quietly places a daffodil on each pupil's desk, explaining that she is giving them something which they are to describe on paper as soon as she says, "Open your eyes". In the meantime they are to notice their thoughts.

Typical responses included:

"When my eyes are closed and then I opened them it felt as though it was the brightest thing that I had seen in my life when I saw it."
"It made me think, I wish that blind people could just open their eyes like some of us done today, the blind people would get a surprise if they could see the nature of our world."

This was followed by reading an extract from *Emma and I* by Sheila Hocken where she describes her feelings when the bandages were removed from her eyes after an operation to restore her sight.

Many of the class were so impressed by this exercise that they repeated it at home where they were able to concentrate on something or someone they considered important.

> "I sat in front of my fish tank with my eyes closed and in about twenty minutes I opened my eyes, and it seemed like a new world. I saw my fish swimming around and all the colours of the fish were lovely, I could sit there for hours and hours on end watching them."
>
> "I emerged from darkness into a world of colour and light. From only being able to hear the chirping of my budgie Casper, I could now see him, and he was beautiful. He had tiny silvery white feathers on his head some tinged with black, and bright black eyes above a small yellow beak. Splashes of purple adorned each cheek, but his body was covered in soft downy feathers of lilac. His wings were smokey grey, white and lilac and his tiny feet were a delicate pink. Yes, he was beautiful."
>
> (Pupil, Seaham Comprehensive)

'I see'

As with other exercises, 'Let Me See!' can be used to fulfil different aims. Tom Limb devised a short script, 'I see', to go with this exercise to help his 8–9 year–old pupils experience empathy for blind people while at the same time getting them used to 'going inwards'.

The first time he did this was shortly after the ecological disaster at Bhopal in India when thousands of people either died or were blinded by an escape of toxic chemical.

Tom referred to this tragedy at the start of the lesson and then suggested that the children should try to imagine what it would be like to lose their sight. In their imaginations they were to take a last look at someone or something they treasured very much. He suggested that the children might like to shut their eyes if they wanted to, but this was not necessary. It was quite a short fantasy, not more than five minutes, and when it was over he asked them to do a drawing of whatever they had seen.

There was tremendous variety in the ideas and images which came up in the fantasy. One girl had seen a pure white rose, another her parents while some boys had played with computers, a toy train set or taken a lingering look at their goldfish and pets. One boy said he found it boring because he was unable to visualise very easily but his friend disagreed strongly, saying how easy and enjoyable he found this exercise.

When asked how this experience related to RE Tom replied that he was primarily preparing the ground by giving the children a number of exercises which got them used to 'going inwards', looking at what is going on inside themselves. Towards the end of the course he would bring in how inwardness is central to religion.

STILLING

> 'In stillness and staying quiet, there lies your strength.'
>
> (Isaiah 30:15)

The ability to calm the body and mind in order to consider the inner self allows the discovery of new channels of concentration and energy. After experiencing total stillness for the first time most people want to repeat the experience.

Bodily relaxation and clearing the mind are recommended by many religious traditions. While stilling is an end in itself for some religious people, for others it is a preparation for worship and prayer.

The ability to still, focus or centre ourselves needs careful attention. Some people find themselves doing it naturally but for others it is an unfamiliar skill which takes time and effort to develop. This can be done in a number of ways — through physical relaxation, breathing exercises, fantasy processes and meditation techniques. These are enjoyable experiences for most pupils who like the sense of peace and the feeling of quiet which is produced. It is through the raising of their own awareness that they have an opportunity to understand religious practices.

> 'Sitting quietly and doing nothing,.
> Spring comes and the grass grows by itself.'
>
> (Zenrin, *The Gospel According to Zen*)

ACTIVITIES

Silence

Purpose

'Silence!' is often used as a command to quieten a class so that another noise, perhaps the teacher talking, can begin. For the religious person, silent meditation can be the means of heightening consciousness and receiving insight. This exercise tries to create a silent space between sounds. It may be used as an introduction to stilling and, when followed by another exercise from this group, to show how silence can be put to use.

Time needed: Ten to fifteen minutes.

Materials needed: none.

Conditions

Some pupils find it difficult and even threatening to be silent for short periods of time. They should be encouraged to express these difficulties. Initially the period of silence should be very short but can be increased gradually as the pupils begin to feel more comfortable.

The situation of many classrooms makes it difficult to achieve total silence. If a quiet room is not available the exercise may still be worthwhile as pupils become aware of, and learn to shut out, external sounds to concentrate on their own thoughts.

Procedure

In a quiet, relaxed voice give the following instructions:

If you think five minutes is too long, try two minutes.

Pause long enough to let them get comfortable.

You should also be silent as you time the exercise. If you are using a clock, make sure its ticking does not disturb anyone.

Discussion can be in pairs, small groups or the entire class.

What I am about to ask you to do is not easy although the instructions sound very simple. In a moment I am going to ask you to **be silent for five minutes.**

1. First of all **make sure you are sitting in a comfortable position** . . . Try to **sit still.** Now **close your eyes**, if you feel you can, but **if not, try to look down** so that you can't see anyone else.
Just use the time to **think about what is happening, how you, and perhaps others, are feeling. We'll talk about this later**. There's no need to check your watch as I **will call time at the end of the five minutes.**
OK. The period of **silence begins NOW.**

2. **Turn to the person nearest to you**, and **spend a few minutes talking about this experience**. As you do so you might want to **consider these questions:**

Drawing out the learning

Unless there has already been class discussion, you may wish to raise these questions again at the end of the session to gain feedback from a larger number of pupils.

What is it like being silent?
What made it easy or difficult to do?
What did you like or not like about it?
What is it like being silent in a group of people?
How does it differ from being silent on your own?
How do you think silence might be of value?

During the discussion you may like to stop the pupils for a moment so that they can reflect on the noise of their conversation in contrast to the previous silence.

Variations

A picture of silence

Instead of talking about the experience, which disturbs the quieter mood induced by the silent period, the pupils could **draw something to express how they felt during the silence**. When they have finished drawing they can **talk about their pictures** and perhaps display them around the room. (Some pupils' responses are shown opposite.)

Silent thoughts

Another possibility is to ask the pupils to **write down the thoughts and images they had during the silence**. These will be very different. They could then **choose one or two thoughts which they don't mind sharing** with the rest of the class. Discussion could continue as for the main exercise. Pupils should of course have the freedom to "pass".

A follow-up exercise to this would be to ask pupils to **concentrate silently for two minutes on one of the ideas or images** which had come up during the exercise.

Most pupils find it difficult to concentrate and they will find their thoughts straying. Tell them this is normal and they should note when the mind begins to wander so that they can gently bring their thoughts back to the topic of concentration. They can then **talk about and compare their experiences.**

> "In this silence we listen for something that our mind has never conceived; we listen as if for a whisper which would be inaudible among the loud noises made by the daily striving and wants of our personality."
>
> (Ferrucci, *What We May Be*)

SILENCE! SILENCE!

I found it quite easy and I blocked out the world. It got harder as it went along. I felt alone and just with God.

I liked the ten minutes silence because I can talk to God.

I felt relaxed and different. It was very quite and peaceful, you had a chance to think about things you wouldn't normally think about. I thought was quite easy although some people were talking and distracting others.

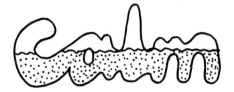

I felt very relaxed, and sort of happy, during the silence. Whilst I was talking to God he made me feel calm and wanted. It was difficult at first but as I started to get into it it became easier. I could speak to God and tell him everything, just as I was speaking to my friends. I felt happy inside because I was able to get rid of all my problems.

Can you remain silent for ten minutes? These third–year pupils at Christ the King Comprehensive, Nottingham, were asked to practise being silent as part of a series of lessons on Christian prayer.

Relax!

Purpose

Learning to relax the body is the first stage in stilling. A short relaxation can be used at the start or end of a lesson to calm the class or as a means of changing pace and mood between activities. This relaxed state is more conducive to learning and is also a preliminary to the experience of stilling for the religious person.

Time needed: Five minutes

Materials needed: None

Conditions

These exercises can be a little embarrassing the first time they are performed as pupils find themselves in a new situation and don't know what to expect. This is natural and may be shown by giggling and silly behaviour. To reduce the number of possible distractions the ideal group size is very small. However it is possible to do the same exercises with very large groups and some teachers have successfully used them in school assemblies.

It helps if the pupils have an idea of what is in store for them. As always, there should be the freedom to withdraw from the exercise for those who prefer not to join in. These activities are usually popular and those who do decide to opt out will probably change their minds when they see how enjoyable relaxation can be. The first few times should not be too long — a couple of minutes or so. The time can be increased gradually as pupils find it easier to relax.

Procedure

BODY POSITION
In a quiet, relaxed voice give the following instructions: If there is a carpeted area available, the pupils could lie down, or they can remain seated at their desks. Some may prefer not to shut their eyes and this should be respected. After the first attempt you could encourage them to find a position which suits them.

Get yourself into a comfortable position. A good position to be in is to **sit up straight, with both feet resting on the floor and your hands in your lap** or on the table in front of you.
Now close your eyes or look down so you can avoid looking at other people. You can peep if you need to but its easier to relax if you don't.

When everyone is comfortable there are a variety of methods which can be used to aid relaxation.

1. TENSING

Some children are not aware of the difference between relaxation and tension. This exercise helps them to notice the contrast between tensed and relaxed muscles. The body can be relaxed by progressively tensing and relaxing different parts and ending with a final tensing of the whole body and then relaxing. It may be easier to do this standing up.

Give the instructions in a slow and even tone.
Pause often.
You can extend this to work right through the body. For a more detailed example see 'Body-breath' on page 83.

Make a tight fist of your hand.
Notice what has happened to your arm.
Relax. Let the fist go.
Now **screw your face up tightly** and quickly **let that tightness or tension go.**

Another idea is for the pupils to stand up and tense all the body, to hold that tension for a few seconds and then relax and become floppy.

2. BREATHING

This can be combined with the other exercises or used on its own. Anyone who has asthma, hay fever or a bad cold may find emphasis on breathing to be unpleasant and they should have the freedom to withdraw.

Pupils could be asked to focus on the breath as it leaves and enters the nose. Or they can imagine all the tension and worries are released with the outgoing breath, while energy and light are breathed in.

Another possibility is to put the hands on the abdomen and notice its rise and fall with every breath.

Allow a minute or so to do this before continuing with your planned lesson.

3. IMAGERY

Visualising pleasant or relaxing images can also assist the stilling process. More ideas are given in the next exercise, 'Clearing the mind'.

Speak in a quiet and even tone of voice.
Pauses should be long enough for the mind to work through the image. Watch for signs of fidgeting which show pupils are ready to move on. Don't drag it out too long, but don't rush either.
Bring them quietly and gently back to the lesson.
You can use all sorts of images, the limit is really your own

I want you to **sit up straight** and **pay attention to your breathing.**
Breathe in slowly and, as you do so, count to four. One . . . two . . . three . . . four . . . Then breathe out, slowly counting to four again.
And repeat. Continue breathing in . . . counting . . . breathing out . . . and counting . . . for a little while.

Imagine you are floating on your back in a warm sea . . . Just lie back and relax . . . It's a salty sea so you are quite safe . . . no one can sink in this water . . . Look at the sky . . . Feel the warmth of the water . . . the warmth of the sunshine . . . Enjoy the gentle movement of the water against your body . . .

When you are ready . . . you can come back to this room . . . in your own time . . . you can open your eyes . . . and stretch if you need to.

imagination. Here are a few more ideas to get you started:

Imagine you have just arrived at your favourite place . . . It may be somewhere you know well or a place you have heard about, or seen in photographs. Where are you? Have a good look around you. What do you see? Notice the details, colours, shapes. What are you doing or what is happening around you? Is anyone else with you? How are you feeling? What are your thoughts? Feel yourself to be part of the scene . . . enjoy it.

Imagine you are watching a cat dozing in the sunshine. Look at it carefully. Notice the details of its colour, shape, and position. Watch carefully in your mind's eye as the cat gently flexes and stretches in its sleep. If you wish you can stroke the cat, and feel the warmth and softness of the fur as you stroke it.

This can be an effective image if there seems to be a lot of tension in the class:

Using your inner eye you can see a lake. Imagine you are standing beside the lake and a storm is raging. Look around and notice the effect of the storm. Watch the waves. Feel the wind. Listen to the sounds. As you are watching the storm slowly dies down, the water is less disturbed, the wind becomes a light breeze. At last the lake is peaceful and still again. Take another look around you and notice the changes . . . spend a few moments watching the scene.

As the skill of visualisation improves, more lengthy images can be used or pupils could be asked to concentrate on seeing one image and holding that image in their minds, not letting their thoughts wander, for as long as possible. A few seconds can be quite an achievement for many people.

Drawing out the learning

Allow a short time to talk in small groups or as a class about their experience.

What was it like for you?
In what ways did you find it easy or difficult to do?
What did you like or not like about it?
How did you feel during the exercise?
How are you feeling now?
What value do you think activities like this might have for you, or for other people?

Imagery is enjoyed by all ages and is a popular exercise used in many schools. These examples of pupils' comments come from Durham.

> **"I felt strange like I was flying. I also felt proud and happy. I felt hungry."**
>
> (Ashley Murray, aged 10, Tanfield Lea Juniors)

> **"I felt a bit embarrassing and shy but so did all the class."**
>
> (Anon. 2nd year, Seaham Comprehensive)

> **"I felt different because I have never been that relaxed in my life when I have been at school."**
>
> (Anon. 3rd year, Seaham Comprehensive)

> **"I think it is very good because if you come in feeling tense you can go out feeling relaxed. It also helps you to think more about the lesson. I would like us to do this every week."**
>
> (Susan Millen, aged 12, Pelton Roseberry Comprehensive)

Clearing the mind

Purpose

A jumble of disconnected thoughts and images frequently occupies our minds. Constantly demanding recognition, this perpetual brainstorm resists our efforts to direct and maintain attention on a single point. Total concentration on stilling is therefore impossible until we are able to clear a space in our minds.

Visualisation can be an enjoyable step towards the stilling of thoughts. By focusing the imagination, this meditation technique creates a channel to unite the often divided energies of the mind. With practice, pupils can improve their ability to clear their minds and so still their thoughts. In this new state of consciousness, the intuition may be freed and new ways of experiencing explored.

Time needed: Ten to twenty minutes.

Materials needed: None

Conditions

There needs to be sufficient space available for everyone to spread out so that they are comfortable and not too close to others. If there is a carpeted area some, if not all, pupils may prefer to lie down. Otherwise they might like to put their arms on the tables so they can rest their heads on them. Eyes should, but do not have to be, closed. Subdued lighting can be used to set the mood.

Any interruptions or outside noises can sometimes be accepted and put aside more easily if their existence is acknowledged quietly by a suitable comment being added to the script.

You can use any of these guidelines or create your own. Always ensure that the class is comfortable and relaxed before starting. Read the instructions slowly and in measured tones, pausing long enough for the scene to work through the pupils' minds. The length of pauses varies but you can get an idea of timing by following the imagery in your own mind. By watching people's movements you can soon learn to gauge the pace and type of instructions to give. Care needs to be taken to bring the class out of the stillness gradually and quietly — allowing time to stretch, move and to re-establish themselves in the room and in the present.

Procedure

MY COMPUTER MIND

Sit still or lie down in a comfortable position. Imagine that your mind is like a computer screen . . . As you watch you can see lots of words and pictures forming . . . These are your thoughts . . . Just watch them for a while . . . You may notice that they change and that you can key in new thoughts which will then appear on the screen . . . Now reach out for the 'break' key . . . you know that when you press this key all the images and words will disappear. OK . . . press the break key . . . now all you can see is a blank screen . . . The screen is clear . . . just watch it . . . If most pictures appear you can press the break key again.

PROBLEM PUDDLES

Get comfortable and relax . . . Now think of a problem or something which worries you . . . You won't have to talk about it . . . There may be a number of things which come to your mind . . . just choose one of them . . . Now imagine that this problem is a puddle of water . . . it's lying on the ground in front of you . . . what shape is it? . . . what colour is it? . . . As you look at the puddle you begin to feel warm and you notice that the sun has come out . . . Watching the puddle you know that the heat from the sun is making the water evaporate . . . as you go on watching the puddle gradually disappears . . . Slowly the heat of the sun dries up the water . . .

WAVES

Get into a comfortable position and relax . . . Now go inside yourself. You are going to see with your inner eye . . . you can see that you are on a beach . . . you are walking along the beach to the seashore . . . you can hear the waves gently lapping the

Instead of writing their name, younger pupils could imagine building a sand castle and watching as the waves slowly lap the edges of the mound of sand and gradually wash it away.

Other ideas

a) A large tent full of people, objects and problems. As you watch a wind comes and blows everything away, leaving the tent open and clear.

b) Gazing down a deep well, slowly looking further and further down until you can see the water at the very bottom. Look at the water for a while and then slowly lift your gaze upwards, noticing that it is getting lighter and lighter.

c) Walking along a path, it's a lovely day, sunny and warm. After a while stop beside a clear pool of water. Throw a stone into the water and watch the ripples. As the ripples subside look at the smooth surface of the water.

sand . . . perhaps you can feel the coarse sand with your bare feet . . . the day is warm and the sun is shining . . . you feel peaceful and comfortable . . . Now you bend down and slowly write your name in the sand . . . see the letters of your name form in the sand . . . Now you can see a wave coming. It's only a small wave . . . it slowly washes up to you and gently flows over and into the letters of your name . . . As the wave flows back into the sea you can see that the sand is clean and smooth again . . . You may like to sit down and watch the waves lapping on the sand . . .

Drawing out the learning

Pupils usually want to talk about what they've been doing. This can be done in pairs, groups or with the whole class. They may prefer to express their reactions and feelings by drawing or writing.

What did you think about that experience?
What happened — if anything?
Did you notice anything in particular?
Was there anything which surprised you?
What were the things you liked, or disliked?
How do you feel right now?

Comments

Guided imagery of this kind is an introduction to fantasy techniques described later.
"I think guided imagery has helped me to relax and understand things and see things from a different side." (Steven Coombe, aged twelve, Pelton Roseberry Comprehensive)

Body–breath

Purpose

This is a more advanced and extended exercise to still the body and concentrate the mind. Attention is focused on the here–and–now, raising awareness of the body and then turning to the breath. In Zen this type of breathing is used almost as a mantra, the repetition of which helps the novice to still the mind more deeply. After doing this exercise pupils often appear to be more alert and attentive.

Time needed: Thirty minutes or more

Materials needed: None

Conditions

Ideally there should be space for everyone who wishes to lie down, although the exercise is also successful when seated. Lighting should not be too bright. Although intended to induce relaxation, turning attention to various parts of the body can also increase tension. You should explain this before starting. Suggest that if anyone notices tension they should give it their full awareness, noting which part of the body is tense and what it feels like. Attention should be paid to how that tension is being created in an effort to relax that part of the body.

   Mention of parts of the body can be embarrassing. Before using this exercise make sure the class is used to and feels comfortable with the stilling process. Any interruptions should be noted before continuing with the exercise.

Procedure

It is not essential to work right through the exercise; some parts could be adapted or omitted, depending on what you consider most appropriate for your pupils.

Allow time for everyone to settle, either sitting or lying in silence. Adopt a relaxed tone of voice, pausing to give time for every one to respond.

1. Get into a comfortable position, and close your eyes.

2. Just spend a moment or two concentrating on your thoughts. **What is going on in your mind right now?** Are you thinking about something that has happened — thoughts of the past — or about something that might happen — in the future?

3. You can return to these thoughts later but I'd like you now to **turn your attention to what is happening HERE. What is going on NOW.**
Be aware that you are in this room . . . taking part in this lesson . . . with these people . . .

4. I am going to ask you to become aware of certain sensations in your body that you are feeling at this present moment.
First get in touch with your body . . . Are you really comfortable? . . . If necessary, see if you can get more comfortable by changing your position slightly.

Depending on your time limit and the response of the group, this can be done fairly quickly or quite slowly.

5. Your awareness is like a searchlight. Whatever you focus your attention on becomes clearer but other things tend to fade . . . Become aware of what you can hear . . . Perhaps you now notice sounds and noises which you had previously missed . . . **While you are doing this you are mostly unaware of the sensations in your hands . . . As I mention your hands, your attention probably moves there** and you become aware of the sensations in your hands . . . As your attention moves there, so **your awareness of sounds fades away . . .**

At this point some pupils may start to get a little embarrassed. You may find it necessary to omit some suggestions or move on more quickly.

6. Now I'm going to ask you to follow my suggestions and allow your attention to shift.
First, **focus your attention on your feet**. How do they feel? Where are the points of contact with the ground, your shoes? Can you flex your toes? And let them relax. **Now tighten the muscles in your legs** . . . hold that tension for a moment . . . and let it go. Be aware of how your clothing touches your legs . . . how does that feel? Now **move your attention up your body to your bottom** . . . tense the muscles . . . and then release the tension . . . Now **do the same with your stomach . . . chest . . . shoulders** . . . Again **be aware of the feel of your clothes on your back . . . your arms . . . and hands** . . . Finish off for yourself by **working upwards, around the face and right up to the top of your head, being aware of each part of the body in turn.**

Pause long enough to let them do this.

7. Now **turn your attention to your breathing.** Take a few deep breaths . . . breathe deeply and let it out slowly . . . **While you are breathing out imagine that all the bad and unpleasant things inside you** . . . your worries, difficulties, aches and pains . . . **are going away with your breath.**
Take another breath . . . breathing in . . . and out. In your mind **count to four while you are breathing in . . . and again as you breathe out.** Breathing in . . . one — two — three — four, and out . . . one — two — three — four.
Pay special attention to breathing in . . . imagine that you are **breathing in goodness . . . comfort . . . warmth . . . whatever you need.**

You might suggest that they imagine this as a warm, white light slowly being breathed into their bodies.

Pause for a short while.

Continue being aware of your breathing. Don't try to control it, just watch. Be aware of air coming in and out of your nostrils . . . observe the breath . . . try to concentrate all your attention on the breath.

When you find your thoughts wandering, don't worry but gently bring them back to your breath.

Let the air breathe you.

Pause.

Pause as long as necessary.

8. Now let the awareness return to your body. In your own time you can begin to move again, wriggle your toes, or stretch slowly. You can **open your eyes when you are ready**.

Drawing out the learning

Before rounding off the session with class feedback, pupils may wish to talk in pairs or small groups about their experience.

What was that experience like for you?
Did you find it difficult or easy to keep your mind following the instructions?
Were there any tensions in your body?
Did they increase or did they go away?
Was your level of awareness any different from normal?
Did anything in particular strike your attention?
How do you feel now?
What is there about this exercise that makes it of value for religious people?

Variation

Step by step
This variation has been used with some success on in–service training courses. While there are obviously constraints which affect its suitability for use in the classroom, you may be interested to try it yourself. It can be used as a follow–on to breathing in the previous exercise. Some pupils may be receptive to this type of walking meditation but it is a serious activity and not suitable for beginners.

By concentrating on the finest detail of very step it becomes easier to keep the mind from wandering and to concentrate on the here and now. With practice this meditation technique can be extended to cover any and every activity of our waking hours. This Buddhist way of mindfulness — Vipassana — is said to create the possibility of insight.

You will need plenty of space to walk around. During this walk you may be more aware than usual of sights and sounds and scents and you will walk much more slowly. Every movement you make should be in slow motion, making the details of each step more obvious.

As you are walking, pay attention to your feet. Notice how you start off on one foot, how the foot moves as it lifts off the ground, how it feels as it swings through the air and then lowers to the ground again.

Then be aware of the precise movements of your other foot. Step by step, notice the slightest detail of every movement.

Don't worry when you find your attention wandering; this is normal. When you find yourself thinking about something other than your walking, just notice what has made your thoughts stray and then bring your awareness back to your walk.

At the end of your walking meditation you could choose to write a Haiku or draw or model something to express your experience.

Haiku

Worrying about how to express an experience can spoil that experience; and yet the experience may evoke great feeling which can be expressed in a few short words.

Haiku is a three–line poetic form originating from Japan. The content is usually derived from nature and illustrates the poet's awareness of the environment. It stems from an experience in which the author opens all the senses to her surroundings. Trying to be aware of everything, she does not discriminate or differentiate but accepts all that comes to her. From this intermingling of the senses it becomes possible to write a haiku without thought or hesitation. The poem is produced spontaneously and captures a point of experience.

While the traditional haiku is composed of seventeen syllables with five syllables in the first and third lines and seven in the middle, pupils should not worry about following the exact form. The idea is to see the poem as a means of reflecting a moment of vivid awareness.

Perhaps the easiest way to demonstrate how to write a haiku is to start with a class brainstorm. Brainstorming one word will produce other words. The next stage is to turn these words into phrases. Then you can use those phrases to compose a haiku.

IN PRACTICE

Let's sit still

Some primary school teachers have indicated that their children find it almost impossible to relax and be still. This problem may be aggravated in open plan schools where there is continuous and noisy activity; therefore the children are not used to silence and the conditions for stilling are difficult, but not impossible, to achieve.

Kathy Raban taught six–year–olds in an open–plan primary school in Leicestershire. Three classes shared the same area, which meant there were over ninety young children in the same space. Fortunately Kathy was able to arrange to take her class into a small but quieter room for short periods each week.

She wanted her class to value stillness and to be capable of going 'inside themselves'. She sees this as a skill which, like sitting still, is not easy to do but can be learned gradually. Silence can be threatening for some children so she made sure that they felt comfortable and safe. The room was lit by natural light since a darkened room may be frightening. Kathy reassured them by telling them what was happening and when they were used to the exercise she suggested she should stop talking so that they could remain silent for a short period of time.

The children sat in a circle in any position they found comfortable. In the centre of the circle was a lighted candle. At first Kathy asked them to watch the candle flame for a period of thirty seconds. She talked to them in a soft and gentle voice and spoke continuously, telling them to look at the flame and then to close their eyes and concentrate on seeing an image of the candle.

Repeating this exercise regularly, Kathy extended the time by adding another thirty seconds each week until they could sit still and quietly for ten minutes. She was able to integrate this practice into a study of the Hindu festival of Divali when the children made clay lamps and meditated on the flame.

While this exercise worked well with Kathy's class, others may find it less successful. Tom Limb teaches eight–year–olds in a Nottingham primary school and has tried a number of different stilling techniques. Looking at the candle flame was not very popular with his class but rather than abandon the idea of stilling altogether he tried other ways. This is his report:

"I wanted them to participate in the decision–making process involved with any activity, including stilling, so I started off by throwing out a challenge. I said, 'Let's practise being quiet. Make the most of it, children, the teacher's here telling you to do nothing special.' Of course I made sure they didn't achieve it. I just said, 'Be quiet!' and they couldn't. They were shuffling all the time so I broke it off and said, 'Ah, I didn't think you could do it.'

Then I offered to help by letting them try different ways of being quiet. I said, 'Perhaps you'll be able to be quiet and feel the quietness more if you listen for it after a lot of noise. Let's make a noise quietly. Find a sound to make and build it up and then when I blow the whistle . . . listen to the silence'. They did that.

Then I suggested they could try something else. 'Let's try lying flat on the floor so that you are not looking at anybody else. Being aware of other people may tempt you to make a noise so look at the ceiling instead. Now let's think about breathing.' They concentrated on their breathing in several ways and then sat up and discussed which was the best way of staying quiet and how it helped them.

In another session they watched the flame of a candle and compared that experience with other methods of stilling they had tried. Just looking at the candle flame didn't seem to work for many of them in that particular group. What did work was counting of breaths when they were lying on their backs, especially when they had their eyes closed. They hadn't particularly noticed that closing their eyes was helping them but they were quieter.

The children learnt a lot. Being still was a new experience for them. They're under pressure to do something all the time; something grown–ups think is purposeful. It's rare for them to sit still and do nothing except be conscious, with others, and perhaps reflect on themselves. I hoped I was offering them a little space in their busy lives when they could reflect, not on action, but on being.

Stilling activities raised their awareness of the difficulty of doing nothing with their bodies and tongues. They became more aware of the differences between people and could accept that, just as some children find it easy to draw a picture and others don't, so some people find it very hard to be quiet. They also fastened on to the notion of centring, finding their centre and being balanced. This had a lot of meaning for them especially when they imagined breathing in through the tummy button and taking that breath to their centre.''

While these children obviously gained in self–understanding and empathy, they were also, to some extent, entering into the world of the religious believer who practises silence in order to hear the 'inner voice'. By adapting exercises intended to raise awareness, both teachers found their own ways of helping children in infant and junior classes to experience inner stillness.

Learning about Buddhism — the Buddhist way

Second year pupils at Usworth Comprehensive School in Washington, Tyne and Wear, had completed traditional work on the Eightfold Path of Buddhism. Their teacher, Joan Formosa, was not satisfied, feeling that they had experienced nothing of the impact of following such a path. She decided to have another go and this time concentrated on 'right mindfulness'. It seemed appropriate to use one of the stilling exercises which would create a new experience for her classes:

"To help the pupils concentrate, I guided them through an awareness of the various parts of their body, starting with breathing and finishing by asking them to be aware of the images behind their eyelids. I was amazed at the stillness and quiet in three of the four classes. In the other group only two pupils giggled for a short time.

I then asked the pupils to write down anything they thought or felt during the time and to choose one thing they could share with the group. This was the first time every pupil responded confidently. Two pupils who have never given an oral answer all year were able to contribute, seemingly without embarrassment.

I felt that I was getting somewhere with the experience but wanted to get back to the Eightfold Path. I therefore asked the pupils why they thought many religions, including Buddhism, suggested that their members should give some time to quiet mindfulness. Their responses were most encouraging — having experienced a short period of stillness, they could now see how it might have some real value."

After hearing of Joan's experience teaching about right mindfulness, another teacher suggested using a statue or image of the Buddha to encourage pupils to reflect on the meaning and significance of the classic pose of meditation. Statues and pictures of the Buddha frequently show him sitting in the lotus position; his face is peaceful and serene. Pupils can focus their attention on the image for a short while before sharing their impressions. If necessary the teacher can guide them to consider the Buddha's facial expression as well as the position he is sitting in. Discussion can draw out the significance of meditation for the believer. Pupils may like to experiment with meditative postures for themselves, using some of the ideas found in the stilling exercises.

Chapter 9

Embodying awareness

INTRODUCTION

When stilling and listening, pupils are asked to be mindful of their own bodies and to notice the use of body language. Now, in Embodying Awareness, time is given to exploring the fact that each of us has a life history which gives us a unique personal identity. This life history is the product of the particular culture and era in which we live.

Experience of the world differs according to whether I am male or female, affluent or poor, my ethnic group, physical appearance, the beliefs of those in charge of my upbringing, as well as the ups and downs of my life. Factors like these determine the aspects of reality that seem important to me. As my awareness develops, it does so in a context which powerfully affects the attitudes and interpretations I bring to my experience. This unique life–history therefore governs what I am likely to notice and what I will probably miss.

If I continually ask myself "Who am I?", the answers can go beyond the external details of my life history, touching on the mystery of human existence. It is at this more profound level that religions approach the question of identity, even to the point of paradox; thus in Buddhism the existence of a "self" is denied.

Since people experience and understand the world in so many different ways, it is often difficult to see the other person's point of view with any sympathy. This is especially true in RE when pupils are asked to respect and appreciate religious beliefs or life–stances that are different from their own. The exercises in this family group are concerned with helping pupils recognise that human awareness is 'embodied'. They can increase their understanding of themselves as unique individuals and begin the practice of empathising with other points of view. The exercises can also open up the more awesome question of ultimate identity.

'What can I do, Muslims? I do not know myself.
I am no Christian, no Jew, no Magian, no Muslim.
Not of the East, not of the West. Not of the land, not of the sea.
Not of the mine of Nature, not of the Circling heavens, Not of earth, not of water, not of air, not of fire . . .
My place placeless, my trace traceless.
Neither body nor soul: all is the life of my Beloved . . .'

(Jalaludin Rumi)

MYSELF: OVERVIEW

> **'If you cannot find it in yourself, where will you go for it?'**
>
> (Chinese proverb)

The aspect of reality that is closest to us is ourselves. We know more about ourselves than anyone else, yet seldom reflect on our own life–history. Religious people, because of their beliefs, tend to expect their lives to have some pattern, meaning or purpose. Often, when they examine their life–journey, they believe that they can discern something of that pattern or meaning.

From another point of view, this everyday self is also utterly mysterious. Beyond the details of name, nationality, life–history and so on, we are still left with a more ultimate question, 'Who is it that has this name, nationality, life–history?' To the devout individual, this is a profoundly religious question, explored through meditation, prayer and theological and philosophical reflection.

The exercises in this section enable pupils to begin to make a practical exploration of these two dimensions of human experience in their own lives.

> **'Lift up the self by the Self, And don't let the self droop down,**
> **For the Self is the self's only friend, And the self is the Self's only foe.'**
>
> (*Bhagavad Gita* Ch 6 v 5)

ACTIVITIES

The question of privacy is one of the issues which can be raised by pupils taking part in these activities. It is easier, more acceptable and safer to talk about the public aspects of ourselves than the private ones, therefore it is important that pupils should not feel obliged to disclose private information. These exercises could be preceded by one which looks at privacy and the appropriateness of disclosure.

Privacy circles

Purpose

This activity is designed to help pupils consider their patterns of privacy and disclosure in relation to their feelings, opinions and actions. It may also raise questions like: "Am I too open?" or, "Am I too withdrawn?"

Time needed: Thirty minutes

Materials needed: Concentric circles (p. 230 can be copied), one for each person.

Privacy circles

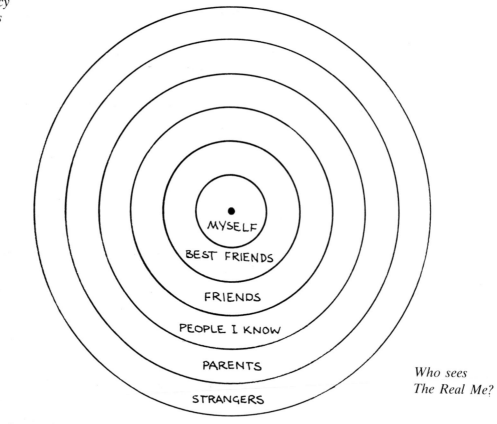

Who sees The Real Me?

Conditions

Questions in Stage 4 should be chosen appropriate to the age and background of the group. There needs to be sufficient space for pupils to have privacy while writing down their responses.

Procedure

Each person receives a set of concentric circles, drawn on a sheet of paper. Explain what each band represents, starting with the outermost one and moving inwards.

1. There are some things in our lives we would be glad to let anybody know — favourite TV shows, games we like, and so on. Even strangers can be told this. Other things we would rather strangers didn't know, but we would tell classmates, or people we work with. Still other things we would reserve for friends. Then there are thoughts and feelings we have, or things we've done or do, which we would tell only our most intimate friends. Finally, there may be some bits of our lives which we wouldn't want to share with anyone; these are reserved for ourselves. There are even some feelings or facts that we don't admit to ourselves and these are acknowledged in the last small circle which is darkened.

2. Write down two things — they could be beliefs, feelings or actions — about yourself which are appropriate to each band of the circle. These should indicate the kind of things which you

would be willing to talk about to the people in that band. The SELF section includes things which you only admit to yourself.

3. When you have finished, **spend a few moments thinking about what you've written down**.

You could substitute any questions you feel appropriate.

4. Now I'd like you to **write down the answers to some questions** I'm going to ask. For example, "Which television programme do you prefer?"
Instead of answering the question, write the keyword of the question, 'TELEVISION', in the band which shows to whom you would be willing to reveal your answer.
Do the same for the rest of these questions:
a) What you cried about last time. (Key word: CRIED)
b) Whether or not you liked one of your parents better than the other. (PARENTS)
c) What you dislike about your best friend. (FRIEND)
d) The details of your spiritual or religious experience. (SPIRITUAL)
e) Details of your feelings about your boyfriend or girlfriend. (FEELINGS)
f) Your dissatisfaction with some part of your body. (BODY)

5. As far as you feel comfortable, tell your partner how you filled in the circles and discuss what made you choose to fill them in the way you did. How alike or unlike are your responses?

Journey of life

Purpose

The concept of pattern and direction in life is common to many aspects of religious belief. The object of this exercise is to consider where life has taken us so far, and to notice some of the beliefs and values that influence our lives.

Time needed: Thirty minutes

Materials needed: Large sheets of paper (preferably A3) and drawing materials

Conditions

Seeing your life recorded on a sheet of paper can be a salutary experience, so this exercise requires a sensitive approach. A lighthearted introductory activity can help to create the right kind of mood, e.g. brainstorming "Life is like . . .", or a metaphor exercise, "If life was a colour, flower, building, etc. it would be . . .". There needs to be enough space for everyone to work on their own.

Procedure

Distribute paper, pens, etc. Make sure everyone can work with some degree of privacy.

Allow a short time.

1. Let's **imagine** for a moment **that life is like a journey** that begins at birth. Take a few moments to **recall the various stages of your journey through life so far**. What are your most vivid memories?

2. Now **spend some time thinking about how your life could be represented on paper as a journey**. For example, have you experienced any ups and downs? What are the turning points in your life — for example, when you started school or began a new hobby? Are there any crossroads in your journey — times when you had to decide what to do next. Don't forget that your life story is continuing and you haven't reached the end of your journey yet.

Ask the class to suggest a selection of possibilities, e.g. a journey across different kinds of terrain or in various types of transport — a plane when flying high, a submarine for the low spots in life, etc.

Allow ten or fifteen minutes.

3. Draw your life as a journey in any way you like.

This process is very personal, therefore, pupils should be given the freedom to select their own partners or remain alone if they wish.

Pupils may be encouraged to thank each other before moving on.
Pupils could suggest other safety rules.

4. In your own time and, **if it feels right for you, choose someone to talk to**. But before you start, let's establish some ground rules.
Don't refuse to listen to someone who brings their journey to you. Listen sensitively to their story.
When you have finished talking about their journey, find someone to share your journey with you. You do not have to share your life journey if you don't want to. You may prefer to spend the time reflecting on your own.

You may prefer to change the questions and/or have them duplicated beforehand.

5. Before discussing the drawings, let's consider a few questions. It might help to write them down.
What do you need to survive on your journey?

Where is your journey leading?
What have been the major turning points?
Do you have a map to help you find your way?

6. When you are ready find a partner and talk about your ideas.

Drawing out the learning

When pupils have had about ten minutes to talk to a friend, it may be appropriate to draw them together in groups to talk about their response to this activity and how it felt to see their lives represented in this way.

The 'Life is like' brainstorm can be used as a lighthearted ending to the session if it has not been used as an introduction.

Variation

Lifeline
Life can be represented as a line which rises and falls according to happy and sad events. For younger pupils, this can be done to represent a much shorter period, e.g. a day or a weekend.

Comment

The 'Journey of Life' can be used when studying the Rites of Passage. Exploring the idea of a map to guide one's path in life can form a useful introduction to a study of a particular religion's tenets. This activity is extended in 'Life is like . . .' on page 126.
Chapter 11 on story also develops the theme of life's journey.

Example

Some six and seven–year–olds from Sproatley Endowed School in North Humberside looked at the journey of life from the point of view of a single day. The teacher gave a simplified version of the instructions, asking the children to draw the ups and downs of their day so far. First year pupils at Bramcote Hills Comprehensive School, Nottingham, used fantasy based on the Mr Men theme to stimulate ideas for their 'Journey of Life'. (Their drawings are shown on page 96.) Their teacher, Viv Peters, gives a brief outline of the lesson.

"Through fantasy the class travels along a path, meeting various characters of their own choice at crossroads or bridges. For example, they might talk to Mr Sad, Mrs Hatred, Miss Giving and decide if they want to take them on their journey or say goodbye to them. As the fantasy continues they can jot down who they accept and who they reject. Afterwards they map out their journey, using thumb–print drawings to represent each character they encountered and then write a little about why they accepted or rejected each one. Finally they are asked to consider what kind of person they might be at the end of the journey, if they have taken on the characters of the people they have met. This leads into a discussion about whether other people become part of us through our relationships with them.

*Pupils' work
Bramcote Hills
School, Nottingham*

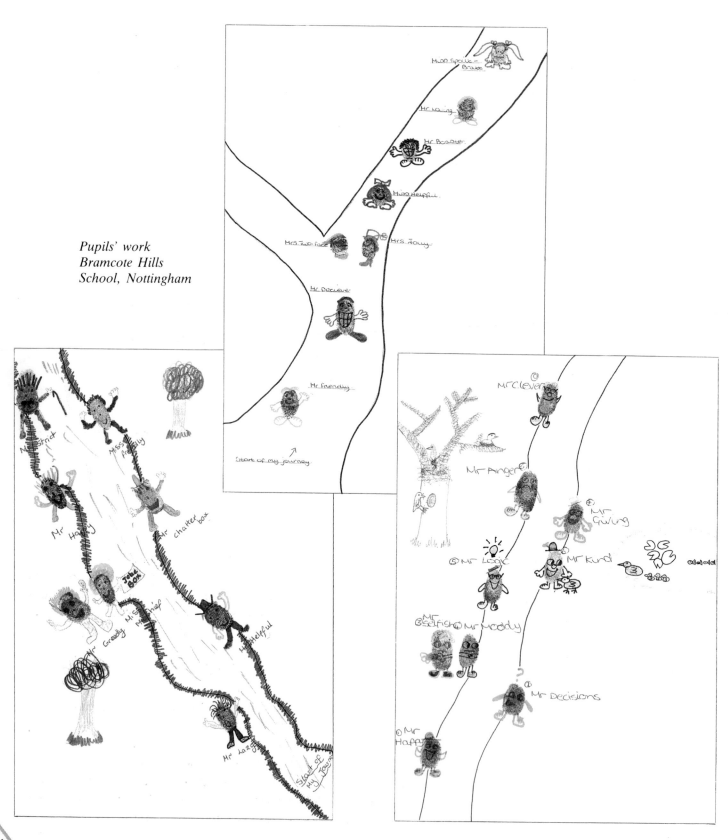

The Real Me

Purpose

The realisation that there may be a difference between the 'person we present to the world' and the 'inner me' is highlighted by this structure. As the exercise involves working with other members of the group the emphasis can also be placed on pupils discovering more about each other rather than learning about themselves.

Time needed: Forty minutes

Materials needed: Index cards, pens, plain paper and drawing materials

Conditions

Pupils working in pairs and small groups should be spaced around the room to ensure some degree of privacy. Materials should be easily available on demand Three pupils could work together if necessary to absorb any odd numbers. It may be more appropriate for younger pupils to begin with Stage 5. Some preliminary discussion about 'inside me' and 'outside me' might be necessary.

Procedure

Arrange the group in pairs. Each person will need an index card and pen or pencil.

You may wish to offer guidance on the type of questions they could ask, e.g. What do you value most? What do you believe in? How would you spend your ideal day?

1. Imagine you want to get to know someone a lot better. You already know some basic facts like name, age and address but want to find out more about them. **Think about the questions you might ask in order to discover the person they feel they really are.**

2. Now **write down five questions** that you could ask that person to discover more about them.

3. When you are ready, **exchange cards with your partner**. Take it in turns to **ask your partner the questions on the card you have just been given. Write down their answers.** You may "pass" on any question which you would rather not answer.

You could ask for any number of questions.
Allow five minutes.
Allow ten minutes.

Allow a short time for some discussion, to begin to draw out the learning.

Ensure everyone has a sheet of plain paper and drawing materials.

It may be appropriate at this point to remind pupils that there is no need to discuss anything they are uncomfortable about.

4. As soon as you have both finished, **swop cards again and have a look at the answers you gave**. You might like to talk about your responses with your partner.

What, if anything, did you discover about yourself from this exercise?
How did it feel to be asked your own questions?
How do you feel about the answers you gave?

5. Fold your sheet of paper in half and open it out again. **In one half draw or write something to represent 'the inside you'** — the person that you feel you are deep down inside.

6. On the other half of the piece of paper, illustrate in any way you like 'the outside you' — the way you present yourself to the world.

7. When you are ready, **talk about your drawing or writing with your partner**.

8. In a few moments I'm going to ask you to team up with two other couples, to **form groups of six**. Then you can **tell that group something about your partner**. But **first check with your partner what you are going to say**.

9. When you are ready join up with another two pairs and take turns to tell the group some of the thoughts expressed by your partner.

Drawing out the learning

How easy was it to represent the inner and outer you?
How similar or dissimilar are your inner and outer self?
What surprises were there for you or for others?

Variations

Inside Me is Outside Me   The inner and outer self can also be expressed through the use of movement or body sculpture. Pupils can be asked to use their bodies to form shapes portraying the 'inside me' and the 'outside me'.

IN PRACTICE

A matrioshka doll is a useful visual aid when trying to explain the inner and outer self. Three teachers explain how they approached The Real Me with the help of this Russian doll.

Discussing dreams with a class of six–year–olds seemed to lead quite naturally to the theme of the inner self. Their teacher, Kathy Raban, introduced the children to the idea that there are lots of different people inside each person, there's the happy person, the sad person, the dreamer, etc. They were all accustomed to stilling exercises so she gave them a minute or two to reflect on what was going on inside them. Then the children cut out paper shaped like a matrioshka doll and drew a picture of their outer selves, showing the clothes they were wearing that day. (The matrioshka or Russian doll is a large wooden doll containing a series of smaller dolls, each decreasing in size.) On the other side of the paper they pictured what-ever they felt was inside themselves.

The matrioshka doll helped Tom Limb explore The Real Me with junior pupils.

"I started the lesson by taking the doll apart as I talked about the different sides of our individual natures. I said that we're all rather like this doll since we each have an outside, exterior, self which everyone can see. Deep down inside, however, we've got a very private self which is what we are when we are on our own. Then there are shades of our personality which are in between the private and the public self. Next we used movement and dance to reflect on the public image of ourselves. The class was in the hall and ready to let off some steam so I played disco music and asked them to show how they behaved at the last school disco. After a few questions to help them consider that side of their character they tried body sculpture to portray their private self.

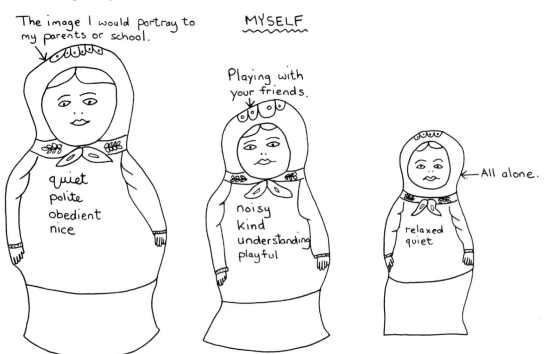

The image I would portray to my parents or school.

MYSELF

Playing with your friends.

All alone.

quiet
polite
obedient
nice

noisy
kind
understanding
playful

relaxed
quiet

They moulded partners into a position which showed what they, the moulder, did in private. Each sculptor admired the work of the other sculptors, spotting readers, games players and computer–buffs. I'd asked them to show me what they do and then think about the way they behaved during that activity. No one opted for abstract positions which showed what sort of people they are. Everyone had the chance to be both model and sculptor as well as look at the work of other people. I asked them what it felt like to model an activity they didn't normally do and then suggested that this could give a glimpse of what it's like to be your partner. The session ended with an exchange of gifts, passing on a quality they felt they possessed to their partners. (See page 172.)

The connection between a Russian doll and the life of the reformed gangster, Nicky Cruz, is not immediately obvious to everyone. However one comprehensive school teacher, Kay Steel, was impressed by this approach when she compared the responses of two first–year mixed ability classes. The topic was 'self' and the scheme of work at Spennymoor Comprehensive School required a study of the life of Nicky Cruz. Normally this was done by reading about and then discussing the life of 'The Gangster who Cried'. That was how the first class, acting as a control group, covered the work.

A second, very similar group, 1U, followed a different method. Their work began with a metaphor exercise, 'Hammer and nail' (see page 131), which introduced them to like–minded pupils. Having found a partner whose choices were similar to their own, they discussed their responses and went on to talk about themselves for two minutes. After a short time reflecting on how they see themselves, pupils again worked with a partner completing statements such as, "If we were animals I'd be a . . . . and you'd be a . . . ." (see page 105). Talking about their choices certainly made them think a little more about themselves and consider the different impression they can make on others. Working alone they each drew a large face, dividing it into two. In one half they drew something to represent the image they thought they showed to others. The other side of the face symbolised how they felt inside.

The matrioshka doll made its appearance in the follow–up lesson to reinforce the idea that we can seem big and strong on the outside while feeling quite different inside. Pupils considered the various images of themselves which they try to project in different circumstances. Picturing themselves as three parts of a Russian doll, they described the image they show to parents and teachers, that which is revealed to friends and finally the way they perceived themselves. When drawing out their learning they explored in some depth why they considered it necessary to reveal particular aspects of themselves to different people.

While both classes read about the lifestory of Nicky Cruz and used brainstorming to explore his character, pupils in 1U were able to build on the experience of these two lessons. Comparison of classwork and examination results revealed that 1U remembered the story more accurately and displayed greater insight and understanding.

"Who am I?"

"Who are *you*?" said the Caterpillar.
This was not an encouraging opening for a conversation. Alice replied, rather shyly, "I — I hardly know, sir, just at present — at least I know who I was when I got up this morning, but I think I must have been changed several times since then."
"What do you mean by that?" said the Caterpillar sternly. "Explain yourself!"

(Lewis Carroll, *Alice in Wonderland*)

Purpose

The search to discover our own personal identity involves asking ourselves the ultimate question, "Who am I?", yet the answer may lie in our experience rather than in words. Since other people can help us in our quest to discover who we are, this activity involves working with a partner. It is based on a zen exercise, using the koan "Who am I?".

Time needed: Forty–five minutes. If time is short, this activity can be divided into two sections. Stage 7 can become the start of the second session.

Materials needed: Paper, pencils, drawing materials. A copy of *Alice in Wonderland* by Lewis Carroll, if required.

Conditions

The answers to the question, "Who am I?" can be deeply personal and the consideration of 'who we are' may be a revealing experience. Pupils should therefore have the opportunity to work with some degree of privacy.

Procedure

A lighthearted way to open this exercise is to read an extract from *Alice in Wonderland*, in which the caterpillar asks Alice "Who are you?".

Explain the instructions clearly so that pupils feel comfortable about the activity. The answer to the question, "Who am I?" is much more than my name, age and address.

1. At times we may all have felt a bit like Alice, feeling unsure about who we really are. During this exercise we are going to **think about the question, "Who am I?"** Perhaps we can help each other to discover some answers.

Arrange the group in pairs and groups of six.

Give out cards/paper and pencils.

2. Find someone you'd like to work with and then join up with two other couples.

3. When everyone is in groups and you know who you'll be working with later, go back to your partner and spread yourselves out around the room.

4. Working with your partner, ask yourself the question, "Who is . . . .?" (partner's name). Think about that question and **write down four answers.**

Allow a short time.

5. Show your list to your partner and talk about the things you wrote down. For example, you might have said: ". . . . is a good runner, a boy, a kind person, has a paper round."

With some groups it may be appropriate to get the partner's permission before sharing what was written.

6. Now **rejoin your group and share these statements** with them, saying how far your partner was satisfied with your ideas.

Allow a short time.

Space out in pairs in order to allow more space for privacy.

7. Go back to your partner again and space yourselves out. **Decide who's going to be A and B.** This time we'll see if you can answer the question yourself — with a little bit of support from your partner.

Stress that A should not suggest answers or comment in any way about B's responses.

8. A, ask B the question, "Who are you?" and write down B's answer. Don't say anything about B's answers, just write them down and then repeat the question. If he or she takes a long time to answer, ask the question again. Use a quiet tone as if you are just reminding your partner of the question.

B, say whatever appears in your mind. If it is difficult to think of an answer, keep trying, often this is when the most appropriate answers come.

Allow seven or eight minutes.

Allow seven or eight minutes.

Make drawing materials and paper available.

Allow ten minutes.

9. When you have written the last answer, **change over so that B asks, "Who are you?", and A writes the answers down.**

10. Now **swap lists with your partner so that you have your own answers**, which were written down by your partner. Quietly **look at your list** on your own for a short while.

11. Choose one answer that seems to be the best description of who you feel you are at this moment. Think about that answer and **imagine it as a symbol or some other form of illustration.**

Now, using the materials available reproduce your chosen statement in any way you like.

Drawing out the learning

Time can be given for pupils to share their drawings with each other if they wish. As this exercise is personal, it is important to make the sharing optional. Pupils may prefer to spend more time on their drawings or sit quietly on their own. An additional activity might take the form of making a badge, using the symbol or drawing. (This could be linked with 'My Badge', see page 140.)

Reactions to this exercise can be explored in the original groups of six, or with their partners. Questions such as, "How did it feel to think about yourself in this way?" and, "What, if anything, have you learnt about yourself?", can be raised. They can also consider how easy it is to answer "Who am I?" when compared with saying who someone else is.

ME AND YOU: OVERVIEW

> **'A person becomes an I through a You.'**
> (Martin Buber)

It is very easy to misunderstand or reject people who appear to be different from ourselves. Quite often this rejection conceals a fear of the unknown. Differences which are to do with religious belief or practice are particularly likely to cause misunderstanding because religions are concerned with fundamental interpretations of reality. It is perhaps notable that many of the most brutal conflicts in the modern world are between people of differing religious beliefs.

RE strives to develop sympathetic understanding of other people's religions and life–stances. It is, therefore, important to develop the skill of empathy, that is, being able to see or imagine ourselves in the other person's place, and in doing so we may learn more about ourselves. The following activities offer ways of exploring and sharing perceptions of each other (see also 'Framing Awareness' activities, page 126).

ACTIVITIES

If I was a . . .

Purpose

This is a light–hearted activity where pupils can look at themselves in a new light, symbolically identifying themselves with physical objects, e.g. types of car, animals, fruit etc. By comparing their choices, they have an opportunity to see different perspectives of themselves and other people.

Exercising the imagination in this way is a useful preliminary to empathy, imagining what it would be like to be someone of a different religion or life–stance. The use of symbols also anticipates the introduction of metaphor in the next family of activities.

Time needed: Thirty minutes

Materials needed: Paper and pens.
For younger pupils a selection of objects or pictures, e.g. a toy car, toy animal, a piece of fruit. Older pupils could be given a prepared worksheet.

Conditions

Young children have difficulty with the abstract nature of symbols, and may need to look at something to stimulate their imaginations. Using physical objects or pictures may help to trigger ideas. Older pupils can play the same game without the use of objects. There should be enough space for everyone to sit comfortably in a circle so that each person is visible to everyone else. You may wish to arrange everyone so that they are sitting with a partner.

Procedure

Young children may need to handle the physical object. It is also helpful if the teacher gives an example, e.g. 'If I was a car, I'd be a racing car/a Rolls Royce etc.'

As other items are passed around the circle, you can ask for a more detailed description of the object.

This part of the exercise adopts the use of metaphor and may be difficult for some pupils. Give a number of examples and try to ensure they say the words 'I am a . . .' along with a description.

The next stage requires the children to work on their own, using their own imagination. It may be necessary to help them by suggesting several possibilities, e.g. flower, piece of clothing etc.

Allow sufficient time to complete this. Younger pupils could draw instead of writing.

1. Everyone sit in a circle. When you are ready, I'm going to ask you to pass this toy car around the circle. When it is your turn, **imagine that you could be a car. What sort of car would you be?** Tell the rest of the group by saying "If I was a car I'd be a . . .".

2. Now we're going to pass round a piece of fruit. As you receive it you say, **"If I was a fruit, I'd be a . . . .". This time try to say a little more about the fruit you have chosen.** For example, "If I was a fruit, I'd be an orange, with a thick skin and plenty of juice inside".

3. Next we'll pass round a toy animal. When it's your turn **tell us which animal you've chosen by saying: 'I am a . . . . [cat, dog, hippo etc.] and I'm . . . .'.**

4. Now, on your own, try to **imagine what you would be like if you were something different. Think of a number of different things** you could be. Then write about the things you have chosen.

5. Have another look at what you have done and **pick the one that you think suits you best.** Then **write** a sentence saying what you like **about the one you chose.**

6. Now **show your partner what you have done** and spend a few moments talking about the things you each chose to be. As you are talking, you might like to consider these questions.

Drawing out the learning

The session should end with a group discussion, giving pupils the chance to hear some of the ideas of the rest of the class. This can also provide an opportunity to begin exploring the implications of seeing the world through somebody else's eyes.

How far does your list compare with your partner's?
Did you choose the same, or similar things? What were the differences between you?
What made you choose those particular things?
Did any of the ideas surprise you?
What did it feel like to say 'I am a . . .'?
Have you learnt anything about yourself or your partner?

Variations

1. It is possible to repeat the same exercise with a partner, this time asking pupils to imagine what their partner would be if they were for example, a television programme, weather, landscape, sound, etc. This activity was devised by Tom Limb, who asked his children to work, if possible, with a friend. A certain amount of sensitivity is necessary on the part of the teacher, since the exercise permits the pupils to comment about other people.

Older pupils could sit silently and complete the worksheet (given on page 108) before comparing and discussing their responses with their partner.

The instructions are as follows:
a) Give out a sheet of paper to each person with the heading 'YOU'RE A . . .' and with five circles drawn on the page.
b) In each of the circles, the children draw and label a picture of what their friend would be, as five of the items mentioned above (or any other chosen examples).
c) The children exchange their sheet with their partner and each chooses the one they like best, writing a sentence beginning: 'I think this one fits me best because . . .'.

2. Both the above exercises can be adapted for use with older pupils, or even adults, and in this case of course the circulation of physical objects can be dispensed with. People can work in pairs using a variety of objects as the source of metaphors, e.g. 'If we were trees, you'd be an oak and I'd be a willow'.

"IF I WAS . . . . YOU'D BE . . . ."

Part A. Without telling your partner what you are writing, fill in the spaces below:

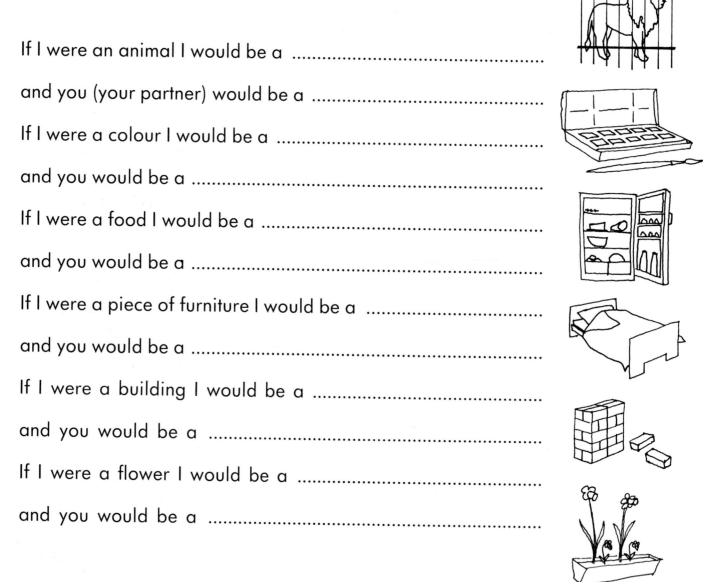

If I were an animal I would be a ....

and you (your partner) would be a ....

If I were a colour I would be a ....

and you would be a ....

If I were a food I would be a ....

and you would be a ....

If I were a piece of furniture I would be a ....

and you would be a ....

If I were a building I would be a ....

and you would be a ....

If I were a flower I would be a ....

and you would be a ....

When you have both finished, compare your answers with your partner.

Now go back to your first answer and talk about it in greater detail with your partner. Help your partner to think about the thoughts and feelings raised by that answer.

When you have finished exploring your first statement move on to the next.

IN PRACTICE

1. # I'm a brown rabbit

"This pair of lessons with 8 and 9 year olds featured in a series called 'Important Things' or 'Deep-down Me'. Most lessons were preceded by a relaxation exercise to help us let the unimportant things go from our minds."

(Tom Limb, Woodborough C.E. School)

Examples of pupils' work

I'm a colour red in the rainbow.

I'm A gold and yellow cover over a corn feild.

I thinck this one fits me Best Because a rainBow Looks nice Beside a sky and I am a bit colour full.

I'm a big gold trumpet

I'M A Brownrabbit

I think this one fits me best because I Like rabbits. I like being Looked after

I'M A....

Content

In a circle we passed round a matchbox car and said "If I were a car, I'd be a......
Then, an apple with some words to "say a bit more about your chosen fruit."
e.g "If I were a fruit I'd be a juicy, plump bunch of purple grapes."
Then, a toy puss, with the change from "If I were.. to "I am a....

Now write down your sentences in the same way. Make six lines in all.
Do a picture of the line which descries you best and write a sentence to say why.

I'm a Flower Sun Flower in the garden.

I think this one fits me best because I am my mum call me sunflower.

I'm A fur soft red and orange bed.

I think this one fitts me best because I like making pepple cumfy.

You're a . . . . . .

"Symbolism is crucial to religion. Language is strained to furnish sufficient metaphors to elucidate religious concepts: e.g. Yahweh = rock, fortress, refuge, strength, shield . . . . or Jesus = lamb, bread, water, vine, light . . . .
The RE teacher is obliged to devise a means of teaching the appreciation of symbolism, the mechanics of the metaphor.
I attempted to do this by beginning with the children's own experience.
The process is designed to sharpen self-awareness and the result is poetic by reason of its imagery."

(Tom Limb
Woodborough C.E. School)

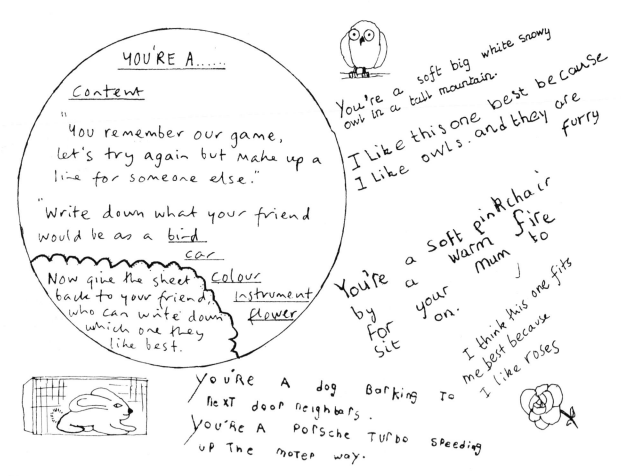

YOU'RE A......

Content

"You remember our game, let's try again but make up a line for someone else."

"Write down what your friend would be as a <u>bird</u>
<u>car</u>
Now give the sheet <u>colour</u>
back to your friend, <u>instrument</u>
who can write down <u>flower</u>
which one they like best.

You're a soft big white snowy owl in a tall mountain.
I Like this one best because I like owls and they are furry

You're a soft pink chair warm fire by a for your mum to for sit on.
I think this one fits me best because I like roses

You'Re A dog Barking To next door neighbors.
You'Re A Porsche Turbo Speeding up The motep way.

You're a black and grey rabbit in a cage.

You're a bright yellow little rose-bush in a big garden

You're a shiny gold little harp played by a world famous musician in a concert.

2. Many young people are troubled by the idea of death, a topic which Ginny Straugheir approached through a study of Hindu belief in reincarnation. In the past pupils were often too shy to disclose their true fears and feelings in front of their classmates but this activity solved the problem.

"I asked each person quickly to jot down their answers to the question, 'if death was a . . . plant . . . animal . . . colour . . . piece of furniture . . . weather . . . sound . . . it would be . . .'". Then sitting in a circle we shared our ideas in turn. (See page 112 for some of their answers about death.)

This proved to be an invaluable stimulus to even the most sceptical boys who were clearly intrigued by their answers. Why did they declare death to be a frog . . . a grandfather clock . . . the colour yellow or pink? Discussion was always animated and pupils felt safe to voice fears and beliefs in a relaxed and uncritical setting.

In this way we were able to raise the topics of out of body experiences, the feelings of *deja vu*, regression, the soul, the importance of the ritual of funerals, children's attendance at funerals or viewing of the body, feelings on the death of a friend, relative or pet, heaven and hell, and so on. Many pupils were grateful for the chance to try to come to terms with their own feelings. Comments from third year pupils at Pelton Roseberry Comprehensive include:

"I was not worried about thinking about death in this way because it seemed harmless and helps you understand."

"I saw everybody's else's view on death and views which I had not even thought about."

"It gave a different outlook on death, instead of looking on it gloomily."

"It made death not seem so frightening. If I thought about death before I couldn't picture it. I now have a better view on death."

"All different ideas, feelings and pains came out of this. I really did discover and find out my own true feelings down inside."

If death was a plant it would be . . . . . .

THISTLE

VENUS FLY TRAP

WEED

BLACK
ROSE

IVY

TREE

CACTUS

If death was an animal it would be . . . . . .

PANTHER

JELLYFISH

VULTURE

COYOTE

HAWK

CROCODILE

WHITE HORSE

If death was a sound it would be . . . . . .

 GUNSHOT

OUT OF TUNE VIOLIN

AN ECHO . . . . . .

DRUMBEAT

EXPLOSION

ALARM

SCREAM

BANG

Walk my walk

Purpose

In many religions, posture is important for meditative practice, recognising the close relationship between bodily and mental states. Awareness of posture is central to certain forms of Hindu and Buddhist meditation and attention is given in Christianity to the correct position for prayer. In this exercise we begin to look at the effects of the posture we adopt when walking. By carefully observing and trying to mirror the movements of another person, opportunities are offered to develop empathy, literally by feeling what it is like to take up the 'stance' of someone else. This activity can also illustrate the influence of posture on personal perception.

After taking part in these activities, many pupils have expressed surprise at how much they discovered about classmates they thought they knew well. Preconceptions are, from time to time, shattered and greater feeling for their fellows may be shown. Drawing out the learning can create opportunities to move on to more explicit areas of RE.

Time needed: Fifteen to twenty minutes

Materials: None

Conditions

This can be done with most age groups, though with older pupils the insights gained are likely to be deeper. The exercise needs enough space for couples to demonstrate their walk to each other. A fairly large room is needed, unobstructed by desks or other furniture. Alternatively it can be done out of doors. Some pupils may feel embarrassed when asked to walk in front of others, therefore, (as always) permission not to take part must be given. Be sensitive in situations where there is a pupil who is physically disabled. This does not automatically disbar the exercise — it may even help to improve understanding of the handicapped person, but obviously the teacher is called upon to make a careful judgement.

Procedure

Or, you could ask the pupils to choose someone they don't know very well, using the exercise to help people get to know each other better.

1. Choose someone you feel happy **to work with**. Decide who is A and who is B. When you are ready, **A, walk across the room** in your normal fashion. Don't worry about it, just go for a short walk. While you are walking **B will watch**. When B has seen enough **stop walking and talk about A's walk**. Try to **notice as much as you can**, for example:

The length of stride
Balance
Speed
Position of arms
The way the head is held
Where the weight is placed —
is it on the heels or the
toes?

This part can cause laughter. Encourage the class to move on from any initial giggles to look more seriously at what they are doing. Discourage any fooling around and deliberate exaggeration of movements.

2. Now **it's B's turn to try to experience your partner's way of walking**. Imagine you are your partner's reflection in a mirror. Reflect A's walk as closely as you can. Try to feel what it is like to walk that way. Talk about it — and then try again.

Allow sufficient time for several attempts to reflect and discuss the partner's walk.

3. Now **try walking together**, both of you walking like A. Then **talk about how it feels to walk like that**.

4. Reverse roles and repeat the exercise.

Drawing out the learning

When the exercise is completed and the pairs have had sufficient time to talk about their experience, bring the group together for a general discussion. This is a chance for everybody to share their experience of walking like somebody else. People are often very surprised to find out how different they feel when they adopt another person's walk.

During the discussion, try to bring out some of the less obvious features, for example, how the world might feel different to someone who walks with their head thrust forward, compared with a person whose head is hanging down.

1. How did it feel to walk another person's walk?

2. What did you learn about your partner?

3. What did you learn about yourself? How do you and your partner differ?

Variations

1. Try asking one pair to walk in the same way across the room. The rest of the group have to decide if the walk is that of A or B.

2. A development of this exercise is to try deepening awareness of our walking, using Buddhist Vipassana methods. This is really more suitable for adults, but it might be worth trying with an interested senior class (see p. 85). The task is to become as sharply aware as possible of the movements involved in walking and in the first instance can be tried for about twenty minutes. Somewhere reasonably quiet should be available.

Comments

These comments are from fourteen and fifteen–year–old boys and girls who initially found the exercise too ridiculous for words. They settled down after the teacher described how successful actors often begin to get into a part by adopting a particular posture and stance which can then provide them with a new outlook and character.

"It was embarrassing, just like being in the school hall with an audience at first."

"It made me really think."

"Everyone has got a different walk and it was like I was taking part of Mandy — it was strange."

"Doing Jeanette's walk it was like I was never getting to the end. I couldn't get there quick enough. I do think I've learnt a bit more about what it means to be Jeanette and we've been friends for years."

"It was hard but I enjoyed it."

"I feel I bang my heels down and I was trying not to do that. I felt tight and funny. I didn't think I walked like that."

"When I tried to do her walk it didn't feel relaxed. It was like she was walking on a tight rope. My arms were doing things they don't usually do."

Framing awareness

It is very easy for us to be blinkered, believing that our picture of reality is so obvious that it is the only possible view. It doesn't always occur to us that what we see is an interpretation of the world around us.

Human experience is framed on the basis of what we learn from others; parents, teachers, friends, the media. It is by adopting the symbols and metaphors dominant in the community in which we grow up that we try to make sense of our own experience. The example of the Necker cube (see page 13) shows that living in an environment full of cuboid shapes is enough to affect the way we see a network of flat lines. Similarly, our images of other people are determined by our culture as well as our individual feelings. We make assumptions about people of the opposite sex, or of another ethnic group, culture or religion, because we see them through the spectacles of our own sex, ethnic group, culture or religion. In the case of religion, this tunnel vision makes it difficult for us to appreciate religious perspectives which are outside our own experience.

It is possible to restructure our experience if we practise using different metaphors and symbols from the ones we normally adopt. But first we have to recognise that there can be other perspectives, with perhaps equal or greater validity than our initial perception. We might even discover that aspects of our self–image change. The first group of exercises uses optical illusions to develop the skill of recognising and changing perspectives. Subsequent structures are designed to increase understanding of the power of metaphor in framing our awareness. When placed in the context of religious education, these activities can help pupils to appreciate the differing perspectives of religious people.

'If the doors of perception were cleansed, everything would appear to man as it is'.

(William Blake)

CHANGING PERSPECTIVES: OVERVIEW

One of the major concerns of religious education is to foster empathy for religious believers. Yet the study of a number of religions can confuse pupils when they are presented with the different and contrasting perspectives of other faiths. RE teachers are accustomed to grappling with contrary and controversial issues. For example, discussions on the meaning of life may highlight the paradoxical perspectives of governments which condemn murder but sanction capital punishment. It is not always obvious that our perception hinges on the story being told at that particular time. "Yes it is wrong to kill — but that's why this murderer must die." It is hard to see things in different ways when our upbringing and cultural conventions train us to organise knowledge in one way. For instance, when asked to repeat the months of the year most people do so chronologically; they find it more difficult reciting them backwards or alphabetically.

There is a tendency to make assumptions when searching for the right, or the best possible, interpretation. Recalling past experiences and expectations to fill in the gaps, our minds try to classify and identify what we perceive. Depending on the assumptions we make, a few lines on a page can become a face for one person, and a vase for someone else. These assumptions, which may be held unconsciously, restrict our perspectives and limit our capacity to understand another point of view.

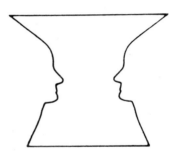

The example of the Necker Cube (see page 13) demonstrates that our initial perception of the cube depends on the story we tell ourselves. If we lived in the 'circular culture' of the Zulus we would probably see it in one dimension, as a series of flat lines. In contrast, our experience persuades us to 'see' this configuration of lines in three dimensions. The position of the cube in relation to ourselves is a little more ambiguous. When we realise that there are at least two ways of seeing the diagram, neither of which holds any monopoly of the truth, then our awareness can switch from one to the other without reaching any conclusion as to which view is correct.

Once they recognise that things can be seen in other ways, pupils may learn to question their perspectives or ways of seeing and perceiving. Illusion and projection activities encourage greater understanding of the ways in which different people can see the same thing. By drawing out the differences it is also possible to point out the uniqueness of each individual. These exercises help to develop the skills of empathy and self–understanding. They can also pave the way for better under-standing of religious language which uses metaphor and riddle, koan and parable to challenge believers to reconsider basic assumptions about the world, other people and themselves.

ACTIVITIES

I'm a soft shoe

Purpose

Identifying oneself with an object can produce unexpected insights as we see ourselves from a new and unusual perspective. This activity picks up a Buddhist notion that to concentrate on an object which is external to ourselves can deepen personal awareness.

Time needed: Thirty minutes

Materials needed: Index cards or small pieces of writing paper

Conditions

You may wish everyone to identify with the same object in which case you could choose any appropriate item, including things not usually found in a classroom. Some groups may benefit from a verbal description of the room, which widens their choice by pointing out that its contents include more than tables and chairs. Seating arrangements should be flexible so that everyone can comfortably observe their selected object, join up with a partner and then return for feedback from the entire group.

Procedure

If you are only using one object make sure everyone can see it clearly. Pause to give time to choose.

Some pupils are unhappy with their eyes closed and this should be respected.

Pause briefly.

1. Sit silently and look around the room. Choose an object to concentrate on. It can be any object you like. **Consider what it would be like if you were that object.** It may be easier for you if you closed your eyes, opening them if you want to remind yourself of anything about that object.

2. Don't just see the object in your imagination. **Try to become the object . . .** what can you see . . . what do you feel . . . can your hear anything . . . what is going on around you?
What is your life like as this object . . . how do you feel about this life?

3. Choose three qualities you think the object possesses and then **write the name of the object and those three qualities on your card**. For example: a shoe — is soft, warm and comfortable.

4. Now **think about whether those qualities describe you**. Give the object your name.

Organise class in pairs.

5. Introduce yourself to your partner using those qualities. For example: "I am Alison, I am soft, warm and comfortable." **Talk about this experience with your partner**, you may like to develop a longer description of yourself as the object.

This stage could be repeated several times.

6. Now **exchange cards with your partner and read out the description on the card, giving your own name first**. "I am Alison, I am a piece of string, I have many uses, I hold things together, I am boring." **Talk about that experience with your partner**, saying how far you felt able to identify with your partner's description.

Drawing out the learning

Preferably arrange the class in a circle so they can all see each other.
Quickly go around the circle saying what you chose to be and anything you may have discovered.
How far did you become really involved in that experience?
To what extent did it provide an accurate description of you or aspects of your life?
What sort of feelings did you experience while doing this activity?
What, if anything, have you discovered about yourself through doing this?

Comment

This process of identifying with an object is technically known as projection. Descriptions are frequently made with a great deal of feeling and seem to suit the people involved. This activity helps pupils get in touch with aspects of themselves which they may not have previously recognised or acknowledged.

Variations

I want to be . . . like you. If you could be someone else, who would you most like to be? List five people, including two people you know, it doesn't matter if the others are living or dead, mythical, fictional, historical, etc. Then for each person on your list write down three qualities or characteristics which you admire, like or value about that person.

  You should now have a list of fifteen qualities which you should reduce to the ten most valued qualities. Write each of those ten characteristics on separate pieces of paper and then throw three of them away. Of the remaining seven take one at random and compare it with another one, throw the one you like least away. Now compare your chosen quality with another taken at random from the five which remain. Continue rejecting one of the attributes until you are left with the quality you value most.

Reflect on the way you selected that value — what was it like to throw things away?

Concentrate on the chosen quality and imagine yourself with this quality — how would your life be different? Think of yourself without that quality . . . and again with it. How do you feel about yourself, about others, how does it help you? Draw your quality.

Join up with three or four others and talk about the qualities you have each brought to the group. Try to be as specific as you can while you consider the ways people with these qualities might behave and write those behaviour patterns around the drawing. Display all the drawings so everyone can see them. What do all these qualities say about the group's notion of the ideal person? This could be rounded off by a group drawing or collage.

Weather or not. A quick taste of changing perspectives can be given in response to a single question. Pupils can ask each other, "What kind of weather do you think I am?" The query usually raises a range of contrasting answers, warm, cloudy, sunny, chilly, and so on, suggesting that the respondents are saying more about themselves than the questioner. The question can utilise an unlimited number of metaphorical possibilities.

IN PRACTICE

Pupils at Middleton St George Primary near Darlington were preparing to follow a day in the life of a monk at St. Bede's Monastery Museum, Jarrow, as part of their cross–curricular study of medieval life. Their teacher, Hazel Bullock, reported later:

"Knowing that part of the workshop time at Jarrow would involve silent, thoughtful reflection, I decided to pursue the theme of meditation further with the class of 22 eight and nine–year–olds.

When everyone was sitting in a circle I introduced the word meditation, describing it as a concentrated thought which could centre on an object or an inner feeling. If meditating on an object they could:
a) think about the physical attributes of that object;
b) put themselves in the place of that object and meditate on how it might feel. We then spent several minutes meditating on the first thing that came to view: the blackboard rubber!

Some of the comments made by the children following the exercise included: "I wouldn't like to be a board rubber as you keep getting your face pushed up against a big black wall and then rubbed on it."
"I thought about how old the rubber must be. It started off black and now it is grey with chalk."

"Each time you think you are going to get a rest, another hand grabs you and pushes you around."

The idea of using meditation to help see things from another point of view came up later, after the group had brainstormed the word 'meditation'. They came up with the idea that if a person hurts your feelings you can use 'meditation' to try and capture how that person might feel having hurt you, i.e. not limiting yourself to how you feel in this situation. They were very excited by this and extremely keen to share their findings with the class.

I am sure this group of children would not have reached this stage of understanding of meditation if it had not been for the experiential approach.

Duck or rabbit?

Purpose

This activity is similar to the exercise using the Necker cube, already mentioned in Chapter 1 (see page 13), but is more suitable for very young children. There are a myriad optical illusions which could be substituted to similar effect. It demonstrates the importance of individuality and the value of being able to see another perspective which is equally valid. (See p. 231 for a larger copy of the diagram below.)

Time needed: Thirty minutes

Materials needed: One copy of duck/rabbit diagram for each person. Drawing materials.

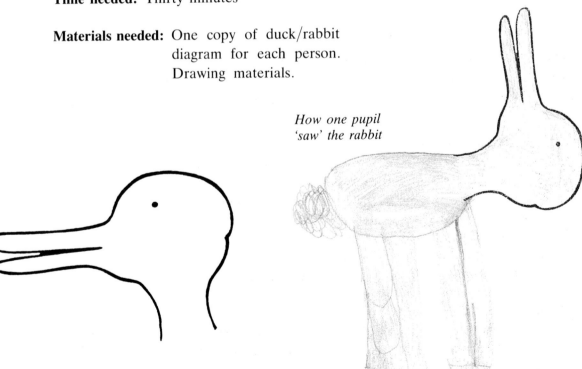

How one pupil 'saw' the rabbit

Conditions

When reproducing the diagram, make sure that the picture is in the centre of a square page so that neither the duck nor the rabbit interpretation becomes obvious. You will need space to display all the completed drawings so that they can be seen by everyone.

Procedure

When handing out copies of the duck/rabbit, present them face down. When everyone has a sheet, explain the process, placing emphasis on the importance of individual interpretation.

1. In a moment **I'm going to give you a piece of paper with part of a picture already drawn on it**. When everyone has got the paper, I'll ask you to **look at it quietly on your own**.

2. Now have a look at the picture and decide what you think it is and then **finish off the drawing**. Don't talk about it or ask anybody else what they think. Don't worry if you see other people drawing something different from you, just carry on and finish your own picture. **There is no right or wrong way to see this picture, YOUR idea is what matters, so draw what you see in the picture**.

Allow ten to fifteen minutes to finish the diagrams.

3. When you've finished, **turn your paper over until we are all ready**.

When everyone has finished or at a time you consider appropriate, display all the pictures and give everyone a few minutes to view them.

Arrange the group into pairs and give each person the opportunity to talk about their responses.

4. Look at all the pictures. Notice if any are different from yours. **Be aware of your reactions** as you look at the pictures and remember those feelings.

5. Talk to your partner and tell them about your reactions while you were doing this exercise.

Drawing out the learning

The way in which the questions are phrased and the depth of enquiry varies according to the age of the pupils. Young children may just be encouraged to notice that other children see the picture in a different way and, with help, they can too.

What did you think when you looked at the picture?
Can you see the picture in any other way?
What, if anything, has this exercise taught you about:
   a) **yourself?**
   b) **yourself and others?**
When else are we likely to see something different from our neighbours?

It may be appropriate to end the exercise with a group discussion about the concept of 'changing perspectives'. Some 'think writing' could be added to the diagrams in the form of a poem or prose.

IN PRACTICE

These two examples of successful work indicate how different perspectives can be illustrated through the use of different media.

Me and my gang. Using three different perspectives of the Necker cube (see page 13), this activity was set up as part of an extended study of apartheid for top band twelve–year–olds. They had previously learnt about the life of Martin Luther King and experienced a change of perspectives when considering the reasons for the bus boycott. (Everyone was paired up so that one partner was seated while the other stood. It was the task of the person left standing to persuade the seated partner, who was feeling footsore and weary, to give up his or her seat. After a few minutes they considered their feelings and reactions and then swopped roles before discussing their experience with the rest of the class.)

This time the desks were moved to create physical barriers, dividing the classroom into three 'territorial' areas. As each pupil entered the room he or she was consigned at random to one of these areas. In this way friendship patterns were broken up and pupils became identified as members of these new corporate groups.

The class discussed the development of friendships and how the interests and behaviour of friends can influence our own actions. Each group was described as a 'gang' and pupils talked about their own experience of gangs — marks of identification, initiation ceremonies, rules, activities, etc.

Still in their territories, each group or gang was privately shown the Necker cube for the first time and told which perspective they ought to see. This was to be their gang's badge. It was up to the gang to decide how to decorate their badge, which must stress the perspective explained to them. They all seemed happy to accept that explanation of the cube to be the only correct way of seeing it.

For several lessons they were given time to organise their gangs and develop an 'image', even to the point of making political addresses in an attempt to persuade others to defect to their gang. Suddenly the territory's dictator (the teacher) declared one gang an illegal organisation. Banned, its members had to disband and join one of the two remaining groups. Reluctant to do so, some members decided to form an underground movement. Others complained of feelings of isolation, injustice, and alienation while some were branded traitors when they happily adapted to their new circumstances.

Insisting that every member of the banned organisation was attached to a recognised gang, the dictator ensured that each group now included two perspectives of the Necker cube. It did not take long for arguments to break out, each convinced that their view was the only possible interpretation. Considerable discussion ensued, provoking many comments from pupils which could be directly applied to their study of apartheid. They had certainly experienced changing perspectives during the work and displayed many mature insights into the consequences of prejudice.

One or the other

A group of eighteen year olds thoroughly enjoyed this 90 minute session. First they were shown a glass containing water up to its half way mark, and asked — is it half full or half empty? That got them going, then they became actively involved, making ink blots and comparing the images they saw in them. Discussion around this activity made it possible to introduce them to the Necker cube, raising considerable interest. Their teacher then read out the story of an old man's encounter with two prospective neighbours. (See below.) Finally they relaxed with a fantasy in which they became a rose bush. The variety of ideas they expressed showed it had been an extremely thought provoking experience.

Perspectives: 'Neighbours'

Once upon a time an old man sat by the side of the road, smoking his pipe, and gazing into the distance, contemplating . . . who–knows–what? Along came a stranger who stopped to pass the time of day. He put down his bundle and took out a sandwich and a bottle of wine, which he forgot to share with the old man. In the course of the conversation, the stranger pointed to the village nestling in the valley below and asked, "What are the people like down there? I'm just moving to that village, you know."

The old man puffed on his pipe, and threw the question back, "What were they like in the town where you used to live, my friend?"

A thundercloud seemed to pass over the stranger's face: "Oh, they were rogues and rascals of the worst sort. Liars, cheats, a pack of knaves they were. I never could get a kind word out of any of them."

Smoke billowed from the old man's pipe, as he shook his head and spoke, "Well then, that's what the people are like in that village down there, my son."

The stranger heaved himself to his feet and walked sadly down the hill. The old man leaned back against the tree for his afternoon nap.

He awoke to see another stranger approaching him. The newcomer smiled and asked if he could share the shade of the stately tree. The old man moved over to make room for him, and gratefully accepted the stranger's offer of an apple and some cheese. As they chatted, the stranger pointed to the hamlet in the valley: "What are the people like in that village?", he asked, "I'm thinking of moving there soon."

A twinkle appeared in the old man's eye, as once again he parried the question. "What were they like where you've just come from, my son?" The stranger's face lit up. "Oh, they're wonderful people, the salt of the earth, not a harsh word nor a dishonest act have I heard of these many years. I only wish I could stay, but it is time for me to move on."

Hiding his pleasure by lighting his pipe, the old man responded, "Well, I'm glad to say that that is exactly how you'll find those people in the village below."

METAPHOR: OVERVIEW

Metaphors are words with distinct meanings which are shifted to a new context and applied in a related, but different, way to give fresh insight. Religions are full of metaphors. If we are to speak meaningfully of the transcendent (which, by definition, is inexpressible) we have to use metaphors. For example, a central idea in Buddhism is *dharma*, sometimes translated as the teachings of the Buddha, or the Path. However, dharma is not just an idea, it has a practical effect on the way a Buddhist experiences reality. Just as the Buddha advocates the 'middle path', so Jesus is described as the 'way', Hindus are on the 'wheel' of samsara and Islam rests on five 'pillars'. In these analogies, familiar words are used in a related yet different sense to present deeper religious meaning.

Lying at the heart of religious language, metaphors create bridges which convey greater understanding; therefore they are essential tools for religious education. It is difficult to say anything without using metaphors — we've just used three: heart, bridges, and tools. Literally speaking, language does not have a heart, but we know exactly what is meant. In all these examples the principle is the same: the accepted meaning of the metaphor or symbol throws new light on an aspect of experience which can then be grasped more firmly.

Neither secular nor religious metaphors are necessarily right or wrong, they are simply the vehicles we use to articulate experience. Metaphorical language is not inferior to the literal, it is different; helping us to explore ideas for which we have no literal means of expression. By presenting alternative models of ourselves and others, metaphors can help pupils to see things from another perspective and offer them possibilities for new insight.

The following exercises encourage pupils to consider how metaphor and symbol can affect their own, and other people's, perceptions of reality. In addition to creating opportunities to increase self–awareness and empathy, the use of metaphor can also assist pupils' understanding and development of religious language. By experimenting with metaphors, particularly with regard to the images we have of ourselves, pupils gain experience in handling symbols used to express perceptions of reality. These activities are preparatory to more explicitly religious metaphors and symbols which are explored in the next family.

> **Reality is what we take to be true.**
> **What we take to be true is what we believe.**
> **What we believe is based on our perceptions.**
> **What we perceive depends upon what we look for.**
> **What we look for depends upon what we think.**
> **What we think depends upon what we perceive.**
> **What we perceive determines what we believe.**
> **What we take to be true is our reality.**
>
> (Gary Zukav, *The Dancing Wu-Lei Masters*)

ACTIVITIES

Life is like . . .

Purpose

Religions offer powerful 'stories' which provide their adherents with an overall perspective and help them find meaning. This activity expands and develops 'The Journey of Life' (see page 93) through the analysis of the effect of metaphorical interpretation. By considering contrasting metaphors of life it explores the notion that our attitudes towards life alter our perceptions. In other words the stories we tell about our lives can change the way we make sense of our experiences.

Time needed: Forty minutes

Materials needed: Large sheets of paper and crayons or felt tip pens for brainstorming. Drawing materials (A3 paper or bigger)

Conditions

There should be enough space for everyone to work in groups of four or five; as well as room for the class to view the completed work of other groups before separating to work as individuals with some degree of privacy.

Some pupils may be unhappy about reflecting on their entire life and could confine their lifeline to a shorter period of last month, week or even the events of one day, or a holiday.

Procedure

Arrange the class in groups of four or five and ensure each group has a sheet of large paper and a heavy crayon or felt tip pen.

If they are unfamiliar with this technique you may prefer to let them practise with a light–hearted topic first.

1. In your groups spend a few minutes brainstorming the phrase "Life is like . . ."
For example Life is like a gift, a sardine tin without the key, hell, a jigsaw, etc. When you have finished we'll display the brainstorms and look at all the ideas. Remember the rules for brainstorming. The aim is to come up with as many ideas as possible and therefore all suggestions should be written down without comment or criticism.
Are there any questions? Then off you go — what is life like?

Allow five or ten minutes then display the sheets of paper so that everyone can see.

Arrange partners.
Allow a few minutes and in the meantime give everyone two or three sheets of drawing paper.

The second drawing could be on a separate piece of paper.

This stage is described in much greater detail in 'Journey of life' on page 93.

Some pupils could be upset by a distressing memory.

Allow sufficient time to finish.

This stage is crucial to the exercise and should be given plenty of time.

2. Look carefully at all the ideas which have been written down by other groups as well as your own. Then choose two of those ideas or metaphors of life. **Choose one which you like and agree with, and pick an idea you don't like.**

3. Find a partner and talk about the two ideas or metaphors you have each chosen.

4. Now either **write or draw about the metaphor you did not like.** When you have finished **turn the paper over and draw or write about the idea you liked best.**

5. Write the date of your birth at the left hand edge of the other piece of paper and put today's date near but not on the right hand edge of the paper.
Now **draw your life line** — a line to represent your life between those two dates. It can go up and down, back and forth, be jagged, curved or straight. Mark any important or special times in your life on the line, perhaps an experience, someone you met or an event which stands out in your memory. If you prefer you can use symbols or a code to represent those important stages in your life. You don't have to tell anyone about them unless you want to.

6. Look carefully at your lifeline, considering its directions and turning points and **notice your feelings** as you are doing this. Then **go back to your partner** and, as far as you feel comfortable, **talk about how you feel about your lifeline.**

7. Have another **look at the drawings or writing you did on your two chosen metaphors**. Take each idea in turn and **thinking about that metaphor, look at your life line again**. Does your life seem any different if you adopt that idea? Do you want to alter your line and redraw it to suit each metaphor you chose?

(*Some examples of pupils' work as part of this activity are given on the next page.*)

Drawing out the learning

First through discussion in pairs and then by sharing their thoughts and ideas with the rest of the class. Attention can be focused on how the perspective we adopt alters our experience and the meanings we give to that experience.

Life is like

chaos

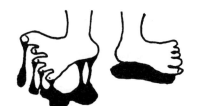

treading treacle

a nightmare

one damned thing
after another

a journey
without a
map

a
problem

a game where nobody
ever explains the rules

an everturning wheel

Pupils' ideas about 'Life'

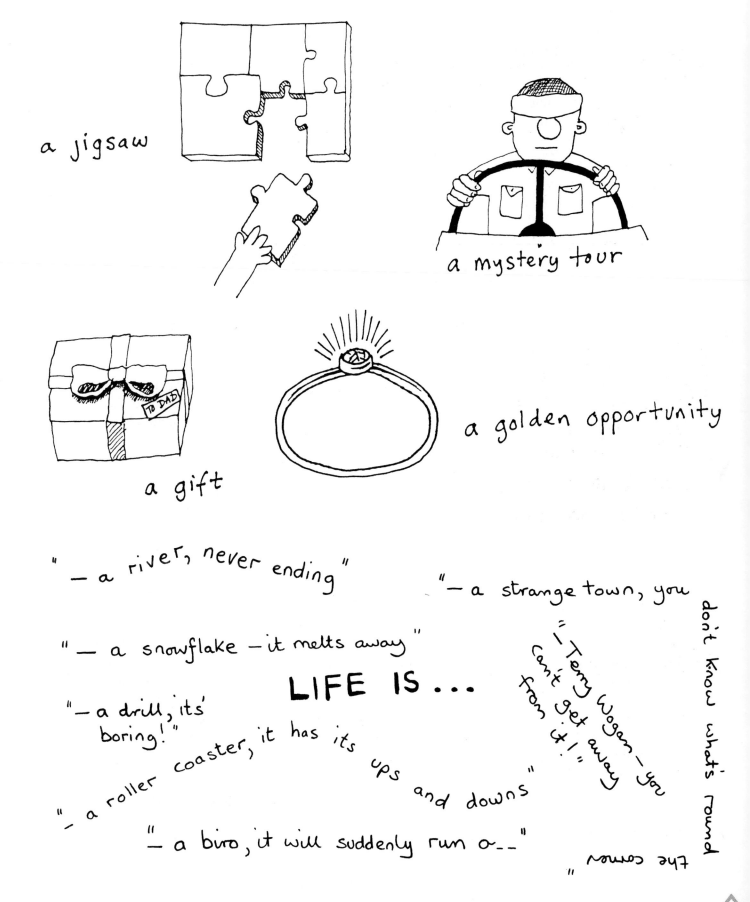

a jigsaw

a mystery tour

a gift

a golden opportunity

" — a river, never ending "

" — a strange town, you

" — a snowflake — it melts away "

LIFE IS . . .

"— a drill, its' boring!"

" — a roller coaster, it has its ups and downs "

" — a biro, it will suddenly run o __ "

" Terry Wogan — you can't get away from it! "

don't know what's round the corner "

Comment

The way we understand our own experience colours our interpretation of the language we speak. Hence no two people speak exactly the same language; placing differing nuances, interpretations and expectations on even the most familiar words.

Brainstorming allows pupils to explore a diversity of concepts connected or associated with a topic which may previously have seemed too simple and obvious for words.

IN PRACTICE

The concept of the Hindu pantheon can be difficult for many pupils who struggle with the symbolism as well as the complex notion of deity. How can so many individual and diverse gods and goddesses encompass all that is good and bad and at the same time remain an aspect of the one god, Brahma? One teacher considered it a 'minor miracle' if half a dozen pupils in her class seemed to understand the complexities of one god having thousands of different faces. The usual methods of chalk, talk and audio visual aids don't always get the message across.

Trying to teach Hinduism to reluctant, not to say recalcitrant, thirteen–year–olds in mixed ability classes was bad karma until they were introduced to experiential learning techniques. Suddenly the study of Hindu beliefs was no longer 'daft, boring and a waste of time', but had become a talking point both in and out of school. RE lessons were being described as 'brilliant, exciting, stimulating, great fun'. Six months later the amount of information recalled and the degree of understanding was exceptionally high compared with the success, or rather failure, rate of traditional methods of teaching about Hindu faith.

In the past, explanations of the Hindu pantheon had prompted many negative and intolerant comments from pupils who failed to see any validity in the symbolism employed in the myths and illustrations of the gods. Now, through the use of brainstorming and metaphor exercises, their tolerance of each other, as well as of beliefs alien to their own culture is much improved. Using the metaphor exercises: 'Hammer and Nail' and 'If I were . . . you would be . . . .' seemed to deepen pupils' understanding of the significance of the iconography. More academic pupils explored the concepts raised by the Necker Cube, which enabled them to relate different interpretations of deity to cultural differences.

A number of pupils commented later,

"This way of working helped us to understand that different people have different views and that our ideas may not always be right. When you brainstorm everyone's ideas are right. No one is wrong".

One girl, noted for her lack of sympathy and understanding, said, "It's not right saying they are stupid for something other people believe in".

Working in small groups, their introduction to Hinduism began by brainstorming on a number of different aspects of 'fire'. At this stage, pupils had no idea that they would be learning about another faith system. They were simply divided into groups which were each given a topic to brainstorm, e.g. a house on fire, a coal fire, a bonfire, a forest fire. They then joined together to produce a class brainstorm on fire. Two pupils jotted down all the ideas generated, both good and bad, on a piece of card which another pupil illustrated with a picture of some kind of fire. By the end of the week, wallcharts produced by six different classes were displayed underneath pictures of a number of Hindu gods.

Next lesson there was considerable interest in the work produced by the other classes and pupils were allowed to discuss the various ideas expressed in the brainstorms. This also gave them an opportunity to look more closely at the pictures of the gods, stimulating their interest so that questions were asked and explanations given. Struck by the contrasting descriptions of fire, each class recognised that fire has many aspects. Whether they are good or bad depends on the story we tell ourselves. For out of the destruction of fire can come new growth and regeneration but, conversely, danger lurks in the comforting warmth of a fire. Yet each tiny spark is both an entity in itself and, at the same time, part of the much wider aspect of fire. Gradually, and of their own volition, they saw a connection between their symbolic expressions and understanding of fire and the symbolic representations of Brahma, "It's a bit like that for all these gods — isn't it, Miss?"

The *Bhagavad Gita* describes Krishna as:

'The soul in the heart of all things; the beginning, the middle and the end; the sun; the moon; the mind; consciousness; the destroyer; the lord of wealth; fire; a mountain; a priest; a vast lake; the word OM; silent prayer; the Himalayas; a tree; a seer; a musician; a horse; an elephant; a king; a thunderbolt; a creator; a serpent; a snake; the ruler of death; a demon; time; the king of beasts; a bird; the wind; a warrior; a fish; the Ganges; knowledge; reason; the sound A; fame; prosperity; speech; memory; intelligence; constancy; forgiveness; a song; a poem; a month; a season; the cleverness in the gambler's dice; beauty; victory; goodness; a poet; a king's sceptre; wise policy; silence; the seed of all things.

Hammer and nail

Purpose

Playing with metaphors encourages pupils to use their imaginations and experiment with different images of how they see themselves. At one level it is a pleasant game used to introduce other work or as a means of mixing to create smaller groups. At a deeper level discussion can reveal how changing the metaphors we use about ourselves may also affect our experience of the world. The activity challenges pupils to reflect on their perceptions and to enlarge their horizons. Experimenting with metaphors here and in 'If I were a . . .' (see page 105) gives practice in using and understanding symbolism, a useful adjunct to the study of metaphor and symbolism which abound in religious expression.

Time needed: Fifteen minutes or more

Materials needed: Writing materials and possibly a prepared worksheet

Conditions

This activity is not intended to be taken too seriously and can generate laughter. There needs to be enough space for pupils to move around the class to compare their answers.

You will probably need to give a few examples to help them get used to the idea of applying contrasting metaphors to themselves. Playing the song 'El Condor Pasa' by Simon and Garfunkel is a relaxing method of introducing this exercise. Children with writing difficulties could put a circle round, or colour in, their choice on a prepared worksheet.

Procedure

Give out a piece of paper or an index card to each person and ask them to write the numbers 1 to 6 down the left hand side of the page. (Larger groups may need more possibilities to choose from and therefore more numbers.) You may wish to introduce the activity by playing 'El Condor Pasa'.

1. Imagine waking up one morning to discover that something rather odd has happened to you. During the night you've turned into something else . . . but it's not as bad as it could be because you did have a little bit of choice in the matter. What we are going to do now is think about some of the things you could have chosen to turn into. For example you might prefer to be a sparrow rather than a snail . . . but of course someone else might want to be a snail. **I'll read out a series of paired words or phrases and for each pair you choose the one you would rather be.** Don't say anything or show anyone your answers just yet and don't worry about what other people are writing down. You choose the one you think you'd rather be. For example I might ask you, "If you could be a lion or an elephant which would you rather be?" If you choose to be a lion just write down the word 'lion', or if your answer is elephant then you write down 'elephant' and forget about the lion. So if you are all ready we'll start now.

Read out six (or more) pairs of alternatives allowing a short time for pupils to write down their choice. Restate the question as you give each set of alternatives. There is no limit to the ideas you could suggest e.g.:

If you could be a . . . hammer or a nail . . . **which would you rather be?**

please or sorry
yes or no
cat or mouse
horse or cart
bacon or egg
a saver or a spender
a tree or a flower
rose or dandelion
popcorn or jelly
swings or roundabout
doughnut or cream cake
red or green
forest or stream
brick or feather

You could give greater choice by using groups of three alternatives, e.g. red, yellow or green; oak, pine or apple tree; bat, ball or net; train, ship, plane.

When everyone has finished writing their answers down:

Allow five or ten minutes (depending on the group size).

A few people may be left on their own and could create a separate group or team up with others who have almost the same answers.

3. Now **compare your answers with everyone else** and try to **find whoever wrote down exactly the same ideas as you.**

4. When you've found someone, or there may be several of you, go and **sit down together and talk about your answers**, and what made you choose them. In what ways do you think you may be alike?

Drawing out the learning

Bring everyone back together for a class discussion.
What was it like when you compared answers with everyone else?
Was there anything which surprised you?
What does it feel like to have different answers from everyone else?
How effective do you think these metaphors can be in describing what you are really like?
What would it feel like to be the things you chose?
What would be different if you were the things you rejected?
What, if anything, have you discovered about yourself or about others?

Variations

I'd rather be. Give everyone a card or piece of paper and ask them to use their own ideas to complete eight to ten sentences using the phrase "I'd rather be a . . . than a . . ." each time. Stress that there is no right or wrong way to do this. When everyone has finished ask them to show their lists to a partner they feel happy working with. They can take it in turns to discuss whether or not they can see any link between the things they would rather be, or would rather not be. They can also consider the reasons for pairing their metaphors and why they chose to be one rather than the other. Does this tell them anything about themselves? How far do their lists compare or contrast with their partner's list? The lists could be presented as a poem or a large drawing which includes the things 'I'd rather be'.

Choices. Giving alternative choices can create a rapid and random method of organising pupils into small groups. This suggestion can also be used to shorten the time it takes to find others with the same answers.

Divide the room into two sections and ask the pupils to choose between say, a lorry or a bicycle, with all the lorries going to one part of the room and the bicycles to the other. They can then choose a partner from fellow lorries and bicycles or, if preferable, team up with someone from the other group, you could continue to subdivide the larger groups by giving more alternatives to choose from.

I could . . . Having selected a number of metaphors, the exercise could be extended by asking pupils to think about what they could do if they became those chosen things, for example, "If I was . . . a computer . . . I could . . . find the answers to all my problems." Encourage them to produce positive rather than destructive or negative ideas.

IN PRACTICE

A mixed ability class of twenty–four seven and eight–year–olds at Skerne Park Junior School, Darlington, were exploring all aspects of food in a cross curricular topic. Rather than choose a different area of work for RE, their teacher, Linda Chapman, developed this scheme using metaphor and guided imagery.

1. Opening sessions

Oral work, expressing our own thoughts and listening to others. Seated in our private circle, tell me, which would *you* rather be?

YES/NO   BACON/EGG   POPCORN/JELLY   APPLE/BANANA   etc.

A multi-choice activity — *you* choose. Now after individual imagining discuss with a partner your feelings and thoughts about the responses you have given.

2. Following sessions

Using imagery, become something else. Indulge in self–forgetfulness. Working with a partner, with the use of metaphor, try to complete the following:

A. If I was a food I would be ....

"A BIG CREAMY CAKE WITH FIVE LAYERS OF JAM AND A BIG, RED CHERRY AND ICING ON TOP,"
NEATH

OR

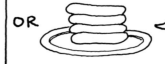

"BIG, LONG, FAT SAUSAGES. I WOULD BE VERY TASTY. I WOULD HAVE GOOD FUN ROLLING ABOUT ON THE PLATE AND WHEN I GET COOKED I WOULD BE VERY HOT."
ANNE

B. If I was a drink I would be ....

SPLASH

"FIZZY LEMONADE. I WOULD BE DRUNK CAREFULLY AND IF YOU SPILT ME I WOULD GET HURT ON THE FLOOR. ALL OF ME WOULD BE WASTED AND I WOULD BE NO MORE."
ELROY

OR

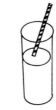

"MILK. I WOULD BE TASTY AND SOFT. MY MILK WOULD HAVE A NICE FLAVOUR."
IRENE

C. If I was a fruit I would be ....

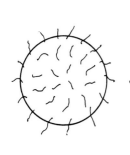

"A BIG, HEAVY HAIRY PEACH. VERY JUICY. WHEN PEOPLE EAT ME, ALL THE JUICE AND JUICY TEXTURE WOULD SQUIRT OUT."
AMY

OR

"A BIG, JUICY BLACK PLUM – TASTY."
SIMON

3. Next step

During the next sessions, I asked all of the children to imagine they were a juicy, rosy red apple. Then they had to react, through drama, as I ate an apple in front of them. The apple I was eating was *their* apple, i.e. themselves. What would they do? How would they feel as I was eating? I would continue to eat the apple until only the core was left and I would drop it on the floor.

These activities would show the children different ways of behaving, open up new ways and avenues of thinking, increase confidence in themselves and allow the children to see more aspects than themselves.

CHILDREN'S WORK

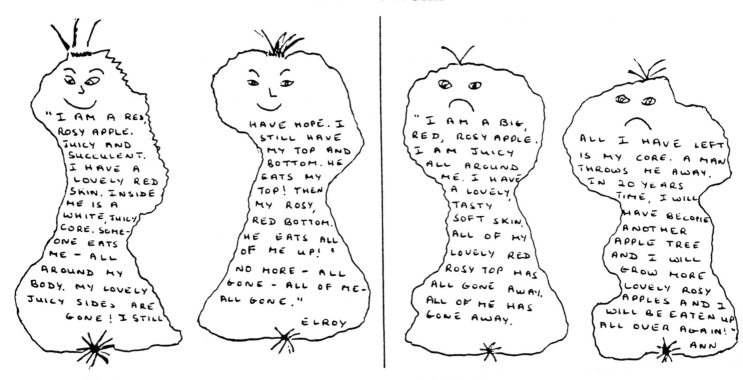

"I AM A RED, ROSY APPLE. JUICY AND SUCCULENT. I HAVE A LOVELY RED SKIN. INSIDE ME IS A WHITE, JUICY CORE. SOME-ONE EATS ME — ALL AROUND MY BODY. MY LOVELY JUICY SIDES ARE GONE! I STILL

HAVE HOPE. I STILL HAVE MY TOP AND BOTTOM. HE EATS MY TOP! THEN MY ROSY, RED BOTTOM. HE EATS ALL OF ME UP! NO MORE — ALL GONE — ALL OF ME- ALL GONE."

ELROY

"I AM A BIG, RED, ROSY APPLE. I AM JUICY ALL AROUND ME. I HAVE A LOVELY, TASTY SOFT SKIN. ALL OF MY LOVELY RED ROSY TOP HAS ALL GONE AWAY. ALL OF ME HAS GONE AWAY.

ALL I HAVE LEFT IS MY CORE. A MAN THROWS ME AWAY. IN 20 YEARS TIME, I WILL HAVE BECOME ANOTHER APPLE TREE AND I WILL GROW MORE LOVELY ROSY APPLES AND I WILL BE EATEN UP ALL OVER AGAIN!"

ANN

Discussions with the children during these sessions led to deep symbolic thoughts and ideas. An apple core was left on the ground, the apple rots away, it dies. What is left inside the core? The children's response — the seeds are left. What will happen to the seeds? Children — they will grow and a new apple tree will come with more apples. These general ideas were expanded to deep beliefs: From decay, death or emptyness a new life can grow. There can be a new start, a new beginning. Through discussions and follow up, the children had uncovered the basis of religious beliefs.

4. Concluding sessions

We tried to look at the difficult ideas of plenty and hunger: once more to go beyond ourselves and to relate to the thoughts and feelings of others. It was easy to imagine being full, having plenty to eat, as we were able to do guided imagery techniques immediately after lunch.

Activity

Eating a three course meal — guided imagery.

E.g. Hot soup and crunchy bread: "How do you feel?"

WHEN I SIP THE SOUP I AM AGLOW AND WARM. IT IS HOT, LOVELY AND SMOOTH

OR

I FELT NICE. A LOVELY WARM FEELING INSIDE ME I HAD A GLOWING TUMMY. IT WAS LOVELY.

The same questions were asked about a roast dinner and a scrumptious pudding. At the end of the meal "How did you feel?" "What did you look like?"

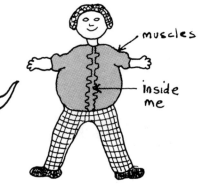

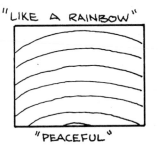
" I FELT STRONG, BIG, LOVELY AND FAT ! "

Other Activities

If fullness and plenty were colours, what colours would they be?
The children chose red, yellow, orange.
If being full were a pattern, what would it be like?

"COLOURFUL"   "SMOOTH"
"NICE TO LOOK AT"

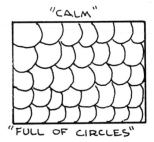
"CALM"
"FULL OF CIRCLES"

"LIKE A RAINBOW"
"PEACEFUL"

The second part of the work was much more difficult, as none of us had ever faced being empty, starved. We tried as best as we could.

Guided imagery: A hot, dusty place, sun beating down, moaning and crying of babies. What would it like to be hungry?

Dramatic interpretations: Children began writhing on the floor, moaning, full of sadness. Others were quite still and silent. It was an emotional experience for us all.

"How did you feel?" "What did you look like?"

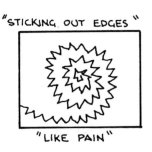
" I FELT HUNGRY AND THIN, BAD, ROTTEN, I WAS WEARING RAGS. FLIES WERE ALL OVER MY FACE. I WAS THINKING OF FOOD ALL OF THE TIME. I WAS LIKE A TRAMP - WITH NOTHING TO EAT."
SIMON

Other Activities

If emptyness and hunger was a colour, what colour would it be?
The children chose black, grey, purple.
If being hungry were a pattern, what would it be like?

"POINTY"
" DARK AND GLOOMY "

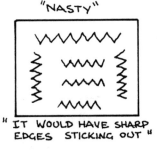
"NASTY"
" IT WOULD HAVE SHARP EDGES STICKING OUT "

"STICKING OUT EDGES "
"LIKE PAIN"

This part of the work was the most difficult but one of the most rewarding aspects of our topic. It needed a lot of support from me, but at the end of it all, we all felt we had gained a little more understanding and thought more deeply about the situation than before.

Extending awareness

The exercises in the previous chapter illustrate the fact that when we put ourselves in someone else's place, the world looks different. Our experience of reality depends very strongly on the perspective from which we view it. In this section we continue to explore the effects of altering our personal perspective, but now we begin entering a realm where the factors that affect experience are the symbols and stories of an entire religious culture.

Even as small children, each of us became aware of the large body of symbols and stories that constructs for us the way we see the world, and this is just as true of secular as it is of religious ways of seeing. It is no accident that almost the first thing we recognise about a religion is the symbol which represents it (Star, Crescent, Cross, Wheel). Within each religious group an extremely rich set of meanings and interpretations of reality has evolved around the central symbols. If we are to have some feeling for that religious perspective we need to enter into it imaginatively; we have to take account of the way in which symbols and stories direct our vision.

Religions face up to the most fundamental of all the questions that human beings can ask: Why is there anything? Why are we here? What should we do? And they do so by telling a story. Religious stories affect every aspect of our awareness because they are about 'Everything'.

Even when we let our minds wander imaginatively in fantasy, we continue to use the symbols supplied to us by our upbringing to provide the materials for our creativity. Thus the imaginative entering into the story of a religion is often used as an exercise for deepening religious awareness, as in the Vision Quest of a number of primal religions, or the Spiritual Exercises of St Ignatius in Roman Catholicism (or even as a means to achieving enlightenment, as in the practices of Shingon Buddhism in Japan).

The exercises which follow can help pupils to gain insight into the power of religious symbol and story to construct reality and to uncover some of the awesome mystery of 'life, the universe and everything'.

> **This is the way It [Brahman] is to be illustrated:**
> **When lightnings have been loosed:**
>   **Aaah!**
> **When that has made the eyes to be closed:**
>   **Aaah!**
>
> (From the *KENA-UPANISHAD*)

> **In the beginning there was nothing but mere appearance, Nothing really existed.**
>
> (A Colombian Indian Belief)

> **Where were you when I laid the foundations of the earth?**
>
> (The Book of Job)

SYMBOLS: OVERVIEW

Religion abounds with symbolism in its rituals, stories, music, art and architecture. Struggling to articulate the inexpressible, religious people of every faith, and throughout the ages, have resorted to symbols in image, gesture and deed. Consequently religious education cannot avoid the study of symbolism as a means of religious expression. Yet this is no easy task since symbols tend to accrue layers of meaning which are not always accessible through detached observation and analysis. It is hard enough to grasp the meanings of our own personal and cultural symbols without having to come to terms with or understand the significance of the symbolism of other cultures and faiths.

Because symbols have many layers of meaning, it is easy to get stuck in one layer to the neglect of other layers. The great teachers of religion constantly warn against this tendency. So, Buddhists are taught to think of their symbols as rafts. The symbols themselves are not transcendent, but they are vehicles used to reach the other shore. It is when religious people fall into the trap of mistaking the symbol for what it represents or expresses that they become superstitious. It is important to note that this can be a problem with secular symbols too, for example, believing that scientific theories about reality describe it directly.

Symbols can excite the imagination. They do not merely act as a sign or represent something else, they actually re–present what is signified, as in the celebration of Passover, or the rituals surrounding the Adi Granth, or Jamrat — stoning the devil at Mina during Hajj, or the transformation of the bread and wine of the Mass into the body and blood of Jesus for some Christians. In this respect the symbol's power lies in its potential to offer a means of spiritual insight.

Yet there can be no standard symbolic meaning. What is true for one person is meaningless to another. Like language, symbols also carry layers of personalised associations and connotations which affect their interpretation and response. The meaning of a symbol can change for an individual and some symbols carry opposite meanings, although one may predominate. The Christian cross recalls the death **and** the resurrection of Jesus, The Hindu swastika, an ancient symbol of good fortune linked with the god Ganesha, is also laden with other emotions when it is associated with the German Nazi party.

Understanding symbolism often requires more than rational thought (which can itself be more a hindrance than an aid to understanding). It has the power to evoke an affective or emotive response and arouse the intuition. Symbols are best left to speak for themselves since efforts to explain them deprive others of the experience of their meaning. Without some degree of personal encounter there is a risk that the symbolism will be dismissed as mere superstition.

ACTIVITIES

My badge

Purpose

This activity uses a popular exercise based on the heraldic shield to help pupils explore the meaning of symbols in their own experience. If wished it can be linked with 'The Journey of Life' and 'Life is Like'. Using different symbols to address various aspects of your own life and comparing them with other symbols adopted by the group offers a useful introduction to subsequent study of explicitly religious symbolism.

Time needed: Thirty minutes
Materials needed: Sheets of paper marked out with a shield or any other badge–like shape. Drawing materials.

Conditions

Some pupils may feel embarrassed by any exercise which asks them to disclose something of their personal lives or character and they should be able to work privately. A little groundwork may be necessary to ensure that pupils understand the word 'symbol' and are able to create their own images.

Procedure

You could begin with a short stilling exercise or a class discussion, asking pupils to recall their lives right back to their earliest memories and taking them a few years into the future. In doing this you should ask them to note the things that make them unique, their special or memorable experiences, characteristics, people they have met, things they have done in the past as well as ambitions and plans for the future.

Distribute badges and explain the idea of a heraldic shield representing aspects of its owner.

1. Think about the best thing that ever happened to you. It might be your greatest success, the most important event in your life . . . like the time you learnt to ride a bicycle . . . something that happened to you that you feel was important. When you've chosen something try to **think of a symbol** you can draw **to represent the best thing that ever happened to you**. You might find it hard to get the right symbol but don't worry about it, just try to avoid using any words to describe it.

They may need to jot down the idea in case they forget it.

2. Remember that symbol because you'll be asked to draw it in a minute or two. But first you need to decide what you will be drawing in the rest of the picture. So now **think about something you are good at** or like about yourself, or something you enjoy or perhaps people say you are good at. Then **decide how you can symbolise that achievement** on your piece of paper.

3. Do the same for something you would like to be better at. It could be something you think you're not very good at just now, or something you are just learning or would like to do but haven't yet had the chance. And again find a symbol to represent that idea.

4. Finally **think of** what you would like to be in the future, **your ambitions**, where you would like to be and what you hope to be doing in the future, say in ten or more years time. When you have chosen that symbol, **think about how you are going to draw four symbols representing your life in the badge**. If you need to change any of the symbols you can do so.

5. Draw one symbol in each section of your badge so that you have all four symbols covering the best event in your life, something you are good at, something you'd like to improve and your ambition for the future.

Allow time for everyone to sketch something in each quadrant and then organise the class in pairs.

6. When you have finished **look at your drawing as a whole and think of a motto** summarising your life to write in the scroll at the bottom of the badge.

Young children can colour in their outlines, cut them out and wear them as a badge.

Drawing out the learning

This can be done in threes, small groups or as a class discussion. Pupils should not be under any pressure to reveal their drawings or to explain their symbols unless they wish to do so.
Which was the easiest symbol you came up with?

And the hardest?

Are there any symbols you are pleased with, or perhaps puzzled by, any you would like to talk about?

In what ways can symbols be a useful way to express information?

What sort of feelings do you have when you look at or think about these symbols?

Are there any symbols which are too private to reveal?

Comment

In some schools this activity has been adapted into a valuable structure for the study of rites of passage, with each quadrant depicting customs and symbols associated with birth, initiation, marriage and death. By adding a fifth sector to the badge, one school devised a visual aid describing the five K's of Sikhism.

Candle and wire

Purpose

This can be a powerful exercise which raises issues about public and personal responses to symbols. It uses two secular symbols which to older pupils may already have certain associations. The exercise accesses a variety of sets of interpretations which can be noted and used as a basis for further discussion and reflection. Such symbols evoke personal images which can be related to religious questions and meanings.

Time needed: Forty–five minutes

Materials needed: A large 'Amnesty' candle. A spiral of barbed wire to fit around the candle. Small and large sheets of paper. Crayons and felt tip pens, or materials for collage.

Conditions

The atmosphere is important. The group should be seated in a circle around a table. Ideally, lighting should be soft and it is important that the exercise is not interrupted by noise or visitors. The group ought to feel secure and fairly confident in each other's company. They should be used to reflective silence and willing to sit quietly and still for some time.

Procedure

All instructions should be given at the outset to avoid disturbing the still and reflective frame of mind which may be generated while pupils are working.

Place a candle on the table in the centre of the group so that it is visible to everyone.

Settle the class, perhaps using a short stilling exercise as an introduction.

A haiku is a three–line poem of seventeen syllables: five — seven — five.

Light the candle.

After a few minutes — the time for each stage depends on the atmosphere within the group as well as the time available.

It does not matter if no one speaks, just move on to the next stage.

Take the candle away and replace it with a spiral of barbed wire.

Allow a short time to meditate.

Now put the lighted candle inside the spiral of wire.

Allow sufficient time.

You may need to increase the lighting in the room, but leave the lit candle in the centre of the wire.

1. We're going to do this meditation exercise together and then work individually. When we have finished the meditation, you can express your thoughts and feelings by drawing or writing a poem or haiku.

2. Will you **sit in silence** please and, **after a few minutes, you will have the chance to talk** about what you have seen, what it means for you, or what it reminds you of, or how you feel.

3. In silence, will you please **look at the candle and notice any feelings and reactions** which may arise as you watch the flame.

4. Would anyone like to say anything? For example, "The lighted candle reminds me of . . .". What about you?

5. Still in silence, will you now meditate on the barbed wire and again **notice your feelings and responses** as you look at it.

6. Does anyone want to say anything about the wire?

7. Now let's **meditate on these two symbols, the candle and the barbed wire,** as we see them together.

8. Without saying anything, collect whatever you need to **draw or write about your feelings**. Please work on your own.

Drawing out the learning

Allow plenty of time for discussion. Poems and paintings can be shared with a partner or small group and perhaps displayed for everyone to see. Discussion can be in small groups or with the whole class.

What were your thoughts and feelings when you looked at the candle on its own? How did those thoughts and feelings compare with your reactions to the barbed wire?

What did the various symbols, the candle, the barbed wire, and the candle inside the wire mean for you?

What did you like about the exercise?

What did you find difficult?

Did anything make a special impression on you?

Was there anything you wanted to say or do, but didn't?

What, if anything, have you discovered from this exercise?

Comment

This exercise could be related to religious festivals: Advent, Easter, Hannukah, Divali, etc., or perhaps during Prisoner of Conscience week, or adopted within a theme on light and darkness.

An understanding and appreciation of the depth and power of many other symbols can be gained through the technique of meditation used in this exercise. Ideas can be collected by brainstorming. Pupils at The Avenue School, Newton Aycliffe, discussed how interpretations of a symbol are affected by the individual's background and culture. They concentrated on the Yin–Yang, a Hopi Indian Maze and the Necker Cube to see how different people might view life. They then linked this activity with 'Life is like . . . .' (page 126).

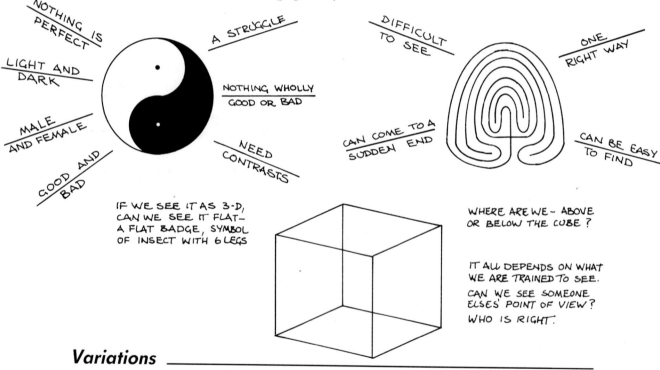

Variations

Appropriate music could be played to complement or contrast each image. Since the music can influence the response and confuse the impact, it may be preferable to remain in silence when a class is introduced to the exercise for the first time. The effect of evocative music can be drawn out in discussion.

IN PRACTICE

Cautious of the potential power of this exercise, one secondary teacher decided to experiment with the first stage of the exercise. A low ability GCSE group of fifteen–year–old girls were studying the saying, "Jesus is the Light of the World". Initial discussion was predictable and superficial until the teacher recalled 'The Candle and the Wire'. She said later:

"The class was thoroughly bored by their course in Christianity. It was the end of the autumn term, and they wanted to relax, so I asked them to bring a candle, an orange, a red ribbon, dried fruit and nuts and orange sticks to their next lesson. I wanted to restore their interest and cooperation, so I gave them twenty minutes to make their own 'Christingles'. This was great fun and the atmosphere improved accordingly.

The next stage was to dim the lighting by closing the blinds and then light each candle. I asked everyone to sit silently and meditate on the candle. They could jot down any thoughts or ideas that occurred to them if they wished, but that was not essential.

After five minutes, they reluctantly gathered into groups. They would have preferred to continue meditating, but time was pressing. Each group brainstormed their ideas and then we spent the last few minutes of the lesson producing a large class brainstorm for display.

Although I was impressed by the variety of ideas expressed, they were 100 per cent on the positive side, so the next lesson we returned to the theme "Jesus is the Light of the World". This time, I scripted a fantasy — taking them through a series of situations which alternated between light and darkness before asking them to brainstorm on "light". (This script was based on ideas suggested by Jan Thompson in *The Christian Faith and its Symbols*.) At last they had seen the light, the fear of being in the spotlight, of being observed by others, of being caught out — ideas which had previously evaded them.

The Christingles made last lesson were brought out of the cupboard and they again meditated, concentrating on the entire symbol of the Christingle. Discussion later centred around the effect of making and keeping the Christingle, its significance, and how effective it is in communicating something about Jesus. Finally, they produced a do–it–yourself Christingle kit, containing materials and instruction leaflet, explaining its origins and meaning.

A year later, I overheard several of that group explaining why candles are used at Christmas. They gave an accurate and detailed account of the symbolism used to express the belief that "Jesus is the Light of the World". Encouraged by this response, I had no hesitation in using the entire candle and wire routine with another senior class studying the work of Amnesty International. They were subdued, although not upset, and preferred not to express their feelings in any permanent form. "To put it down on paper just wouldn't say what I want to say," was one boy's explanation. But it didn't stop him, and others, from returning later to ask how they could support "prisoners of conscience"."

A class of twelve–year–olds were about to start a course on symbolism in religion. It was a sunny summer's day and the previous class had used leaves as an aid to meditation. It had generated a relaxed atmosphere and the teacher was not looking forward to changing mood to introduce the next topic.

Thinking on her feet, as teachers often do, she quickly concealed the leaves as the next class entered. Following the instructions for 'Let me see', p. 66, she asked each member of the class to meditate on a leaf and practise visualising it. As they did so, many allusions and similes came to mind which they noted before returning to the task in hand. Then they drew their leaf from memory, and jotted down some of their thoughts about the leaf around the drawing. Finally, they shared their most striking ideas with the rest of the class. Suddenly, there was a vibrant discussion about symbolism and the power of ostensibly latent meanings. The lesson was so successful that the class subsequently asked if they could repeat the experience with other objects. It was a useful way of sharing differing perspectives and proved a valuable introduction to symbols in religion.

Religious symbolism encompasses such a vast wealth of material that it is impossible to provide a small number of activities which would answer everybody's needs. Individual teachers will adapt and invent activities as required. One teacher who criticised 'Candle and Wire', admitted later that it was through decrying that activity that the idea germinated for the following series of lessons.

SYMBOLS AND WORSHIP

The aim: To introduce first year secondary pupils to the concept of Ancestral Worship. It was part of a much larger scheme studying various aspects of deity and it was hoped that this work would lead on to consideration of worship. However, as the work progressed, it became obvious that the pupils were focusing their attention on the value and meaning of the symbols they thought appropriate in an ancestral shrine.

Group: Top and middle band eleven to twelve–year–olds, eighty–five pupils in three separate classes. Afterwards sixty–four were enthusiastic about the work. Of the others, sixteen did not like working with the opposite sex and fifteen had no particular likes or dislikes.

Time: Six lessons of thirty–five minutes.

Brief: To establish a family group of four to six pupils with at least two members of each sex in every group. After initial moans, the boys and girls worked extremely well together. Classroom furniture was arranged so that each family could sit together around the kitchen table to discuss their plans. They were asked to imagine that a much–loved relative had died, an imaginary relative, code–named Great–Great–Grandpa Ken, and they were to spend some time as a family deciding what was special about him.

The family wants to create a special place where they can remember Great–Great–Grandpa Ken and they are to plan the things they will keep there as reminders of this life. As they planned their shrines, photographs of ancestral shrines in the Far East were passed around, leading to a discussion of the practice of leaving symbols and replicas of items which the dead may need to live happily in their after–life. They were then asked to prepare their family shrine, making and collecting any items they wished to include.

Finally, when everything was completed, they were asked to stand quietly for a short time, looking at their own shrine and reflecting on its meaning and importance for them. Later, many commented that this experience had taken the form of a prayer to Great–Great–Grandpa Ken.

Drawing out the learning

There was a great deal of curiosity about other families' shrines and everyone was given the chance to look at and talk about the work of their classmates. In class discussion they displayed a sensitive and, at times, critical approach towards the beliefs of others. Comparison was made with the practice of putting fresh flowers on the grave of a long deceased relative. It was recognised that a shrine can take many physical forms or be confined to the imagination and that the process of preparing something like a shrine is both universal and therapeutic. Most importantly this work had apparently provided the pupils with an opportunity to experience the importance of a symbol while at the same time realising that the same symbol was meaningless to others.

Photographs were taken of each shrine and used to create a wall display. This fascinated other pupils as well as giving the first years a chance to see what the other two classes had done in their lessons on ancestral worship.

Responses

In general the shrines contained flowers, books, favourite foods and drinks, tobacco and matches, spectacles, photographs, watch, money, credit cards, pools coupons, newspapers and false teeth. One group used cardboard to build a Viking longboat to represent a burial ship, while another family constructed a pyramid. Criticised for their lack of conformity, they raised the point that the contents of a shrine will differ according to the time and culture of its people.

Comments about their activities and experiences during this work were recorded in the pupils' RE diaries. They included the following:

"I think I became a bit involved with this lesson and expressed things I might have expressed if he had died really."

"These things remind me of great great grandad Ken sitting in a chair with his glasses on, smoking and reading his paper. The dried flowers and grasses remind me of when we were on holiday and we had a picnic in a field of long grass. It helps me to make myself happy if I am sad."

"I feel that his spirit is among the contents of the shrine."

"Going to the shrine helps me to relax and calms me when I have some problems on my mind."

"I feel I am closer to him than ever I was."

"I can talk there because he might be able to hear me."

STORY: OVERVIEW

Children love 'story time' and like to hear a favourite story again and again, taking possession of it and making it their own. As children grow up stories are neglected. In secondary schools at least, they are frequently reduced to being subjects of literary criticism. Yet we never grow out of story–telling, constantly telling ourselves stories in order to make sense of and categorise everyday experiences.

Stories are a powerful and an essential part of our communication system. They transcend time and place, extending our experiences and sympathies by allowing us to be both participant and spectator within the story. Stories 'stretch' reality. By giving the imagination free rein they can extend our sense of what is possible and lead us along paths we might not see if restricted to rational thought. Such stories are devices for learning.

Religions abound with stories intended as vehicles for teaching and challenge. Often part of the community's oral tradition, these stories employ metaphor, symbol, fantasy and drama to express and interpret the intangible. They offer layers of meaning which require reflection before they are uncovered. The original context of some teaching narratives has been forgotten so that they are now regarded as fairy tales, while familiarity has robbed other stories of their power to surprise. These folk tales and fairy stories can be seen as childish or mildly amusing, yet they can shed light on our past and present experience and say something about the real world. Different patterns and new interpretations can emerge as we grow and change, becoming more adept at unwrapping the various layers of meaning.

There are numerous collections of tales from different cultures and religions which provide fruitful sources of stories for RE. Story–telling provides listeners with time to picture the events as they occur and then, in later discussion, to share reactions and points of interest. Talking about a story can lead to deeper consideration of aspects which may have been missed or glossed over, and to the noting of personal patterns of response and perception. The stories challenge listeners to self–discovery and ethical decision–making while offering opportunities for an increased understanding of religion. The sagas, myths, parables and poems of religious traditions go beyond rational thought. They appeal to the world of inner experiences, to the personal, intuitive aspects of the mind, and they create openings for new awareness. For example the sayings and stories of Zen Buddhism are used to jolt awareness; to wake people up to new meanings and possibilities.

Useful collections of stories include the Jataka Tales for Buddhism; *Zen Flesh, Zen Bones* by Paul Reps; *The Song of the Bird* by A. De Mello, and the collections of Sufi stories by Idries Shah: *Caravan of Dreams, The Pleasantries of the Incredible Mulla Nasruddin*, amongst others.

ACTIVITIES

Purpose

Religions are packed with stories — perhaps because the narrative is a means of saying what is otherwise unspeakable. All good stories have layers and depths of meaning which do not appear immediately, but need to be reflected upon. These suggestions help pupils 'mine' the depths of a story and see in it their own interests and concerns. Working in this way can reveal the process in which a hearer or reader moves from being aware of a simple allegory to perceive much deeper and more paradoxical meanings.

Time needed: varies according to each story

Materials needed: writing materials

Conditions

The conditions you choose to adopt will, of course, depend on the ability, mood and maturity of the pupils as well as the kind of story you are using.

The group needs to be comfortable and able to hear clearly the story being told to them. Establishing a relaxed and receptive mood is therefore important. You may wish to tell some short stories twice to give pupils the chance to notice any subtlety. Whenever possible *tell* the story rather than read it. If you do read it aloud, look up often to catch the eyes and mood of your listeners.

Procedure

Make sure the class is sitting comfortably. You may wish to organise partners and groups of four to minimise disruption later. To avoid spoiling the impact of the story, give the instructions before you start to tell or read the story. In some cases, it could be appropriate to give a resumé or an introduction to the story first.

You may prefer not to reveal the title of some stories until the end of the session.

Offer a couple of starting points to indicate the sort of things to look out for. Be careful not to restrict ideas which might occur to them.

1. Is everybody comfortable? When you're ready, **I am going to tell you a short story** called . . . . . When it is finished, I'd like you to **think about what you have heard.**
While you're listening, you might like to **watch out for . . . and there might be other points you particularly notice.** Are there any questions?

Tell/read the story.
Some pupils may like to listen with their eyes closed.

This will depend on age, etc.

Encourage them to report their own perceptions of the story, and not ideas you or others in the group may have suggested.

Open up discussion to provide feedback for the entire group. Take one point from each group in turn. You may need to watch time restrictions to ensure each group has a chance to report back.

2. Can everybody hear me clearly?

3. Sit quietly for a few minutes and **think about the story** you've just heard.

4. Now, if you are ready, **turn to a partner and compare your thoughts and ideas about the story.**

5. Join up with another pair to do the same thing again, sharing your thoughts and observations, and then **write down a list of your group's ideas.**

6. Going round each group in turn, **what were the points your particular group noticed** or talked about?

Drawing out the learning

Activities such as these help pupils to focus on the story and think more deeply about what they have seen.

1. Stories
a) **Titled:** Pupils can brainstorm possible titles for a story and select the best three.
b) **Questioned:** Groups of pupils can compose questions they would like to ask about the story. These can be swapped with another group who try to answer each other's questions.
c) **Given proverbs:** Proverbial sayings appropriate to a particular story can be suggested or invented. Again, the best can be chosen by the whole group.
d) **Expressed in different media:** It is important to provide non–verbal means of expression. Pupils' responses can be given in paint, clay, collage or mime. In this way, a mood or shades of meaning can be explored which might not be caught in words. This can be expressed by picturing a scene or sequence, or adopting a more symbolic form of image, e.g. a mandala, or even acting the story out to develop a ritual.

2. Suggestions for working on a text
Each group could have a different story to work on, or different parts of a longer story which can then be re–assembled by the class.
a) **Decimate: Print the text with every tenth word blotted out.** Give copies to the class and let them work in pairs to fill in the missing words.

b) Jigsaw: Cut up the text into sections and distribute the story in its sections among groups of four to six. After reading out their section to the others, pupils can decide on the proper order and stick the pieces to a backing sheet. They can also provide an illustration to accompany their own section. The completed work can be assembled and displayed.

c) Commentary: For short pithy stories **the text can be printed out, leaving broad margins** in which pupils can write any question, comment or reference that comes to mind. You may need to start them off with a few examples from a different text from the one they are working on. Their marginal notes can then be compared with a partner's. The comparison and questioning prompts further insights and new ways of seeing that otherwise might have been missed. They could join up with another pair and write up their combined commentary for display. Older pupils could be asked to notice the way their ideas progressed from an individual's first thoughts to the group's final analysis.

3. Our own lives as stories

Pupils can be encouraged to tell part of their own life story with a drawing which serves to tease out more details — as I draw I remember more and as I tell my memories I can elaborate further on my drawing.

A fascinating way to work on your own story is to see it as a journey or quest. The quest is a powerful metaphor for human life and is central to many kinds of narrative: myth, saga, fairy story, religious history, novel and science fiction. A central character makes a journey to somewhere for something. The quest provides a medium for relating and reflecting on the past and present and so raises questions about future goals.

The poet, W. H. Auden, provides a richer and more complex framework for understanding a quest. He maintains that each quest story has: a hero or heroine; a journey through space or time; a series of testings the hero or heroine must undergo; helpers who assist the main character in the time of trial; hinderers who make the task more difficult; a final goal or treasure.

When working on a quest story, pupils can identify examples of each of these characteristics. Exploring their findings in class will reveal further levels and meanings in the stories used.

Procedure

1. Explain to the class that the theme of journey is important in books, films and T.V. series. Give some examples and ask pupils to work in pairs to find other examples for themselves.

2. Ask for a couple of examples from each group. Explain that journey stories are quest stories: a journey undertaken by someone to somewhere for something. Ask the group to identify these features in their chosen examples.

3. Then allow them to discuss and comment briefly on the ideas raised. Are there any exceptions?

4. Explain that quests have six characteristics.

Hero or heroine	Journey
Testings of hero or heroine	Helpers in the testings
Hinderers who bring on the testings	The Goal or Treasure

Work these through with a well–known quest, e.g. Jason, The Wizard of Oz, and ask the class to do the same with their own examples.

5. Ask for more examples and consider whether there are any exceptions. Perhaps a goal to lose rather than gain?

6. Working individually, ask them to **imagine** that they are the hero/heroine. What is their own journey, testings, helpers, hinderers, goal or treasure? They are to take time and write a sentence or paragraph about each element or, if they prefer, draw or symbolise these aspects.

7. Their quest can be graphically expressed on a large piece of paper, to include the main characters and events of their personal journey.

8. Suggest they show and talk about the picture to a partner if they wish. They can move around to look at the work of others and share if appropriate.

9. Further reflection could be stimulated by considering the nature of the goal — what happens when the goal is achieved? Is the quest then finished? What goals can never be fully attained? Why are hinderers and helpers the same people in some stories? Did anyone find this in their own quest?

This activity could be part of a more extensive scheme with detailed work on journey: the longest, most exciting journeys made; consideration of the preparations; the element of risk in a journey — setting aside the secure and unfamiliar to experience the new wider horizon; feelings of hope and anxiety.

It could be followed by an exploration of journey in religion:

- The Buddha's early life as a quest.
- Islam and Muhammad's flight from Mecca to Medina.
- The parables of Jesus — the pearl of great price and the treasure hidden in the field — as typifying the demands of a journey to set aside what is known in order to search for something greater.
- Pilgrimage: the journey to the sacred place to bring back into everyday life something of the holiness of that place of pilgrimage.

FANTASY: OVERVIEW

'Stop day-dreaming and get on with some work' is a familiar classroom admonition supporting the assumption that fantasy is a waste of time. Yet there is increasing evidence that fantasy can be an important aid to learning and understanding since it helps to attune the intuitive, creative and affective sides of ourselves. Many successful writers, scientists, artists and composers admit that their best work comes through 'playing around' with ideas in fantasy.

In what might be described as 'waking dreams', scripted fantasy is a technique which guides the imagination. It can be tightly controlled or offer freedom for the imagination to range around the subject suggested by the guide. In this respect, guided fantasy differs from dreams where the subject matter is determined by the dreamer's unconscious. Through fantasy activities pupils can learn to respect what goes on in their own and other people's mind as they discover their uniqueness by exploring individual, original and creative thoughts.

Fantasy is a tool in the search for meaning since it draws upon the imaging aspects of the self and speaks in the language of symbols. It allows us to approach areas of our personality which lie beyond the immediate conscious mind and so has the potential to deepen our knowledge and understanding of who we are.

The creative nature of guided fantasy has long been understood in the religious traditions of the world. In Japanese Shingon Buddhism the progression through a long series of guided fantasies is central to the achievement of enlightenment. In the Christian tradition the spiritual exercises of St Ignatius Loyola use a series of imaginative visualisations as a means of deepening spiritual awareness.

These traditions use fantasy to deepen spirituality within a particular religious point of view. However, teachers of religious education are in a very different situation and, in state schools, are not in the business of advocating any particular beliefs. For the purposes of RE, fantasy is a tool which can offer opportunities for sensitive and imaginative insight into the pupil's own self. At the same time it can increase empathic understanding of the lives of believers. On a cautionary note, fantasy is not a means of creating a religious or spiritual exercise in the classroom. Teachers should never attempt to interpret any pupil's fantasy experience.

The activities begin with a simple script created as a revision aid for pupils studying Islam. Other fantasies provide greater freedom to explore deeper and universal questions of existence. Although it is not essential, it is helpful if pupils have had some practice at stilling exercises. They need space to sit or lie comfortably and undisturbed throughout the fantasy and should be allowed to return gently to the reality of the classroom. It should always be clear that if anyone wants to stop participating in the fantasy at any stage they can do so quite simply by opening their eyes. They should not disturb anyone else. When they are ready to return to the fantasy they can close their eyes and begin to concentrate on the instructions. Pupils unused to this experience may giggle and fidget nervously but this is rarely a sign of lack of co-operation. Persevere and complete the fantasy before declaring it a failure — you may be pleasantly surprised.

Comment

Teachers who have no prior experience of the use of fantasy in the classroom are advised to try out some of the stilling exercises described in Chapter 8 before attempting the more extensive guided imagery given in the following scripts. A more detailed exposition of the use of fantasy is given in 'Guided Imagery and religious education', in Part four. (See page 223.)

'Many cultures throughout history have employed fantasy as the traditional place where man transcends himself, communicates with God, and where ultimate truths are revealed.'

(Anthony de Mello)

SCRIPTING A GUIDED FANTASY

Guided fantasies can be created from almost anything — from an apple core, to a blackboard rubber, to the search for the Holy Grail. The material is as wide as your imagination can determine. However, for religious education, the richest resources are the stories and symbols of the major world faiths.

All guided fantasy needs to begin with a time of relaxation and stilling before embarking on the fantasy. Following or noticing the breath and counting the breaths are two traditional methods of doing this.

When the atmosphere is relaxed and quiet, you can begin the guided fantasy. The story is told in such a manner that the participants can identify with features or characters or are part of the story as themselves. Stress is laid on the experiences of the senses through questions — how does it feel, can you hear anything, what colour is it, etc.? Sometimes added insight can be obtained by asking the children to become different aspects of the fantasy (even objects) and seeing the fantasy from a different perspective. The story could be further explored by giving a voice to characters or objects and getting them to talk to each other or the participant.

The fantasy is conducted in the present tense as if it were happening now, and all questions are framed in the present. It is also helpful to make questions as open as possible, so that the participants are not too confined in the responses they can give. Some people find that being directed in a script produces a negative blocking response. They are helped by couching the script in tentative terms. For instance, instead of saying, "You are standing in a meadow", it might be more appropriate to say, "I would like to invite you to imagine you are standing in a meadow".

By the end of the fantasy, we hope that the participants will be relaxed and deeply involved in their own story. They need to be brought back from this as gently as they were taken in. Concentrating on breathing, bodily sensations, envisaging the room and their part in it, are appropriate means of re–emerging.

ACTIVITIES

Pilgrimage

Purpose

The relevance of fantasy work to RE is not always immediately clear. However, with careful scripting, fantasy can be used to reinforce more traditional ways of learning, offering pupils an opportunity to delve into the atmosphere of a situation.

This script, produced by Philip Doughty of Wilsthorpe School, Long Eaton in Derbyshire, was devised to help fifth year examination candidates gain a deeper understanding of the meaning of pilgrimage for a Muslim during the Hajj. It was used as a revision exercise.

Time needed: Thirty minutes.

Materials needed: Four or five slides to stimulate the imagination are preferable, but not essential, e.g. frames from 'Religion in Human Experience — Islam', produced by ARGUS. (Available in most Teachers' Centres.) Projector and screen.

Conditions

As with all fantasy work, pupils should be able to sit comfortably without disturbance for some time. They need to be familiar with the main events and vocabulary describing the Islamic pilgrimage and have previously viewed some form of visual account of the Hajj.

Procedure

If using slides, make sure all equipment is ready and working before commencing the fantasy. Pupils should be sitting, or perhaps lying down, comfortably in a relaxed position, preferably with eyes closed, except when looking at the screen. Always pause long enough for the scene to work through people's minds. Imagining the scene yourself is a guide to the length of time you need, but you will also need to keep an eye on pupils' reactions.

You may wish to begin with a short stilling exercise.

Suggest slides showing:
Clouds seen from above.
Allow a moment for pupils to re-orientate before continuing the fantasy.

Inside the mosque at Jeddah.

Sit quietly . . . breathe slowly . . .

Imagine you are in an aircraft . . . you are very tired and look out of the window . . . (please look towards the screen) . . . you begin to drift into a dream . . . (please look away again) . . . I am so tired . . . I can remember the excitement of the last week . . . the journey out . . . the crowded streets . . . meeting my guide . . . putting on my white garment . . . everyone dressed alike . . . some rich . . . some poor . . . men . . . women . . . kings . . . peasants . . . black . . . white . . . yellow . . . all assemble . . . equal before God . . . then we left the chaos and noise and went into a mosque in Jeddah . . . (please look towards the screen) . . . inside the mosque . . . I can see the backs of people wearing similar white garments . . . (please

Ka'aba from street level.

Arafat.

Clouds.

look away again) . . . then we travelled by bus to Mecca . . . passed the Hira cave . . . the very place where Muhammad received his first call to prophethood . . . we eventually arrived in Mecca . . . at long last . . . I could hardly wait . . . the crowds . . . everyone the same . . . all making for the entrance to the Ka'aba . . . as we got nearer I was so excited . . . after all these years . . . the saving . . . the photographs and here I am . . . (please look towards the screen) . . . the Ka'aba . . . how magnificent it looks in the sunlight . . . the contrast between the white minarets . . . the blue sky . . . and the black and gold of the Ka'aba . . . (please look away again) . . . seven times we went around the holy stone . . . I forgot all about my aching feet . . . I can remember little about Sa'i' but the next great event I remember was at Arafat . . . we travelled by bus . . . many walked the eighteen miles in the blistering heat . . . we arrived early enough to see the huge plain of Arafat filling up with pilgrims . . . and we eventually made the short journey up the Mount of Mercy . . . what a view . . . (please look towards the screen) . . . of Arafat and tents . . . (please look away again) . . . here we assembled for prayers to ask for forgiveness and God's help and guidance . . . I will never forget the view . . . as far as I could see . . . white tents . . . Much later we threw stones at the pillar in Mina . . . but I cannot remember these things so clearly as I can hear the voices inside the plane . . . (please look towards the screen) . . . we are almost home now . . . (please look away again) . . . as the plane lands . . . we say goodbye to our fellow travellers . . . and we return to the classroom.

Drawing out the learning

The class then answered the question — what memories of your week in Mecca are strongest?

Comment

There is some evidence to show that rehearsal in fantasy of certain lesson content aids recall. (See *Transpersonal Education*, eds. G. Hendricks and J. Fadiman). Philip Doughty has devised many scripts for use with secondary pupils of all ages and abilities. Other examples include asking first years to imagine they are young Hebrews getting ready to follow Moses in the Exodus. He guides them through the excitement and frustrations of preparing to leave Egypt. The fantasy is backed up by the use of text books and a celebration of the Passover meal as part of a theme on festivals. First year lessons on Founders include imagery based on the revelation of suffering to the Buddha. Pupils often comment that fantasy helps their studies come to life.

How does your garden grow?

Purpose

The image of a garden is a fruitful one for exploring ideas of personal growth. Other exercises where pupils focus on one specific image of a tree or flower can be used in a similar way.

Time needed: Thirty to forty minutes

Materials needed: Large sheets of paper and coloured crayons.

Conditions

Pupils need to be accustomed to stilling and to be able to settle for an extended period of time. There should be space for everyone to sit, or lie down, comfortably and without disturbance. As with most fantasy scripts this can be shortened, or modified, to suit the needs and circumstances of the group.

Procedure

There are frequent pauses to allow time for the scene to work through people's minds. The time needed can be gauged by watching pupils' reactions and imagining the scene for yourself.

Begin with a short relaxation and centring exercise.

Some people do not like the idea of a wall and this stage could be omitted.

Imagine you are walking down a path which leads to a wall . . . Stand in front of the wall and look at it for a few moments . . . try touching it . . . it is solid and strong . . . you know that behind this wall is a secret garden which is waiting for you to explore it. This garden is yours. As you look at the wall more closely you see a door . . . what does the door look like? Find a way to open the door — perhaps you have to say some words . . . perhaps the door opens by itself . . . Go through the door and into the garden and stand and look at the garden.

Now begin to explore this garden . . . it is your garden and yours to explore in peace.

What kind of plants grow there . . . perhaps there are paths to follow . . . or maybe the garden is without paths? Choose which way you want to go . . . I will offer you some suggestions . . . you may choose to follow these . . . or you may prefer to follow your own ideas and ignore my suggestions . . .

Look at the general layout of the garden . . . is it organised . . . formal . . . wild . . . or well cared for? . . .

Look at the plants growing there . . . perhaps they are grouped together . . . or lots of varieties mixed up . . . new seedlings . . . mature plants . . . trees . . . shrubs . . . flowers . . . vegetables . . . herbs . . . fruit . . .

Take some time to explore . . . any hidden areas . . . woodland . . . watery boggy bits . . .

Now stand back and take a long look at the garden . . . are there any changes you would like to make? . . . Perhaps you would like to create more space in the garden or put in more plants . . . Decide what you would like to do . . . Remember too that some changes will take a long time to show . . .

This garden is yours to visit whenever you wish . . . say goodbye to the garden and go to the door in the wall . . . is there any message you would like to give your garden . . . or anything you would like to do? When you are ready open the door and leave the garden . . . and come back to this room . . . Using a large sheet of paper, draw the garden you have just visited . . . take your time. You may also like to write down your feelings about this garden . . . are you worried about it . . . pleased . . . peaceful . . . anxious to make changes? . . . Start when you are ready.

Drawing out the learning ——

Pupils can talk about their work with a partner, taking five minutes or so each.

Anna

My rose is one big rose that is alone. It is a beautiful pink rose. My rose has a bird flying near it. The sky is clear and the grass is green. It is a lovely day and my rose is getting warm. My rose has a lovely smell. I feel like my rose because it is neat and I am neat. There is a bird by it and I like birds. And I think my rose is beautiful. The sun shows it has been a lovely summers morning.

IN PRACTICE

Varying the theme of growth to include transformation, which is a central notion of religion, Kathy Raban was able to use fantasy to explore the parables of Jesus with infants.

Class

While teaching at Newcroft Primary School, Shepshed, Leicestershire, I had a class of five– to six–year–old children, most in their first year at school. At this age reading and writing are just beginning, but the inner images are not.

Topic

We were doing a topic on 'growing things' which included germinating all kinds of seeds in the classroom and watching some wonderful time–lapse films of seeds growing. For part of the topic I decided to use the parable of the seed growing secretly as the basis for a guided inner journey.

Setting

We were lucky enough to have a quiet withdrawing room (the school is open–plan) which is carpeted and curtained.

Procedure

I settled the children, curled up rather than stretched out. When they were relaxed I introduced the parable by asking the children to imagine that they were a seed being jostled in the farmer's sack — as at all stages, I asked how this felt and encouraged the children to explore the possibilities of positive and negative reactions so that they would feel that whatever images came up were acceptable.

Then I talked the children through:
a) being scattered and falling deep into the earth — stressing the feeling of the earth and being buried in a dark moist medium;
b) the feeling of the hard shell of the seed gradually softening;
c) the seed swelling and the emergence of roots and shoots;

d) the feeling of growing through the soil and the first sight of daylight;
e) finally I asked, "What kind of seed are you, what do you grow into?"

Drawing out the learning

The talking and sharing afterwards was very 'fruitful'. The children grew into a tremendous variety of plants from pine trees to red roses; several kinds of fruit trees and mustard and cress. Most of them were happy with what they grew into.

Tom Limb adapted the script to encourage his junior pupils to become a tree.

The wise person

(This activity has been adapted from *Awareness* by J. O. Stevens.)

Purpose

This fantasy employs techniques which bypass the rational or conscious mind. Pupils may discover that they have inner resources when considering issues which perplex them.

Time needed: Forty minutes

Materials needed: drawing or modelling materials

Conditions

Pupils should be familiar with the practice of guided imagery and able to remain quiet for about fifteen minutes while the script is read out to them. This script suggests pupils identify with parts of the fantasy; the skill of identification may require some practice, for example, 'I'm a soft shoe' (see page 118). There needs to be enough room for everyone to sit or lie down comfortably without being disturbed by other people. While it is better to try to avoid any interruptions and external noise, scripted fantasy can be very successful under quite adverse conditions. Some groups may prefer lighting to be subdued. Choose a suitable stilling exercise to relax the group before starting this script.

Materials should be easily accessible so that pupils can start their drawing or modelling as soon as they are ready and without disturbance. They should have privacy to get on with their work.

Drawing out the learning

This can be a very personal experience. Some pupils are loathe to return to the reality of the classroom and others need time to readjust after their fantasy experience. A quiet period of drawing or modelling some aspect of their fantasy can provide them with a focus for reflection. This can be followed by talking about this work to a partner. Some pupils will be happy to have their models and pictures displayed.

Procedure

This is quite a long fantasy and can be shortened if necessary. For example, omitting Stages 4 and 5 and ending at Stage 7. There are frequent pauses giving time for the scene to work through people's minds. One way of gauging the length of each pause is to allow the fantasy to run through your own mind as you read out the script. Watching pupils' reactions can also be a useful guide.

Make sure everyone is settled in a comfortable position either sitting or lying down if appropriate before you begin.

Invite the group to close their eyes but do not insist that they do so if they feel uncomfortable. Begin with a breathing or short, guided imagery exercise to help everybody relax. Adopt a quiet, soothing tone of voice which is loud enough for everyone to hear.

To shorten the fantasy, Stages 4 and 5 could be omitted.

1. "I want you to imagine that you are walking up a trail through the mountains at night. There is a full moon which lets you see the path easily . . . and you can also see quite a lot of your surroundings . . . What is this trail like? . . . What else can you see around you? . . . How do you feel as you walk up the mountain trail? . . . Just ahead there is a small side path that leads up higher to a cave that is the home of a very wise person who can tell you the answer to any question. . . . Turn off on to this side trail and walk towards the wise person's cave . . . Notice how your surroundings change as you move up this trail . . . and come closer to the cave . . .

2. When you arrive at the cave . . . you may see a small campfire in front of the cave, and you'll just be able to make out someone sitting in the firelight . . . Go up to the fire, put some more wood on it, and sit quietly . . . As the fire burns more brightly you will be able to see this wise person more clearly . . . Take some time to really become aware of aspects of this wise person. Look at the clothes . . . the body . . . the face . . . the eyes . . .

3. Ask the wise person a question that is important to you. As you ask this question, watch the wise person and see what reaction is given . . . Perhaps the answer is in words . . . or with a gesture or facial expression, or you might be shown something . . . What kind of answer comes?

4. Now become the wise person . . . What is it like being this wise person? . . . How do you feel, and what is your life like? . . . How do you feel towards this visitor? . . . What do you say to your visitor — whether in words, gestures or actions? . . .

5. Become yourself again and continue talking with the wise person. Do you understand what is said to you? . . . Do you have any other questions to ask? . . . How do you feel towards the wise person?

   Now become the wise person again, and continue this conversation . . . Is there anything else you can say to your visitor? . . . Become yourself again.

6. You will soon have to say goodbye to the wise person . . . Say anything else you want to before you leave . . . You see the wise person reach into a bag and search for

something very special to give to you . . . The wise person takes your gift out of the bag and gives it to you to take home with you . . . Look at the gift . . . How do you feel towards the wise person now? . . . Say how you feel . . . and slowly say goodbye . . .

7. Now turn away, and start walking back down the mountain path, carrying your gift with you . . . Look at the path carefully, so that you will remember your way back to the wise person when you want to visit again . . . Be aware of your surroundings . . . and how you feel.

This fantasy could be curtailed by going straight to Stage 10, omitting Stages 8 and 9.

8. Keep your eyes closed, and bring your gift with you as you return to this room . . . Take some time now to examine this gift in more detail . . . What is it? Discover more about it . . . Touch it . . . smell it . . . turn it over in your hands and look at it carefully . . .

9. Now become this gift. Identify with it and describe yourself. What are you like as this gift? . . . How do you feel as this thing? . . . What are your qualities? . . . What do you do, or how can you be used or appreciated? . . .

    Now become yourself again and look at the gift . . . see if you can discover even more about it . . . Do you notice any change in it, or anything that you didn't notice before? . . . Now put this gift away carefully and safely in your memory . . . and say goodbye to it for now . . .

10. Gradually become aware of yourself in this room now . . . When you are ready open your eyes and you can stretch if you want to.

11. In your own time, try to express something of your experience during the fantasy by drawing (or modelling). When you have finished, you can show it to a partner if you want to."

IN PRACTICE

Junior school teacher Tom Limb used this fantasy when considering ultimate questions. First, the class of eight to nine–year–olds talked about real and imaginary wise people — who are they? This was followed by a poem about impossible questions, which was read out to the class. Then in fantasy, Tom guided the children to meet a wise person and ask a really hard question. They were asked to notice any answers they received so they could write them down later, e.g. "Why did God make the world? — Because he did!" In the ensuing lively discussion, the idea of producing a wall–chart evolved. The children suggested a picture of a wizard surrounded by lots of brainteasers, but they insisted there should be no answers written down.

Journey to the stars

Purpose

Awe and wonder are never very far from the awareness of the religious person. This exercise can give a vivid reminder of the vastness of the universe in which we find ourselves, and opens up ultimate questions about the place of human beings in the midst of such grandeur. It can also be seen as a way of 'putting things into perspective'.

Time needed: Forty minutes

Materials needed: Drawing or writing materials

Conditions

This is best done with a group which has been together for some time and in which there is an atmosphere of trust. If there is a carpeted room available, pupils may wish to lie on the floor; otherwise they should be seated so that they are able to remain alert and relaxed for some time. The exercise assumes some basic information about geography and cosmology, which may mean it is unsuitable for some groups. Alternatively, the exercise could be prefaced by looking at the location of the British Isles as well as photographs of the earth seen from space, pictures of the solar system and astronomical photographs of galaxies. These should assist the imagination of pupils during the fantasy.

Procedure

Drawing materials should be handed out or readily available, so the quiet mood of the fantasy is not broken until pupils are ready to speak. You may wish to organise the class into pairs before beginning the fantasy, in order to avoid any possible disruption when trying to draw out the learning.

Make sure that members of the group are spread out so that each person has a sense of having some private space.

It is important to take time for centring, otherwise it will be very difficult to avoid the distractions pupils bring into the classroom with them.

Pause long enough for pupils to work through each stage of the imagery.

1. Choose a place in the room where you feel comfortable and either sit on a chair or lie on the floor. If you are sitting on a chair, make sure that your back is straight and your feet rest firmly on the floor so that you can remain both comfortable and alert for several minutes.

2. At the end of the fantasy, take a few minutes to express your experience on paper in some way — by drawing or perhaps writing a poem or a description.

3. We'll begin by centring ourselves for a minute or two. If you feel comfortable doing so, it is best to close your eyes. Start by being aware of your breathing, observing the difference between the feeling of the in–breath from the out–breath . . . Now become aware of your body, taking each part in turn, starting with the feet . . . ankles . . . lower legs . . . knees . . . thighs . . . pelvis . . . lower back . . . abdomen . . . chest . . . shoulders . . . upper arms . . . elbows . . . lower arms . . . hands . . . fingers . . . back to the neck . . . the back of the head . . . the ears . . . forehead . . . eyes . . . face . . . jaw.

4. I want you to begin by being aware of your own body, lying or sitting in this room . . . Now become aware in your imagination, perhaps by picturing in your mind's eye, that you are part of a group of people sharing this room . . . And now move

Insert name of town or village you are in.

Monitor pupils' movements to gauge an appropriate time to suggest they return to the room.

your awareness beyond the room to take in the fact that we are sharing a building with many other people. People who, at this moment, are doing other things . . . and be aware that the building we are in is only one of a number of buildings . . . roads . . . fields in the area, where other people are involved in their own tasks . . . Become aware in your mind's eye of (name of town) perhaps by imagining yourself rising above it and seeing it lying below you . . . Notice the detail of what is going on . . . the people walking in the streets . . . vehicles . . . the shape of the town or village . . . Now rise further until you can see the whole county, with its towns, villages, fields, hills and be aware that you are part of that . . . Higher still, you can see the entire country, as if you were looking down on it from space . . . Continuing to rise up . . . until you can see the continent of Europe.

Gradually the whole world comes into view . . . the other continents Asia . . . Africa . . . North and South America . . . Australia . . . the white of the polar ice caps . . . be aware of all the people inhabiting the planet, and that you are a part of that . . . Moving further away, you see the Earth becoming smaller . . . with its Moon circling round it . . . then the other planets . . . all of them circling round a vast, bright Sun . . . to form the Solar system, of which you are a part . . . And you are so far away that the Earth has vanished and the sun is one small star amongst millions forming the galaxy of the Milky Way . . . Now there is no more 'up' or 'down'; you become aware that there are galaxies of stars all around you, stretching to infinity, and that you are a part of all that . . . take some time to be aware of this infinity . . . And when you are ready, open your eyes and be aware that you are back in this room.

5. Stay quiet for a little while longer and try to express your experience of the fantasy on paper — it could be with a drawing, a symbol, a poem or any other way you think appropriate.

Drawing out the learning

This exercise can be very powerful in its effects; often pupils are deeply moved by the realisation that they 'belong to the universe'. Therefore it is important to retain an atmosphere of relaxed quietness after the guided fantasy is over. Allow plenty of time for pupils to share their experience with a partner. Pupils usually appreciate an opportunity for general feedback from the whole class. Questions they may like to consider include:

What parts of the fantasy did you find easy to get into? What parts were difficult? What sort of things did you see or experience? How did you feel during the exercise? What kind of effect could that fantasy have on the way people feel about who they are?

It may be appropriate at this point to illustrate from sacred texts some of the ways in which the world's religions have responded to awe and wonder at the universe.

> **When I see the heavens, the work of your hands,**
> **The moon and stars which you arranged,**
> **What is man that you should keep him in mind,**
> **Mortal man that you care for him?**
>
> (Psalm 8)

> **His, through his might, are these snow-covered mountains, and men call sea and Rasa* his possession;**
> **His arms are these, his are these heavenly regions.**
> **What god shall we adore with our oblation?**
> **By him the heavens are strong and earth is steadfast, by him light's realm and sky-vault are supported;**
> **By him the regions in mid-air were measured;**
> **What god shall we adore with our oblation?**
>
> (*Rig Veda X*, 121, 4–5)

(*According to the Hindu mythology of the *Rig Veda*, Rasa is the river which encompasses the earth and the atmosphere.)

Comment

The variety of responses evoked from a mixed ability group of fourteen–year–olds intrigued them so much that they pestered their teacher to repeat 'Journey to the Stars' on other occasions. No matter how often they took part, they never seemed to tire of this fantasy which continued to provide them with scope for further discussion and reflection. Many pupils enjoyed drawing some of their ideas and fantasies (see next page).

Examples of pupils' work

When I was out in space there was total blackness. I could see my body floating around looking at earth and planets (the earth and planets were colourful). I was totally alone but I didn't feel alone or afraid it was a nice feeling, a feeling that although I was by myself I was still part of things my family my friends and where I live.

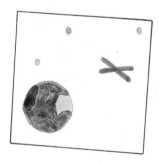

✗ my body

Michelle Lyons

AS I BECAME MORE RELAXED I COULD SEE MYSELF GLOWING AND AS I LOOKED ROUND I COULD SEE TWO MORE PEOPLE GLOWING. AS I LIFTED MY BODY ABOVE THE SCHOOL I COULD SEE ONLY THREE MORE PEOPLE GLOWING IN THE WHOLE SCHOOL AS I LIFTED MYSELF HIGHER I REALISED WHY I WAS GLOWING IT WAS BECAUSE I WAS A STAR. I SAW THE TOWNS AND COUNTRY AROUND ME AND AS I WENT HIGHER THE THINGS GOT SMALLER. IT BECAME DARKER AND I BECAME COLDER. THEN I DID A SLOW HEAD FIRST DIVE BACK INTO MY BODY AND WOKE. WHILE I WAS GLOWING I NOTICED THE PEOPLE AROUND ME WERE IN GREY COCOONS AND THE COLOUR OF THE WORLD WAS GONE JUST DIM PASTELS AND FIVE GLOWING BODIES. THE COCOONS WERE LIKE BUTTERFLIES WAITING TO HATCH FROM A DEAD COCOON LIFELESS AND GREY.

AMANDA CLARK

Mandy Richson

The figure in the picture is me. I felt light, a bit like a cake when its incorporated air. I was floating away from the planet. The planet is earth, round it was bright colours like yellow, orange and red. The rest of the picture was dark. I was floating away, I kept going until the Earth was the size of a pin head, but the colours were just as bright. Then I just floated so far I found myself back in the classroom.

Endings

> **We shall not cease from exploration**
> **And the end of all our exploring**
> **Will be to arrive where we started**
> **And to know the place for the first time.**
>
> (T. S. Eliot)

All good things come to an end sooner or later. It may be the end of an activity which has been appreciated as a valuable learning experience or the end of term when pupils and teacher have to say goodbye to one another.

Experiental learning often depends on the assistance and cooperation of others in the class. In some activities pupils will have delved quite deeply into their feelings, relying on the support of their classmates. They may need time to reorientate themselves and adjust before moving on to other things. Discovering and accepting that your own contribution is valued by others can boost morale and enhance the climate within the classroom.

There may also be a sense of regret that the group is about to part and some pupils may feel embarrassed by a desire to do something to mark the occasion. At such times, the introduction of a structure to help them express their appreciation provides an opportunity to end on a positive note. The following activities are suitable for groups which know each other well and are able to show sensitivity towards other people's feelings.

Know me through my hands

Purpose

This activity works well as the final session of a series of lessons, but it can also be used to round off a single exercise. It gives members of a class a chance to share positive statements about each other and take away a symbolic memory of their part in the group; something which is special to each individual and of which they can be proud.

There are obvious links with Embodying Awareness; the emphasis on individuals' positive qualities, abilities or skills — those attributes which are special or unique to them, and the part played by others was identify those qualities.

Time needed: Thirty minutes

Materials needed: Large sheets of plain paper and coloured pens or crayons.

Conditions

This should be used with groups who know each other fairly well. The risk of anyone's feelings being hurt by an insensitive comment is lessened if pupils work in small groups where the author of a hurtful comment is likely to be identified. It is, therefore, not appropriate for use with a group which harbours hostility, although it can sometimes be helpful where there is evidence of some negative feelings. Asking people to find something positive to say about others can lead them towards discovering value in people they thought they did not particularly like.

Procedure

It may be appropriate to move on to this exercise from an activity in which the pupils have already been working in groups. Otherwise organise the class into groups of about half a dozen. The exercise can be introduced by talking about the positive qualities that everyone possesses. Often these are not mentioned, either because we take them for granted, or out of shyness or embarrassment. Yet we all like to hear good things about ourselves, even if it is sometimes embarrassing to receive a compliment.

Give out a large sheet of plain paper to every pupil and make sure a variety of felt tip pens or crayons is available for each group.

In small groups it is not always necessary to include a name. Anonymous drawings can be displayed so that everyone sees the completed comments.

1. Take your sheet of paper, and **draw round the outline of one of your hands**. Make sure it is in the middle of the paper. Then spend a few minutes colouring in the drawing of your hand in any way that you like. Try to make it represent you or the way you are feeling. Put your name somewhere in the drawing.

Allow time to reflect.

Emphasise that the focus is on writing something positive about each person. Asking pupils to sign their name at the end of a comment reduces the risk of insensitivity.

This stage can be omitted if felt inappropriate.

2. Think of the others in your group. How have they helped you? What quality do your like about them? What are their particular strong points?

3. In your small group, look at everybody's drawings. In turn, **write down on each person's drawing something you like about that person**. You may like to **sign your name at the end of your comment**. You might want to say something about a skill you admire, or something that person has said or done, or any other positive comment which comes to mind.

4. When everybody has finished, walk round the room and add positive comments to the drawings of people in other groups.

5. Now **take back your own drawing** and read the comments on it. **Talk about your drawing and its comments**, with the other members **in your small group**.

It may be helpful to end with a large group discussion, but a determined attempt to 'draw out the learning' is not always relevant to what is intended to be a convivial exercise.

Variations

I like me
Children could do the drawing on their own, as an exercise in self–appreciation. In this case, they write appreciative comments about themselves, beginning, "What I like about me is . . . .". They can write the comments inside the fingers on their drawing.

Paper chain
The second half of the exercise could be done on its own. Pupils write their name at the top of a sheet of paper which is then passed round the class. Starting at the bottom of the page, each person writes a positive comment, signs it and then folds the paper over to conceal their statement from the next writer. When the papers are returned to their owners, they can choose which comment about themselves they like best.

Compliments
Sitting in a circle, members of the group take turns to compliment each other verbally in some way. Both giving and receiving compliments can be embarrassing at the time and it is sometimes hard to accept a compliment gracefully. However, pupils should be encouraged to acknowledge the comment with a positive reply, e.g. "Thank you, I didn't realise that" *or*, "Somebody else has said the same," *or* "I'm pleased you said that".

IN PRACTICE

With the aid of an ink pad, Tom Limb asked his eight–year–olds at Woodborough Woods C.E. School, Nottingham to put their hand–print on to paper and draw around it. After examining their hand–print for some time, they wrote about the pictures they saw in their hands. This was an interesting introduction to other work on metaphors.

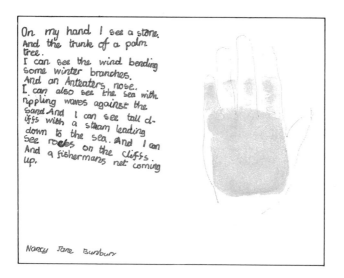

On my hand I see a stone.
And the trunk of a palm tree.
I can see the wind bending some winter branches.
And an Anteaters nose.
I can also see the sea with rippling waves against the sand And I can see tall cliffs with a stream leading down to the sea. And I can see rocks on the cliffs.
And a fishermans net coming up.

Nancy Jane Bunbury

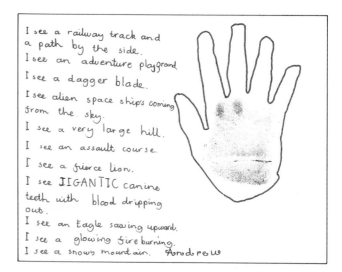

I see a railway track and a path by the side.
I see an adventure playground
I see a dagger blade.
I see alien space ship's coming from the sky.
I see a very large hill.
I see an assault course.
I see a fierce lion.
I see JIGANTIC canine teeth with blood dripping out.
I see an Eagle sawing upward.
I see a glowing fire burning.
I see a snowy mountain.   Andrew

ACTIVITIES

Giving gifts

Purpose

This activity creates an opportunity to show sensitivity towards, and appreciation of, others in the group. It symbolically offers the experience of giving and receiving gifts. The gifts may recognise an individual's hopes and aspirations or may be offered as tokens of that person's value to us. It is normally used to round off an activity or a course where the group has worked well together, but can also be employed as an introduction to explicitly religious concepts of charisma, sacrifice or worship.

Time needed: Thirty minutes

Materials needed: Index cards or paper, felt tips or pens.

Conditions

This is an exercise that needs plenty of space, so furniture may need to be moved to one side, ensuring sufficient chairs are spaced around the room to provide each couple with somewhere to sit. The class should know each other well before trying the exercise, and the teacher needs to watch out for the insensitive joker who may unwittingly hurt someone's feelings.

Procedure

Distribute writing or drawing materials.

You may wish pupils to remain in small groups, which were operating in a previous exercise, or to choose a series of partners at random. Any milling activity would do; the suggestion here is a form of blindman's buff, but you need to remember that some people feel uncomfortable when asked to close their eyes, and should be given the option to remain sighted.

A suitable introduction to this activity would be to discuss how giving someone a really appropriate present can be as pleasurable as receiving a gift ourselves. Pupils may be keen to talk about the best and worst presents they've received and, from that discussion, it may be possible to draw out the point that material goods are not always the gifts we value most.

Some people will prefer to keep their eyes open and this should be respected.

1. Would everyone please **stand up and**, if you feel comfortable, **close your eyes**. When you are ready, start to **move round the room**, trying to keep your eyes shut, and **stretching your hands out in front of you**. When you come into **contact** with **another pair of hands, open your eyes** and find somewhere to **sit down with your partner**.

Emphasise the importance of choosing something positive which their partner would appreciate.

2. Consider what you know of your partner, and on a card, **write down or draw the gift you think he or she would like to receive**.

3. Now **exchange your gifts** and try to **explain why you chose that particular gift** for your partner.

If working with small groups, Stages 2 and 3 will have to be repeated a number of times so that everyone has given and received several gifts. It is also appropriate to repeat the exercise several times when working with the entire class.

Drawing out the learning

Ask the class to sit in a circle to talk about their experiences. Other questions can be asked to draw out the aims and objectives of a specific lesson.

What were the gifts you received?

How did it feel to receive gifts? Which did you like most and why?

How did it feel to give gifts? How did you choose what to give?

Comment

It is important that the giver explains the rationale for the gift before the receiver jumps to conclusions. One couple came to blows over the gift of a Siamese cat — something the donor had always wanted. Unfortunately her partner was terrified of cats and regarded the gift as a death wish.

Variation

Today

Giving and receiving gifts involves a certain amount of risk and self disclosure. In this variation pupils have the chance to reflect on an activity or course and, if they wish, share their own feelings with the group. This may be the entire class or a smaller number of pupils, perhaps a friendship group.

Ask everyone to sit in a circle and invite them to make a positive statement, beginning with the words: "Today I have . . .", or "This term/in the last few weeks I have . . .", etc. The teacher will probably have to start the ball rolling with a few examples. Nobody needs to speak unless they want to and there is no formal structure, e.g. going round the circle, which might pressurise a pupil to speak against his or her wishes.

Statements can be about something they liked about that day's work, something they feel they achieved, thanking others for helping in some way.

IN PRACTICE

Loving lollipops

This variation was developed by Kathy Raban and her class of six-year-olds. It is designed to encourage them to think in a positive way, to see that their thoughts can be powerful and to stretch their imaginations. Since it focuses on projecting positive images, it can contribute to a caring atmosphere within the classroom, even among egocentric infants.

"I told the children to get into pairs and then took one from each pair out of the room. Each child was given a word which they could easily visualise: a cat or a ball or something like that. When they returned to the room, they sat and held hands with their partner and tried to send the word across. This was done in silence.

It seemed to work well. They sat there and concentrated and were absolutely silent. They were really working hard on sending this across. After a while I said, "Now you can tell your partner the word," and some got it every time. That was probably coincidence, I don't know, but enough got it to be able to make the point:

"Well your thoughts are quite powerful, and if you can send the picture across to somebody else, just think what else you can do with your thoughts, and how important it is that you have good thoughts towards everybody else."

I've been able to build on that concept about the power of thought and how it can change you and the environment round you. That works well with my children, who accept this as a bit of magic. The fact that even a few have managed to communicate their word, leads them to think they've done it by transferring thought. Whether they have or not, I don't know, but they are prepared to take the point that I make about thoughts being quite powerful.

I followed it on with the suggestion, "Let's send loving thoughts to one another." We sat in a circle and I asked them to hold hands, which was the worst thing I've ever tried to do. Another group would sit and hold hands wonderfully well, but in this particular group, two or three of them can't hold hands without it being a real hassle. So instead, we sat close to one another ready to send loving thoughts.

I asked them for an image, "What would be a loving thing to send everybody?" In the end, they agreed on a lollipop. So everybody imagined a lollipop being sent to everybody else."

Giving and receiving gifts

Through a centring exercise, Joan Formosa asked pupils from Biddick School, Washington, Tyne and Wear, to focus on a quality which they thought would help them survive the bustle and excitement of Christmas preparations.

This was the first taste of experiential learning for the class of fourteen to fifteen–year–olds. She found the group "amazingly responsive" so she suggested that pupils could give these qualities to their classmates as Christmas gifts.

Joan reported later:

"Each pupil was given the chance to reject a gift and those who did gave articulate reasons for doing so. One boy in the class offered a very quiet girl the gift of self–confidence and she accepted it rather reluctantly. I was moved when another student offered her the gift of friendship and support while she was learning to use her new gift of confidence. Another pupil was offered the gift of modesty but rejected it saying you needed to think you were good to get on in this world, nobody was going to help a loser. I was saddened by this response but the group accepted it and continued to offer the boy other qualities until he accepted the gift of 'being able to understand others'. By the end of the session every pupil had both given and received a gift. This was particularly impressive as I did not put any pressure on the group to include everyone, it simply came about naturally."

PART THREE

Applications and implications

Sequencing in the secondary school

"My syllabus is content–based and doesn't lend itself to that kind of teaching," or so some teachers thought when they were first introduced to the activities outlined in Part 2. Brian Netto was Head of RE at Frank Wheldon Comprehensive School in Nottingham where the county Agreed Syllabus, 'Quest', stresses content. He has drawn up this outline syllabus which provides an indication of where individual activities could be used, alongside more traditional modes of teaching, to enhance and complement the learning.

The activities in this book are not intended to be isolated entities, used by the teacher 'for a change', as a source of entertainment or diversion. They are intended to be integral to any religious education course, though by no means a substitute for a school's scheme of work or syllabus. It is important to remember that many of the structures can be appropriate in a variety of different contexts (for example, guided imagery can be used in lower school work on 'signs and symbols' as well as in upper school studies of 'myself and the universe').

Clearly, it is impossible to produce a syllabus which will satisfy the needs, interests and resources of each and every RE department. The intention of producing this outline is to indicate some of the possibilities in sequencing the activities within already existing syllabuses. This syllabus is multi–faith, and focuses on content*. It deliberately assumes RE is taught as a separate subject, but it also lends itself to integrated, interdisciplinary approaches. The outline is not meant to be exhaustive or prescriptive; omission of elements of the course will depend on such factors as time and the interest of the students.

The syllabus for years 4 and 5 represents the contribution of RE to a core Personal, Social and Moral Education course. Many of the activities suggested could equally be of use in a GCSE course.

The experiential activities are all described elsewhere in the book. The teacher is recommended to look at these in more detail in order to understand the link being made with the syllabus.

A note on terminology
In this syllabus, the word 'religion' is taken to mean any consistent, coherent, ethical life–stance which may be theistic or non–theistic, and thus allows the inclusion of Humanism, Marxism and so on.

Brian Netto

---

* In 'Integrating with an Agreed Syllabus', Maureen Potter explains how experiential learning is of value when following a syllabus based on concepts, skills and attitudes.

An outline multi–faith syllabus

	General Aims	Ideas		Questions	Experiential Activities
YEAR ONE	To raise awareness and understanding of: 1. religion.	1	religion is a universal phenomenon, found in all parts of the world.	1 (*i*) What is a religion? (*ii*) How do religions begin?	'Walk my walk.' 'Journey to the stars.'
	2. ultimate questions and fundamental values.	2(a) (b)	religions raise questions about what is most important. religions provide the basis for that which is of ultimate value in life.	2 (*i*) What questions and values are raised by religious stories? (*ii*) What are the most important and valuable things in life?	'Life is like . . .' 'If death were a plant . . .'. Guided imagery, 'Clearing the mind'. 'Who am I?'
	3. sacred ritual.	3	religions involve prescribed actions.	3 (*i*) What actions are characteristic of religious people? Dance, special movements, special body positions (*ii*) What are rites of passage? Do they involve special rituals?	Listening exercises: 'Radio Gaga.' 'Take no notice.'
	4. celebration.	4	religions involve special events and occasions, for celebration and commemoration.	4 (*i*) Why do people celebrate? (*ii*) What sorts of occasions do people celebrate? (*iii*) What is a religious festival?	'Giving gifts.' Listening exercises: 'Just a minute.' 'Pay attention.' 'That's what I said.'
	5. sacred space.	5	religions involve places and objects which are regarded as sacred and special.	5 (*i*) Why do people have special places or objects? (*ii*) What is a sacred space? (*iii*) What is a place of worship?	'How does your garden grow?' Guided imagery, 'Clearing the mind'.

	General Aims	Ideas		Questions	Experiential Activities
YEAR TWO	To raise awareness and understanding of: 1. community and family in religion.	1	religious ideas affect the way families and communities are organised.	1 (*i*) What different types of religious community are there? (Muslim **umma**, Buddhist **sangha**, etc.) (*ii*) What types of family units are encouraged by religions?	'Know me through my hands.'
	2. religious founder, messenger or leader.	2	many religions look to special people, for who they were and what they did.	2 (*i*) What are the differences between founders, messengers, prophets and leaders? (*ii*) What sorts of stories are told of these special people? (*iii*) What makes these people special?	'Wise person' fantasy.
	3. religious practice, in terms of meditation and worship.	3	religious people practise their tradition individually and collectively.	3 (*i*) What is worship? (*ii*) Why do people come together in worship? (*iii*) Why do people worship alone?	'Clearing the mind.' 'Relax.' 'Body-breath.'
	4. symbol.	4	religion is often expressed through symbols, which can be of many kinds.	4 (*i*) What is a symbol? (*ii*) What different forms of symbol are there? (artefact, ritual, language, etc.)	'If I was a . . .' 'Hammer and nail — which would you rather be?' 'My badge.' 'I'm a tree.' 'Symbols of life.' 'Let me see!'
	5. pilgrimage.	5	many religious people go on special journeys to sacred sites, for a variety of reasons.	5 (*i*) Why do people go on pilgrimage? (*ii*) Why do some people regard life as a journey?	'Journey of life.' 'Journey and quest stories.' 'Pilgrimage.'
	6. belief.	6	the beliefs which we hold can structure our perspectives on life.	6 (*i*) How do people develop belief? (*ii*) In what ways might belief structure our perspective on life?	'Necker cube.' 'Be aware.' 'Duck or rabbit?' 'I'm a soft shoe.'

	General Aims	Ideas		Questions		Experiential Activities
YEAR THREE	To raise awareness and understanding of two religious traditions. (As an example, a systematic study of Hinduism is illustrated.) 1. the nature and origins of Hinduism.	1	Hinduism is an evolving tradition, embracing many diverse ideas and practices.	1 (i)	What are the origins of Hinduism? (ii) Why are there no founders or prophets, similar to other religions, in Hinduism.	In this section, the activities referred to are ones more familiar to RE teachers, exploring the explicit dimension of religion.
	2. some key concepts in Hinduism (**dharma, samsara, Karma, moksa, maya**, etc).	2	There are some unifying ideas which pervade all of the Hindu tradition.	2 (i)	What do Hindus believe about the nature of reality and the goal of life?	Stories and myths retold.
	3. the life cycle in Hinduism — **asrama.**	3	The life cycle of the Hindu illustrates some major themes in Hinduism.	3 (i)	What are the major stages in the life–cycle of Hinduism?	Life–line (cyclical).
	4. stories and writings of Hinduism — e.g. Rig-Veda, Laws of Manu, Upanishads, Mahabharata (Bhagavad-gita), Puranas, Ramayana, etc.	4	There is a variety of literature, symbolism and meaning in Hindu writings.	4 (i)	What are some of the major themes and ideas embodied in Hindu mythology, legal writings, devotional literature, stories, legends, poetry, etc?	Artefacts and iconography. 'Let me see!'
	5. the lives of revered Hindus — e.g. Gandhi, Vivekananda, Ramakrishna, Caitanya, Tagore, etc.	5	Many contemporary and past Hindus have had profound effects on human thinking and action.	5 (i)	What effects have the lives of revered Hindu saints had on human thinking and action?	
	6. Hindu belief and practices.	6	Hindu beliefs are embodied in the daily life and ritual practices, meditation, puja, etc.	6 (i)	What are the main forms of Hindu practice?	Visit to a temple/home. Reconstruction of a puja, using taped music/chants, incense. Demonstration of yoga, asana and pranayama.

General Aims	Ideas	Questions	Experiential Activities
YEARS 4 & 5 RE IN A PSME COURSE To raise awareness and understanding of: 1. religious views of the self/person.	1(a) Religious traditions have views about the individual which include concepts like spiritual, soul, atman/Brahman, anatta, etc. (b) these ideas are embodied in particular practices, such as acupuncture, yoga, meditation, tai–ch'i, faith healing, etc. (c) different ideas of the self result in different approaches to life.	1 (i) How are religious views of the person different from humanist views? (ii) What religious practices provide insights into views of the self? (iii) How do different views of the self change people's attitudes towards life?	'Who am I?'/'The Real Me.' 'Privacy circles.'
2. religious views of the individual in relation to other people.	2 Religious traditions have developed codes of conduct, and principles by which to live one's life.	2 (i) What 'golden rules' do religions have with regard to treatment of other people? (ii) What different types of religious community are there? (e.g. **Khalsa, sangha, umma,** commune, etc.) (iii) How does religion affect the way people organise themselves into groups?	'Candle and wire.'
3. religious views of the individual in relation to the universe.	3(a) Religious traditions are fundamentally concerned about questions of ultimate value, meaning and purpose. (b) religious traditions have developed holistic views about the relationship between the individual and the universe.	3 (i) What do religions have to say about questions of life and death, the soul, immortality, rebirth, reincarnation, salvation, enlightenment, etc.? (ii) What do religions have to say about the relationship between the individual and the universe, the microcosm and the macrocosm?	'Journey to the stars' — guided fantasy.

Chapter

14

Integrating with an Agreed Syllabus

During the 1980s a number of local education author-ities recommended a conceptual approach to religious education. The Durham County Agreed Syllabus of Religious Education, 'Growing in Understanding', was one of the first to emphasise the concepts, skills and attitudes involved in understanding religion. In 1985 Durham agreed to pilot the materials produced by the Religious Experience Research Project. This pilot project was initiated in twelve schools with such success that the approach has been introduced to teachers throughout the county. Maureen Potter, Durham County Adviser for RE, explains how experiential learning techniques are beneficial in implementing a conceptual agreed syllabus.

The concepts

With the publication of 'Growing in Understanding' in 1982, Durham moved away from the idea of a content–based syllabus to one which is directed towards the development of concepts involved in understanding religions. The syllabus defines a concept as a 'fundamental idea' and goes on to state:

> *'In religion the comprehension of a concept comes not only through the intellect but also through the emotions, the imagination and through experience — it is an "empathetic awareness".'*

The factual body of knowledge is neither excluded nor devalued but the experience of each child and the way that experience is expressed and interpreted is regarded as equally important.

In order to develop the concepts certain skills are also required. A number of these may be termed 'affective' skills which are not measurable by tra-ditional methods of assessment. However, these are the skills which are essential in developing religious understanding as well as personal and social compe-tency. The conceptual approach is not just a method of teaching but is rather a process of learning which sets out to involve young people in the particular process of becoming religiously educated.

Six of the ten concepts to be investigated and explored (the **A** concepts) stem from basic human experience and can be identified as the implicit aspect of religion: awe and wonder; self; relationship with other persons; personal qualities; corporate identity; relationship to the natural world. The other concepts are concerned with basic themes or patterns found in one or more religions. These are the **B** concepts which represent the explicit aspects of religion — universality of religion; deity; worship, ritual, sacrifice, symbolism, prayer, religious language; and belief, faith and commitment. These concepts are interdependent and each one can be deepened and broadened with each age group from five to sixteen years. In a conceptual approach there is no beginning or end but a continuing spiral of experiences designed to provide a basis on which young people may build further.

Teachers welcomed this approach which emphasises the spiritual dimension as well as the religious approach to life. At the same time they expressed concern that their existing teaching methods and resources would not be sufficient to fulfil the demands of their new syllabus.

The Durham Pilot Project

Early in 1985 I met David Hay and Alison Jones of the Religious Experience Research Project (now the Religious Experience and Education Project [REEP]) and felt that their work in experiential learning techniques could be beneficial in implementing the Durham Agreed Syllabus. There are two aspects of the syllabus in which the 'experiential' dimension of religion is particularly prominent.

(a) The investigation of the idea of a spiritual dimension to life.

(b) The development of the skill of entering imaginatively into the experience, intentions, beliefs and desires of other people.

Phenomenology has strengthened teaching in the ethical, social, doctrinal, ritual and mythological dimensions of religion but the 'experiential' dimension needs to be explored with the additional technique of experiential, or active, learning. The principle reason for developing the ideas of REEP in Durham is to advance pupils' understanding of the experiential dimension of religion.

Having gained the approval of the Director of Education, I began to plan a pilot project to run for one year in six primary and six secondary schools. The initial letter of invitation to headteachers explained what I perceived to be the benefits of being involved in this pilot project.

'. . . The immediate benefit to the school is that the teaching of religious education will be enhanced by developing materials in support of the Durham RE Agreed Syllabus concept A1, 'Awe and Wonder'. This is a difficult aspect of RE but there is a growing belief that it is an essential element to explore if we are to develop the spiritual area of experience presented in 'Curriculum 5–16'.

The wider implication of involvement is that the work of this project may be seen as part of the school's life skills or personal, social, moral education programme. Pupils will engage in classroom activities which are designed to develop personal skills associated with emotions, feelings, intuition and uncertainty when faced with paradox. These skills, which are difficult to handle in school, and therefore often neglected, are essential to becoming a whole person . . .'

At the start of the new academic year, Alison Jones came to Durham to lead a two–day introductory course for the twelve participating teachers. Prior to that inaugural meeting each teacher received a background information sheet expounding the reasons why we need to develop experiential learning techniques in Durham.

The rationale was rooted within the Agreed Syllabus which states that one of the two basic areas of investigation is 'the idea of a spiritual dimension to life'. Pointing out that this approach is in line with statements in paragraph 78 of the DES document, 'The Curriculum 5–16', I went on to say:

'. . . The spiritual dimension forms an important element in the 'A' concepts in our syllabus, particularly A1 — Awe and Wonder and A2 — Self. We require a methodology to explore the "spiritual".

Through this pilot project we hope to develop learning techniques which will help us to bridge that gap between the study of religion and the experience of religion. This is very important if we are intent on developing in our pupils the skill of "entering imaginatively into the experience, intentions, beliefs and desires of other people". In experiential learning pupils can become "participant observers", enhancing their ability to empathise.

In developing religious understanding we need to show that, for many people, a religious view of life is important. It is the task of the RE teacher to *open the pupil's mind and experience to this whilst appreciating that there is an important boundary — whether the pupil takes the next step of accepting cognitively that way of life and becoming a believer is not the concern of the teacher'.* (David Hay BJRE Vol. 7, No. 3, Summer 1985)

Awe, wonder, self–awareness, relationships with others and the natural world are difficult areas to deal with in the classroom. We need to develop pupils' reflective skills, to make credible their intuitive responses and give value to emotion and feeling in human experience.'

Two further points which were persuasive were the aspect of continuity and the teacher's role as facilitator. Firstly, the REEP approach is equally relevant for RE for primary and secondary schools. This supports the continuity of 'Growing in Understanding' which emphasises that a religious concept is:

'. . . capable of exploration and understanding at different depths. The same basic principle or idea may be explored by infants as well as by sixth form students, the academically less able as well as by the academically gifted, though obviously at different levels and in different ways . . .'

Secondly, in experiential learning the teacher becomes a 'facilitator' rather than one who transmits information, so that the centre of learning switches from the teacher to the pupil. I consider that this change in emphasis is crucial if we are intent on creating a receptivity to the spiritual dimension in the classroom.

The twelve teachers continued using experiential learning techniques and recording reactions. Their enthusiasm prompted the interest of other teachers who requested more information. Within a few months the local association of RE teachers held a successful evening meeting when one of the primary teachers introduced members to some of the activities and showed examples of pupils' work.

A year after the project began only one infant teacher had withdrawn and the others were writing up their experiences for a booklet sent out to every school in the county. The pilot project indicated that experiential learning can help pupils grow in their understanding of religion, so the next stage was to formalise this approach and make it available to every interested teacher. Several six-week courses were arranged with teachers volunteering to attend their local teachers' centre one evening each week. Each course was over-subscribed despite the pressure of many new initiatives and demands on teachers in schools.

Since then primary and secondary teachers throughout the county have continued to use, adapt and develop the exercises in many different ways. Examples of some of their work can be found throughout this book. Their work would seem to suggest that experiential learning is a useful tool in a religious education curriculum which attempts to explore the spiritual and experiential dimensions of religion.

Maureen Potter

Chapter 15

Thematic RE in the primary school

Thematic planning is part of a common approach to learning in many primary schools. This can create difficulties when trying to provide a balanced religious education. Jo Moxon explains how it is possible to achieve that balance when integrating explicit and implicit RE with other areas of the curriculum.

There are several approaches when planning religious education in the primary school curriculum. One possibility draws RE out of a chosen topic or theme which governs most aspects of the curriculum for a set period, perhaps half a term or a full term. An alternative approach might include having a separate theme for RE which does not correspond to the topic used in other curriculum areas. It might be the case that the school has developed an RE scheme giving guidance about appropriate topics to be covered by each age group.

Whatever the approach, planning RE can present difficulties for the teacher of young children. One danger is that thematic planning may result in RE being reduced to the presentation of a well-known story or a moral discussion. This approach can also fail to introduce children to the reality of religion by integrating it out of existence. Being confined to a set scheme may prevent spontaneous investigation that naturally arises from the children's experience. Yet a balanced picture of what it means to be religious can be presented at a level appropriate to even the youngest children in school.

Primary teachers need to consider carefully objective ways in which children can be introduced to:

1. explicit religious practice, i.e. what religious people do;

and

2. implicit religious ideals, e.g. what religious people believe, how they feel, why they do the things they do.

1. Children can be introduced to explicit features of religion through the use of the senses. In this way they are using first-hand experience when discovering more about religious buildings, clothes, food, music, ritual, artefacts and so on. This approach depends upon the teacher becoming familiar with aspects of explicit religion which are appropriate to the topic or theme in hand. It also needs to be supported by resources which allow first-hand (or very good second-hand) experience. For example, a collection of artefacts or a visit or visitor provide first-hand experience while the use of audio-visual aids is secondary.

2. Helping children to experience the implicit elements of RE involves exploration of their own spiritual dimension. At some time in their lives most people ask questions like "Who am I?", "What happens when someone dies?", "What is life all about?". Some people find the answers to these questions in their religion. These and other spiritual concerns can be explored in the classroom in a way which is non-confessional, inter-active and meaningful for young children. Experiential learning in RE offers many possibilities through which these issues can be handled effectively.

Spiritual education of this nature plays a vital role in RE and, hand in hand with the explicit dimension, helps children to build a picture of the whole nature of religion. For many primary teachers experiential methods have provided a vehicle through which the inner dimension of religon can be experienced. This becomes possible without assuming belief on the part of the pupils or expecting them to cross the threshold of commitment.

It is possible for children to acquire knowledge and experiences of both explicit and implicit religion from their earliest years in school. This can be done either in an integrated way (related to general themes that inspire many other curriculum areas) or through themes that are specifically chosen for religious education. Thematic planning for RE should include, wherever possible, examples of explicit religious practice and some deep thinking and questioning. This kind of reflection is particularly enhanced by experiential learning methods and activities.

A groundplan for structuring a theme for RE might include some explicit work such as:
a) a relevant example from religious literature;
b) mention of an appropriate religious ceremony or custom;
c) a visit to a religious building or inviting someone into the classroom to discuss a particular aspect of their belief or spiritual awareness.

Implicit work might include:
a) some experiential exercises centred on a relevant aspect of the chosen theme;

b) activities which involve the children making meaningful contact with each other, the rest of the school or the local community.

I have used the following groundplan for structuring many RE themes. It has become a useful checklist for me, ensuring that both explicit and implicit aspects of religious education are being presented. If I find that a general theme used to inspire other areas of the curriculum does not fulfil the requirements of the groundplan then I adopt a separate RE theme for that period.

Example of a groundplan which may be used to structure the religious element of a chosen topic theme.

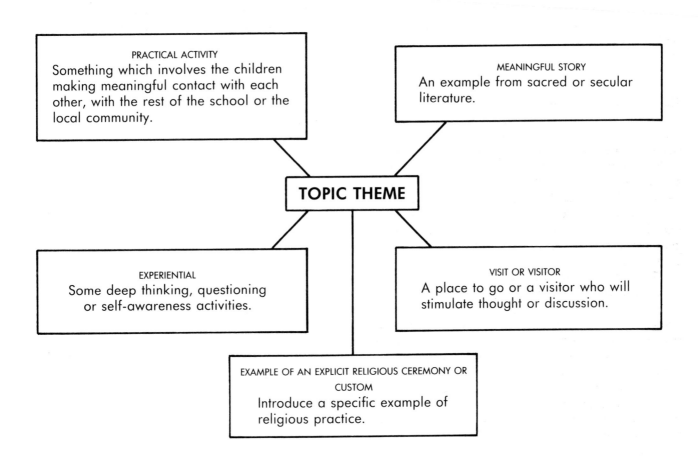

PRACTICAL ACTIVITY
Something which involves the children making meaningful contact with each other, with the rest of the school or the local community.

MEANINGFUL STORY
An example from sacred or secular literature.

TOPIC THEME

EXPERIENTIAL
Some deep thinking, questioning or self-awareness activities.

VISIT OR VISITOR
A place to go or a visitor who will stimulate thought or discussion.

EXAMPLE OF AN EXPLICIT RELIGIOUS CEREMONY OR CUSTOM
Introduce a specific example of religious practice.

A groundplan showing only the RE elements of one of the most successful themes, *stones*, is included here as an example. This was part of a much wider topic which encompassed many curriculum areas with five and six year olds.

Sample groundplan used to plan the religious element of the topic theme 'stones'.

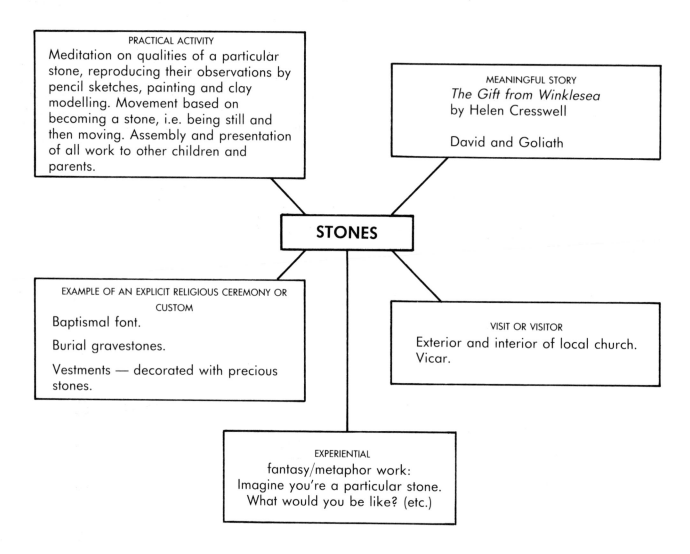

PRACTICAL ACTIVITY

Meditation on qualities of a particular stone, reproducing their observations by pencil sketches, painting and clay modelling. Movement based on becoming a stone, i.e. being still and then moving. Assembly and presentation of all work to other children and parents.

MEANINGFUL STORY
The Gift from Winklesea
by Helen Cresswell

David and Goliath

STONES

EXAMPLE OF AN EXPLICIT RELIGIOUS CEREMONY OR CUSTOM

Baptismal font.

Burial gravestones.

Vestments — decorated with precious stones.

VISIT OR VISITOR
Exterior and interior of local church. Vicar.

EXPERIENTIAL
fantasy/metaphor work:
Imagine you're a particular stone.
What would you be like? (etc.)

I led a short meditation based on the stones that the children had been handling and sketching. The children imagined they became their stone, using their bodies to create a very meaningful movement sequence. They wrote some short, but heart–felt comments about what it felt like to be a stone.

A selection of experiential activities was used to establish a climate in which cooperative learning could take place. The ongoing approach to learning included the regular use of listening, stilling and self-awareness exercises. These 'Raising Awareness' activities were accompanied by inter–active ways of processing learning as part of the general daily routine. This provided the children with the means to allow their inner thoughts and feelings to be explored and expressed in RE using ways which were already familiar to them.

In my experience, the application of experiential learning methods to thematic RE enhances the presentation of implicit religious concepts. It helps me to achieve balance in my approach. The study of religion cannot be reduced to a moral story or discussion. Neither can it ignore the whole realm of spiritual awareness by becoming a clinical analysis of what religious people do.

The area of recommendation termed 'the spiritual' in the DES document, 'Curriculum 5–16', filled many teachers with feelings of apprehension. I feel that experiential learning makes a vital contribution by offering ways to approach this aspect of the curriculum. In my own teaching of RE I have discovered that the work helps to improve children's relationships with each other and heightens their awareness of themselves and of their value as people.

Jo Moxon

"I AM A ROCK AND I LIKE MYSELF"

Andrew Sinclair
if I was a flint I would have sharp points

Justin Seddon
I am a rock and I like my self.

Victoria
I am a purple and yellow stone and I have some black stripes

Gareth Charlton
I want to be a flint stone and I am little

David Burns
I am a big big stone.

Relevance of experiential learning in Catholic schools

A member of a teaching order, the Sisters of Mercy, Sister Margaret Mary Ryan has taught in primary schools for more than twenty years. Charles Reilly has taught RE for a similar length of time and is head of department in a large Catholic comprehensive school. Their links with the Religious Experience and Education Project go back to 1984 when they were involved in developing and testing the exercises on themselves and with their pupils. Although long accustomed to traditional teaching methods they have both found their lessons transformed by the introduction of experiential learning techniques.

The primary setting

The publication of the Documents of Vatican Council II (1962–1965), which gave rise to the greater participation of the laity through the use of the vernacular, also provided an opportunity and the freedom to involve children in a more active way in religious education.

The daily RE lesson in many Catholic primary schools traditionally comprised the learning by rote of questions and answers from the Catechism of Christian Doctrine, reading and recalling stories from the Old and New Testament, and the learning of responses, prayers and hymns so that children could participate in an adult–orientated liturgy. Now, awareness of other religions is also brought to the children so that they can learn to appreciate God's calling of people, in different ways, to knowledge of Him. While the understanding of what was learned by rote

may not always have been clear, their religious education was not a daily dead half–hour. In a Catholic school, Christianity is a way of life, a philosophy. It is like a gold thread running through the whole day giving life a purpose and goal. I regard parents as the prime teachers, and children find the school is an extension of the home. This unity of thought and doctrine between Catholic homes and the school gives a security and solidarity to the children's lives.

It was round about 1967 that I took my first step in using experiential methods of teaching and learning. Working in an ordinary London primary school with a group of eight to eleven–year–olds who formed a 'special class' with learning difficulties, I began with assemblies. The success of these was evident because of the sense of achievement and sheer enjoyment of the children. Other Junior teachers began to use these forms of assemblies and eventually the whole school adopted them.

Since I moved from London to Nottingham in the early 1970s, the 'Veritas' religious syllabus was published in Ireland, adapted for use in England, and is now in wide circulation in Catholic primary schools. It is an excellent syllabus and ideal for experiential learning. It is used to great effect throughout my present primary school of nine classes. The use of this resource book has been the second big step in my new approach.

The third step came with my introduction to the Religious Experience Research Project (now REEP). It broadened my understanding of teachers' varying approaches to religious education and their interpretations of the meaning of religion and spirituality. It affirmed much of what I was already doing, which I found encouraging. Most of all, the exercises opened up a vast range of experiences from which the children could learn. I have used this material with the Junior age range, seven to eleven–year–olds, and invited parents and teachers to participate. I have never experienced any negative response or reaction.

What I see as the degree of involvement of the children, the quality of work and their comments, proves to me, if proof were needed, that this method has enormous value in a Catholic primary school. I attribute this to their willingness to enter into the activities, an atmosphere of relaxed participation, their awareness of another's care for them, their enjoyment of sharing and listening to each other and above all freedom from compulsion and coercion.

Through the adaptation and use of exercises within the 'Veritas' RE syllabus, teaching is enhanced and pupils affirmed. Each exercise which I use ends with prayer, silent or vocalised. There have been many growth points:

- The children are encouraged to be open and willing to share, at different times, with individuals, small groups and the whole class.

- There is honesty in recognising the gifts and talents in oneself and in others and in the willingness to use them in order to enrich our lives.

- They are more able and willing to express emotion, for example, anger, frustration, hurt, jealousy, tenderness, love, joy, etc., through drama, drawing, poetry and movement.

- The children grow in their awareness of inner resources.

- There is a raised level of tolerance, leading to the acceptance of oneself and of others, and this is expressed by their sympathetic and empathetic attitudes.

- The children appreciate having time for silence.

- There is often a sense of awe and wonder.

- This approach helps them to understand their faith at their own level.

Saint Irenaeus said that, 'The glory of God is humankind fully alive'. The aim and objective of my use of experiential learning is to enable children and myself, in our struggle to be truly human, to reach holiness which is wholeness.

Sister Margaret Mary Ryan

The secondary setting

For me, RE in a Catholic comprehensive school has two aims. The first is to develop the subject in a dynamic, academic way which will assist young people to become theologically literate. The second aim is to develop young people spiritually. While I am sure these two aims are in the forefront of the minds of others who teach in church schools, in my experience the second aim often gets left out.

For many years most of my teaching was what I term cerebral in approach. While realising that emotions and feelings were very important, I did not have the necessary guidance to use and train them effectively in the RE lesson. I now see experiential learning as giving the practical direction and assistance needed in supporting spiritual development.

What, one may ask, is the benefit of these awareness activities in our schools? I certainly questioned their usefulness at first. After the initial frustration of not being able to get into the exercises, soon I began to experience peace and a sense of wellbeing. The attempt to quieten the mind and attain some sort of silence, through concentration on body sensations or breathing, brought me a new power. So now I begin all my RE lessons with a brief period of silence, followed by a prayer. There are so many distractions for people in our noisy world, especially for young people, that any attempt to silence the mind, even for a short time, is beneficial in itself.

Meditation is not a matter of advanced techniques in prayer but a way of listening. We have the example of Jesus who sought solitude when he knew there were going to be demands on him. He had a need for solitude because he was human. Human beings need to be alone, silent and still. What we need above all is 'inner space' — space to make sense of what is going on around us; space to face ourselves, our fears, and have the time to reflect on our feelings. Silent reflection which identifies inner feelings is a necessary preparation for an encounter with Christ.

For me the greatest benefit of the experiential approach is that it helps young people to pray. There is no prayer without silence and I found myself becoming more aware of this fact when I took part in the development of the exercises during the two years' research. Prayer is quiet repose. It is not thinking profound thoughts, but just being still in His Presence.

Thomas Merton in his book, *The sign of Jonas*, says, 'When you gain interior silence you can carry it around with you in the world and pray everywhere.' He also notes, 'It is absurd to talk about interior silence when there is no exterior silence.' Prayer pulls us away from self and challenges us to a new adventure with God. God is beyond our feelings and emotions and hopes, yet He is at the very centre of all of it. So we need to begin with the self.

I feel that using the REEP exercises will help our young people to become more aware of their interior world. If this method is used sensitively in our church schools, we can open up and prepare the way for enrichment by the Spirit. To the young people who tell me that they get nothing out of the exercises, I assure them of the intrinsic value of doing nothing. I also remind them of the old peasant who is supposed to have said, 'Sometimes I sits and thinks, and sometimes I just sits.'

Charles Reilly

'Waiting patiently in expectation is the foundation of the spiritual life.'

(Simone Weil, *First and Last Notebooks*)

Slow learners

After ten years teaching RE in comprehensive schools, Ted Huddleston was awarded the St. Luke's Foundation Research Fellowship at Exeter University to study the religious education of children with special educational needs. Here he concentrates on slow learners as he explains how experiential learning can help pupils with learning difficulties and gives some hints for success in the classroom. First he provides a definition of the term 'slow learners'.

Characteristics of slow learners

Slow learners are pupils who, in one way or another, are not achieving as much as the majority of people of the same age. Rather than having physical or sensory disabilities, they simply find it more difficult than others to learn the basic skills. Their level of attainment in reading, writing, numeracy, social and communication skills is both lower and reached more slowly.

For a few people the difficulty seems restricted to one particular group of skills, such as reading–writing–spelling, otherwise their progress is normal. These are 'children with specific learning difficulties'[1]. They are comparatively rare, and may need extra help of quite a specialised nature.

Much more frequent are learning difficulties which extend over a range of activities to varying degrees. These 'children with mild or moderate learning difficulties'[2] all need some form of extra help. They are often grouped together and labelled 'less able' or

'remedial' as if they all share the same problems, although the range and extent of help required by each person varies enormously.

Educational psychologists[3] usually attribute the wider range of learning difficulties to two different, but interconnected, underlying features.

1. A generally lower level of cognitive and linguistic functioning

Slow learners are said to have more difficulty with activities which involve thinking or reasoning. Tending to have less imagination and creativity, they are inefficient at problem solving. Linguistically, they have more difficulty listening, understanding what they have heard and expressing themselves in spoken vocabulary. They learn more slowly, generally finding it more difficult to concentrate, remember and transfer what they have learned to new situations. Inclined to be more egocentric, they have difficulty forming abstract concepts and seeing other people's points of view.

2. Expectations of failure

Children learn to expect failure if they cannot live up to educational standards which are too high for them. They also learn to expect failure if others expect them to fail. Reluctant to expose their perceived inadequacy when the going gets more difficult, they often prefer to seek refuge by withdrawing into quiet isolation, or becoming aggressive or disruptive, (though not all disruptive children are slow learners). Avoidance or disruptive behaviour can result in further failure, reinforcing lower expectations and creating a vicious circle which becomes increasingly difficult to break.

That is the theory — what happens in the classroom? How can a teacher identify the extra practical help a particular individual is likely to need? Hard and fast judgements are dangerous, but when a child begins to give cause for concern a checklist[4], like the following, can help.

Compare:
- i) spoken and written language — are they of the same poor standard?
- ii) content and spelling of written work — are they of the same poor standard?
- iii) language and number work — are they of the same poor standard?
- iv) reading and spelling — are they of the same poor standard?
- v) ability and performance — does he or she seem to be trying as hard as possible?

Ask:
other teachers if they have observed the same.

Slow learners and experiential RE

Some approaches to religious education are more suited than others to the needs of slow learners. The kind of person–centred experiential approach outlined in this book seems to possess a number of general advantages:

1. **Its subject–matter is the ordinary human experience of the pupils themselves**. Everyone has something they can contribute regardless of their level of cognitive or linguistic functioning. In addition, it builds on something they find intrinsically interesting — their own experience.

2. **It requires the development of personal qualities which are not directly linked to levels of cognitive or linguistic functioning**, e.g. trust, openness and acceptance. A slow learner can be just as trusting as the most gifted child in the class.

3. **It maximises opportunities for success through a variety of learning experiences**. By encompassing any, and every, means of stimulus and expression — from relaxation exercises to brainstorming, art to body sculpture, music to poetry as well as talking — it minimises the usual emphasis on reading and writing which slow learners find especially difficult. Pupils can participate at various levels without the fear of failure since these learning experiences do not demand a specific degree of cognitive or linguistic functioning. The variety of experiences which are offered also benefits slow learners who have less difficulty with some activities than with others.

4. **It minimises opportunities for failure since there are no right or wrong answers**. It is not possible to apply terms like 'true' or 'false' to human experience. All human experience is individual and every individual is different, therefore each person's experience is valid because it is true for them. Slow learners never need to fear being wrong when describing their experience.

Extra help is still required

While a person–centred experiential approach to religious education possesses a number of general advantages for slow learners, it cannot by itself eliminate all the difficulties they face; nor does it completely obviate their need for extra help in the classroom.

Take language, for example. However hard you try, it is impossible to eliminate language, in some form or other, from classroom teaching. Language is the chief medium for both instruction and expression and this immediately disadvantages those pupils whose language development is poor. They can have difficulty understanding the teacher's instructions and explanations, they don't always comprehend what others in the group are saying, and they struggle to find words to express their own feelings. Thought is inextricably connected to language and similarly impossible to avoid. Activities in religious education aim to stimulate conscious reflection on personal experience. That reflection depends, amongst other things, on the ability to think about our own thoughts and feelings and to 'look at' ourselves from the outside. This skill is more developed in some people than in others, as is the ability to transfer what has been learned from one situation to another. Some children learn in smaller steps and need greater repetition of learning experiences before they can learn.

In the same way, an approach in which there are no right or wrong answers may reduce the possibility of low expectations arising or being reinforced, but it cannot entirely eliminate it from happening in practice. Try as you might to impress upon them that everyone's experience is equally valuable, some children soon come to perceive that their peers are 'better' talkers. From this perception, it is only a short step for them to equate 'better' talking with 'better' answers. It is not uncommon for slow–learning pupils to feel intimidated in class discussions and simply parrot what others say, for fear of being wrong or being shown up as inarticulate. Unfortunately, once children have learned to expect failure, they need a great deal of extra help to unlearn it.

How, then, can a person–centred experiential approach to religious education provide slow learners with at least some of the extra help they need? There is no perfect solution but experience has shown that a number of general strategies may help.

a) Learn to identify slow learners' difficulties

Labelling someone as 'lazy' or 'disruptive' is too easy. It also militates against the possibility of creating an open, accepting atmosphere. If you cannot accept these pupils for what they really are — people who have more difficulty learning than others — then in turn, they will find it even more difficult to accept others for what they are. It does not take an expert to recognise some of the everyday characteristics of individual slow learners (see above checklist), though it does take a little time and a little experience. Keeping records can help, too.

b) Take small steps

Slow learners can learn to tackle more complex, and emotionally difficult, work by building up to it in small stages. For example, Kathy Raban extended the time children could concentrate on a stilling exercise from thirty seconds to ten minutes.

c) Repeat what is important

Slow learners generally need more opportunities than other pupils to learn to do the same thing. Sometimes straightforward repetition is best. You may have to explain patiently, time and time again, that there are no wrong answers and that their experience is just as valuable as the next person's. Sometimes direct repetition is unhelpful and learning is achieved by repeating the same lesson in a variety of different ways. For example, both a story and a relaxation exercise may help a child to differentiate between her public exterior and her private interior self.

d) Explain what you are doing

Explain why you are doing things, as well as what to do. (If you can't do this it's probably because *you* don't know what you are doing either!) Slow learners need more direction in order to understand what to do and also to grasp the point of doing it, so check that they do understand before you proceed.

e) Create a secure atmosphere

Many slow learners need a greater sense of security than others before they can take the risk of trying anything new. This feeling of security can be developed in the classroom by making it clear that they are valued for themselves and not devalued for what they

cannot do. There are a number of ways to help pupils feel more secure. For example, stories and guided fantasy can be used to allow people to project their feelings on to characters in imaginary situations. Instead of referring to 'me' or 'myself', they can talk about the feelings and experiences of the imaginary characters. In this way they can distance themselves from sensitive issues by reflecting upon them vicariously. In addition, the chance to opt out of activities without having to give explanations gives pupils a genuine opportunity to avoid situations they find too painful or embarrassing.

f) Individualise

Slow learners are all individuals who need differing amounts of extra help in different ways. Where possible, special allowance should be made for each pupil's needs by teaching in smaller stages, with more repetition, increased explanation, greater security and so on.

g) Help with basic skills

Basic educational skills, particularly those of reading and writing, are important aspects of the social life of our culture. They cannot be avoided. Slow learners need, and expect, help with essential skills rather than to be told that it is not important. This may mean sometimes writing things down for them, for example in a brainstorming exercise. At other times, it means restricting the demand for writing to a level the pupils can achieve. They could try a Japanese haiku or attempt a cinquaine, a simple five–lined poetic form consisting of 1, 2, 3, 4, and 1 words to the line respectively.

h) Keep an open mind

Far too little is understood about why some pupils in school fail to do what the majority of people of the same age can do, particularly in the complex field of religious education. In a short account like this there is always the danger of oversimplification. Try, therefore, to avoid making hard and fast decisions about what individual children can or cannot do. Instead, proceed with caution, be observant and subject your judgements about others to frequent scrutiny.

Ted Huddleston

Colour of my dreams

I'm a really rotten reader
the worst in all the class,
the sort of rotten reader
that makes you want to laugh.

I'm last in all the readin' tests,
my score's not on the page
and when I read to teacher
she gets in such a rage.

She says I cannot form my words
she says I can't build up
and that I don't know phonics
— and don't know c-a-t from k-u-p.

They say that I'm dyslectic
(that's a word they've just found out)
. . . but when I get some plasticine
I know what that's about.

I make these scary monsters
I draw these secret lands
and get my hair all sticky
and paint on all me hands.

I make these super models,
I build these smashing towers
that reach up to the ceiling
— and take me hours and hours.

I paint these lovely pictures
in thick green drippy paint
that gets all on the carpet —
and makes the cleaners faint.

I build great magic forests
weave bushes out of string
and paint pink panderellos
and birds that really sing.

I play my world of real believe
I play it every day
and teachers stand and watch me
but don't know what to say.

They give me diagnostic tests,
they try out reading schemes,
but none of them will ever know
the colour of my dreams.

Peter Dixon

References

1. *Special Educational Needs*, Report of the Warnock Committee, H.M.S.O.: London 1978.

2. *ibid.*

3. For an introduction to this field see, for example.

   Ainscow, M. & Tweddle, D. A., *Preventing Classroom Failure: An Objectives Approach*, Wiley: London, 1979.

   Bell, P. & Kerry, T., *Teaching Slow Learners in mixed ability classes*, Macmillan: Basingstoke, 1982.

   Chazan, M., 'Children with learning difficulties', in Chazan, M., Moore, T., Williams, P. & Wright, J., *The practice of educational psychology*, Longman: London, 1974.

   Gulliford, R., *Teaching Children with Learning Difficulties*, NFER-Nelson, 1985.

   Haigh, G., *Teaching slow learners*, Temple Smith: London, 1977.

   Taylor, R., *Ways and Means 2: Children with Learning Difficulties*, Somerset Education Authority, 1981.

4. Bell and Kerry (above) is particularly helpful.

Multi–faith RE and experiential learning

Traditional methods of teaching RE, which present religion as a body of knowledge to be transmitted and learnt, often fail to promote any understanding of the living faiths they seek to represent. In this article, Brian Netto argues that experiential learning provides an effective approach to multi–faith RE. He begins with a popular Eastern parable which can be related to the study of religion through religious education.

Studying religion — a modern parable for religious educators

'Six blind people set out to discover for themselves true knowledge. They are instructed by a wise teacher to search out a mysterious beast, called "elephant", which is the source of all wisdom. On their journey, each one stumbles across an elephant. One blind person grabs hold of a leg and thinks that what she holds is like a tree–trunk, firm and solid. The second takes hold of the tail and concludes that it is like a rope; the third holds the elephant's trunk and says that what he has found is like a huge snake; the fourth passes his hands along a tusk and proclaims that truth is smooth and sharp; the fifth touches an ear and believes it is like a ship's sail; the sixth holds the rasping tongue and knows that it is wet and warm.'

It is noteworthy that none of the people in the parable discovers what gives life to the elephant, what animates it. They each develop partial views, and even collectively they are unable to find true knowledge.

A similar situation has developed in multi–faith RE where, in the past, religious traditions have been conceived as bodies of information to be transmitted by the teacher for students and children to compile and learn. This approach to the study of religion is underpinned by an ideology of cultural and religious transmission which is offensive to most of these traditions.

The changing nature of religious education

One problem is that when trying to understand anything new, we tend to superimpose our own presuppositions which are conditioned by personal experience of religious or secular life. Historically, British society and culture have evolved through and from a Christian standpoint. Resultant views about religion, education and religious education have been governed by these structures. Consequently models of religion in the past have tended to superimpose structures which are inappropriate — structures which often tell us more about the author than the tradition being studied.

In the case of RE in the British state education system, the majority community is Christian (at least nominally and effectively), or secular. This community generated an approach to RE which was underpinned by a process of cultural assimilation and integration. What was taught were only those aspects of other communities which were regarded as compatible with the values, beliefs and lifestyles of the host community. The result was often a Christian perspective on 'other' religions. This approach has often regarded 'religion' as something distinct from the 'secular'. In contrast, many religious people see the world as intrinsically religious, so that *all* aspects of life are always within a religious framework.

Phenomenology of religion

The approach to religious education advocated in this book breaks away from this sort of model. The Religious Experience and Education Project is based on the phenomenological approach to RE and provides teachers with ways of communicating the spiritual insights of the religious traditions of the world. Experiential learning uses the tools of phenomenology, in particular the device of 'bracketing out', or putting aside, our personal assumptions when attempting to understand the religious life of another person. This helps to develop the skill of 'seeing' or perceiving this life world through the eyes of that person.

Phenomenology is not obviously rooted in any particular theological or religious tradition. Its main assumption is that one has to participate in that life world, albeit in a provisional way, in order to understand the life world and religious meaning of another person. In other words, the process of understanding a religion is rooted in the experience of the pupil. It is determined by the experience of the faith and not just a study of its underlying concepts. As we move towards a truly pluralist democracy, the individual faith communities are beginning to develop political power, to define and represent themselves. Now the tendency is to allow those faith communities to set their own agendas and produce their own resources.

Phenomenology is primarily concerned with *understanding* — understanding the nature and source of religion(s), and understanding oneself in relation to religion. In aiming to develop understanding, empathy and respect for different religious traditions, phenomenology transcends questions of indoctrination and the undermining of the faith which may be raised when a critical or analytical approach is stressed.

The aims of the Project as compatible with the aims of modern multi–faith RE

A religiously educated person is not defined as someone equipped with a vast amount of information about a variety of traditions. The exercises in this book attempt to explore the often hidden dimensions of religion — their spiritual cores, while the learning model rejects the view that the child is a passive recipient of a transmitted body of knowledge. This deficit model of the individual is replaced by a child–centred 'holistic' model which affirms the pupil in his or her own process of growth. Pupils begin to participate in the process of education, are enabled to change their environment, make decisions, and so on.

In this approach, linear 'quest' models, which see life as a journey towards a particular goal, are balanced by cyclical models which view development in terms of 'wholeness' and integration. The work of REEP has drawn on the experiences of a wide range of religious traditions and peoples as well as contemporary forms of humanistic psychotherapies. Its exemplars are multi–faith and the flexibility of its framework allows the teacher to incorporate insights and ideas drawn from other traditions. As such, its aims, perspectives, activities and techniques are integral to a fully multi–faith religious education which is reduced to a dry 'naming of parts' without them.

Brian Netto

Chapter 19

Movement, music and massage

Perhaps you find the title of this section surprising in a book about religious education. Movement, music and massage are not traditionally considered to be appropriate vehicles for RE but they do represent aspects of spirituality which can be explored in the classroom.

Since ancient times religion has been expressed through dance and music which reflected the resonances and rhythms of life. The power of the massaging hands was also known and is still acknowledged in some faiths today, for example in the ritual of laying on of hands. These practices are based upon the concept that body, mind and spirit are inseparable aspects of the same human essence. Thus, each has an irreplaceable role on the path to spiritual growth.

'Movement and rhythms are something that pertain right through the cellular level down to the subatomic state. It exists in the universe — pulsars and stars that recede, let alone planets that circle, and it exists in every cell of our bodies, where molecules of matter pass to and fro through cell membranes. Thus the whole of our lives and the universe in which we live and the matter of which we are made, is dependent upon and permeated by movement and rhythm to keep it in existence.'

(Wethered)

Movement

Movement offers a way of knowing ourselves and others; the inner impulse can be perceived in the outer expression. For example, through movement we can know ourselves as strong and forceful or gentle and tender. Movement can extend possibilities too. It can become possible to know, and give expression to, deeper aspects of the self. Movement can link the individual with the universal. For instance, the theological notion of creation out of chaos can be worked out in contrasting movement phrases, the performance of which links the individual to the universal concept.

Movement is not only knowing but communicating. It can give an opportunity to explore some of the issues that arise out of being creatures that exist in relationship — issues such as acceptance, rejection, encountering, avoiding, supporting and opposing. For example, the last theme might involve various situations in which the body is either supported·by others or pushing against others.

It is through rhythm we can participate in the very life of the universe; feel it pulsing in our veins. Through rhythm we can glimpse the vision of the mystic who sees that all things are one, that there is no division between us and the universe we call home. There are many kinds of rhythm. One example is the urgent, exuberant rhythm of creation, as portrayed by the Hindu, Shiva Nataraja. With a background of drumming a repetitive sequence of stamping, gesturing and turning, this potent symbol of the recurring cycle of life and death could be appreciated through movement. The seasons, the waxing and waning of the moon (parallelling the waxing and waning seasons of human life), the rhythm of death and rebirth can all be known through movement.

It is good to work in a medium which is not verbal

in our over–intellectualised and wordy world and to remember that words are not sufficient to capture the spiritual. It is the real literal and carnal body which must be resensitized and educated in the sacredness which has hidden in its feelings.

Music and sound

Pir Vilyat Khan, head of the Sufi order in the West, suggests that through music we plug into the 'software' of the universe. Its forms express the meaningfulness and orderliness of the cosmos, and give form to the thinking and the feeling behind it — music is perfection made audible. In this way it acts as a bridge between our senses which perceive it and our spiritual self which grasps its significance. For instance, J. S. Bach described his music as a blueprint for understanding the ordered nature of life where themes had a certain amount of freedom to develop, yet the whole blended harmoniously together. A piece of Bach introduced to children with this explanation, and possibly in conjunction with the journey to the stars fantasy or even an elementary lesson in astronomy, could create for children something of the sense of order and purpose that the religious believer sees in the working of the universe.

Scientists are beginning to discover that certain frequencies have healing effects on cells of the body. The vibrations and tonal effects of different kinds of music can affect not only physical but physic states too. For teachers this can mean that music can be a door to unlock the spiritual. Through music we can enter into states of mind which parallel the religious, such as peace, harmony, glorification. For example, you might like to try a music meditation (devised by Malcolm Lazarus of the Wrekin Trust) which is in four parts of five minutes each. The first consists of 'emptying' through dancing as vigorously as possible to loud, beat music. The second part involves standing with arms held out and singing along with the Halleluiah Chorus from Handel's *Messiah*. The third section is tenderly humming to Pachelbel's *Kanon* and finally, five minutes of silence.

We can enter the spiritual not only through music which is outside us, but also through our own inner music. Eastern traditions have developed the use of *mantra* which is the constant repetition of a sound or a word. Many of these involve vibrations and resonances in the body which have the sensation of linking with the resonances of energies beyond the individual person. Sound and meaning become associated through constant repetition. You might try getting a group to hum continuously for a short period of time, asking them to concentrate on the physical vibration rather than the sound. This could be presented with the idea of some religious believers that all matter is one and the vibration takes you out of yourself to feel temporarily part of everything that is. Repeating one's first name can be a fascinating experience; many new levels of meaning and feeling about yourself can emerge.

Massage

Massage is another neglected avenue to the sacred which, because of its sexual overtones, has had its spiritual aspects overlooked and ignored. It belongs to the same religious traditions as laying on of hands where we are more able to appreciate the spiritual nature of human touch. It is a beautiful expression of caring and healing from one human being to another. To touch another in an atmosphere of reverence is to convey acceptance and concern on a level deeper than words. Obviously the scope available in a classroom is limited but the benefits of breaking through the no–touching barrier are enormous. I have often ended a session with children sitting in a circle facing the back of the person in front and gently kneading the shoulders and upper back of the person. Faces can be stroked with thumbs, or heads simply held, especially around the temples. A useful book for beginners is *The Massage Book* by George Dowring.

The sacred needs to be rediscovered in what moves and touches us. What a tragedy if religious education neglects the precious gifts of body and senses with the rich potential for spiritual development which they contain.

Kathy Raban

Useful books
Crandall, Joanne, *Self Transformation Through Music*, The Theosophical Publishing House, Wheaton, USA, 1986.

Hamel, Peter Michael, *Through Music to the Self*. Glement, 1976.

Lingerman, Hal A., *The Healing Energies of Music*, The Theosophical Publishing House, Wheaton, USA, 1983.

Dychtwald, Ken, *Bodymind*, Wildwood House, 1977. A discussion of the connection of body, mind and spirit and the story of self that the body can tell.

Keen, Sam, *To a Dancing God*, Collins Fontana, 1970. He argues for a 'visceral theology', a theology based on wisdom of the body.

Dunlop, Valerie Preston, *A Handbook of Dance Education*, MacDonald & Evans, 1963. Basic movement theory for education.

Dowring, George, *The Massage Book*, Penguin Books, 1974.

Tapes of suitable music from many different cultures can be obtained through WOMAD, who produce world music tapes for schools. Address: 3rd Floor, 85 Park Street, Bristol, BS1 5JN.

PART FOUR

Background papers

Religious experience in modern Britain

This article, first published by New Society *in April 1987, sets out to answer the question: How religious are the British people in the latter part of the twentieth century?*
As director of the Alister Hardy Research Centre, David Hay collaborated with Gordon Heald, director of Gallup Poll, London, to produce this summary of a survey they conducted into contemporary religious experience.

How religious are the British? By 'religious' we mean something deeper than whether people attend services, believe the tenets of the various religious creeds or obey their commandments. What interests us is something much less tangible, the inner life, the secret arena that most of us don't often like to share with others.

Up until 1985 we were able to predict confidently that about a third of all adults would claim that they'd had some such experience. A poll conducted for the Alister Hardy Research Centre at Manchester College, Oxford, by Gallup in 1985, suggested that approximately 15 000 000 Britons would say that at least once or twice in their lives they have 'been aware of, or influenced by a presence or power, whether they call it God or not, which is different from their everyday selves'.

In 1986 we set out to find out the proportions of the population reporting different *kinds* of experience falling into this category, and how they related to conventional religion. To guide us we had the files of the Alister Hardy Research Centre (AHRC) which now contain over five thousand written accounts sent in as a response to advertisements in the media. On this basis we were able to predict what the major categories of experience were likely to be and we inserted questions about them in a Gallup Omnibus Survey.

The results showed that nearly half the adult population of Britain believe they have had a religious or transcendental experience. That is the conclusion to be drawn from the overall positive response rate of 48 per cent, which parallels trends in the United States.

The figures for in–depth surveys of specific groups in the population are more astonishing. Structured interviews with random samples of postgraduate students, citizens of Nottingham and, most recently, nurses in two large Leeds hospitals, all show a positive response rate of over 60 per cent. We will argue later that it may signal the breaking of a taboo. The classification of the results into types also allows us to give a thumbnail sketch of the nature and distribution of the 'religious experience' of contemporary British people.

TABLE 1: National frequency of report of different types of experience

TOTAL POSITIVE RESPONSE	48%
TYPES:	
Patterning of events	29%
Awareness of the presence of God	27%
Awareness of receiving help in answer to prayer	25%
Awareness of a guiding presence not called God	22%
Awareness of the presence of the dead	18%
Awareness of a sacred presence in nature	16%
Awareness of an evil presence	12%
Experiencing that all things are 'One'	5%

Patterning

The most commonly reported experience, just nudging 'awareness of the presence of God' out of first place, is the sense that there is a patterning to the events of life. This is rather unlike all other types in that it does not necessarily (though it may) involve a direct awareness of a sacred or transcendent presence.

Characteristically it includes an experience of 'synchronicity' and of course often such experiences are trivial. Thus, the psychologist Carl Jung illustrates the notion by the example of someone who happens to notice the serial number on his streetcar ticket. On arrival home he receives a telephone call during which the same number is mentioned; and in the evening he buys a theatre ticket which again has that number. It is when conjunctions of this kind are associated with non-trivial events in a way that assists the individual, that they tend to be interpreted religiously:

'. . . The experiences of the last six months have . . . confirmed my deep conviction that God is directly and indirectly guiding my life . . . As well as being absolutely convinced of Divine Guidance in the larger issues of my life, I feel this guidance strongly even in some of the smaller events . . . the pattern of my life seems to be a mosaic, in which everything, including seeming disasters, eventually turn to good . . .'

(*This example and the others quoted in the article are drawn from the files of AHRC*)

The numinous

Britain may be highly secularised on the surface, but the next three categories illustrate clearly the continuing influence of Western monotheism. Awareness of the presence of God, particularly during prayer, is so basic to Christian devotion, that it is not surprising that it is very commonly reported. We know from a number of in–depth studies that the occasions that tend to be recalled most vividly are when the individual is in some kind of distress:

'. . . I had an experience seven years ago that changed my whole life. I had lost my husband six months before and my courage at the same time. I felt life would be useless if fear were allowed to govern me. One evening, with no preparation, as sudden and dynamic as the revelation to Saul of Tarsus, I knew that I was in the presence of God, and that he would never leave me nor forsake me and that he loved me with a love beyond imagination — no matter what I did . . .'

But you don't have to be conventionally religious to believe that you've had one of these experiences. Many people, perhaps angry or irritated by the religious institutions, do not wish to label the presence. Nevertheless their descriptions of their experiences have a numinous quality similar to those directly identified as theistic:

'. . . I . . . know that since I concluded some years ago that my mind could not accept a personal God

. . . I seem to have become more aware of this all-pervading power which to me is strength, comfort, joy, goodness . . .'

The dead

In many societies, religion involves a cult of the dead or of the ancestors. It is tempting to speculate that, so to speak, the raw material for such a cult lies in quite commonplace human experience. Not far short of a fifth of the British populace believe they have been aware of the presence of the dead. Quite often it's a close relative, recently deceased. But the power of the Western theological tradition probably directs attention away from these experiences as a source of religious belief and, especially among the well–educated, may make them taboo.

There is evidence that experiences of the dead are reported more commonly by less well–educated people. Dr. David Lewis of the AHRC who did the survey of the experiences of nurses in Leeds, found that when he split the sample in two according to educational level, the better educated group were more likely to report experiences of the presence of God whilst the less well educated reported more contacts with the dead.

Nature mysticism

The European Romantic tradition, mediated in England especially by Wordsworth, gives permission to the religious intellectual, and Nature mysticism is not uncommonly reported by university graduates. Sixteen per cent of the national sample claimed to have been aware of a sacred presence in nature at some time in their lives. The following is typical:

'. . . As a child in the country, I wandered by myself sometimes but was rather afraid when I became conscious of solitude and silence. I became increasingly aware of a Presence which I associated with nature around me. In my adolescence I gave It the name 'God', and aimed at being alone to commune with It . . .'

Evil

It is a curious fact, remarked on by the sociologist Peter Berger, that at a time when religious interpretations of reality are often seen as implausible, a lot of credence is given to manifestations of evil or occult forces. Berger explains this in a Freudian manner (though Freud would hardly have approved!) as evidence for the bizarre return of repressed religion. Twelve per cent of the sample reported an awareness of an evil presence. About a third of them interpreted their experience religiously, though the connection was sometimes rather oblique:

'. . . Suddenly I became aware of a sense of the uttermost evil . . . I was enveloped by this revolting force, so vile and rotting I could almost taste the evil. I recall that I managed by a great effort to stretch out my right hand and with my index finger I traced the shape of the Cross in the air. Immediately on my doing this the evil enveloping me fell away completely . . .'

Mysticism

Mystical experience, much beloved by academic students of religious experience, was claimed by only five per cent of the sample. The following is typical:

'. . . I've been doing some TM [Transcendental Meditation, as taught by the Maharishi Mahesh Yogi] recently and I find occasionally as my thoughts become more and more refined, there's a feeling of being part of a whole. It's a very physical awareness of myself as an organism which relates to a greater organism.

In the past, some theorists of religion have seen this as the most fundamental aspect of a 'common core' of religious experience. If that view has any substance, we would have to conclude from the results of our survey that the monotheistic bias of British culture still has a dominating role in affecting the manifestation of experience. As in the case of some other categories, there is evidence from detailed survey work in Nottingham that 'mysticism' is something to which well educated people are more prone, perhaps because they are more likely to be aware of Eastern religious traditions.

The taboo on religious experience

What kind of interpretations can we make of this array of human experience? One question that we have been dodging so far is whether the experiences we have been describing can truly be called 'religious'. That is because it is very difficult to give a simple answer. The people we interview have the same problem (Table 2).

TABLE 2: Percentages of people interpreting their experiences religiously

Awareness of the presence of God	80%
Awareness of receiving help in answer to prayer	79%
Awareness of a sacred presence in nature	61%
Awareness of a kindly presence looking after/guiding	58%
Experiencing that all things are One	55%
Awareness of an evil presence	38%
Awareness of the presence of someone who has died	35%
Patterning of events	32%

At one end of the scale, some people don't even wish to call an awareness of the presence of God a religious experience. From in-depth survey work we know that the common reason for this is anger with the religious institution, which is perceived as a dead husk, remote from the intense reality of direct spiritual encounter. That sounds to us like a religious anger.

At the other end of the scale, an extraordinary patterning of events is quite often interpreted religiously, sometimes because the patterning itself is experienced as pervaded by a presence. But for others, who presumably have a prior religious belief, it seems to be based on a deduction from the improbability of the patterning.

We are inclined to think that this ambiguity of interpretation reflects a profound ambivalence in contemporary society about the status of religion. At least since the eighteenth century, when interpretations of reality began to be dominated by the rationalism of the Enlightenment, Europeans have been uncertain whether religion is the cure for a disease of the spirit, or is itself the disease.

In this survey we have some evidence about

ambiguous feelings. For one thing, we have found that, as with the results of earlier studies by the Alister Hardy Research Centre, most of these experiences took place when people were alone (Table 3). Now of course it is true that solitude is traditionally recommended as most appropriate for prayer and meditation. But, quite apart from Durkheim's explanation for religious experience as fundamentally a social phenomenon, the emphasis on communal worship in Western religion would lead us to expect it to play a far larger part in the manifestation of experience.

TABLE 3: *Percentage of people reporting the experience taking place when they were alone*

Awareness of receiving help in answer to prayer	76%
Awareness of the presence of someone who has died	75%
Experiencing that all things are One	69%
Awareness of a kindly presence looking after/guiding	68%
Patterning of events	66%
Awareness of the presence of God	64%
Awareness of a sacred presence in nature	64%
Awareness of an evil presence	61%

In fact, at least in contemporary society, the presence of other people is usually seen as an inhibitor. (An exception to this is amongst the membership of those charismatic or radical cults which emphasise 'experience'. But our figures demonstrate that though colourful, they represent only a small proportion of those claiming religious experience. Indeed, almost half of the positive respondents never attend a place of worship.)

The extreme privacy which surrounds many of the experiences is further demonstrated when we ask people whether they have told anyone else about them (Table 4). Extraordinarily high proportions have never told anyone else at all.

TABLE 4: *Percentage saying 'No' in answer to the question, 'Have you told anyone else about your experience?'*

Awareness of a sacred presence in nature	44%
Awareness of receiving help in answer to prayer	42%
Experiencing that all things are One	40%
Awareness of a kindly presence looking after/guiding	39%
Awareness of the presence of God	38%
Patterning of events	33%
Awareness of the presence of someone who has died	28%
Awareness of an evil presence	28%

From other work, we know that this reticence is unlikely to be because the experiences are too trivial to merit a mention in conversation. On the contrary, people often count them as among the most significant events in their lives. What appears to be producing the silence is a taboo on revealing the very existence of such a dimension in one's life. Overwhelmingly, people believe they will be thought mad or stupid if they admit it.

Their anxiety may be justified, but research does not support the sneerers. The stereotype is contradicted by the majority of the evidence collected in Britain and the United States over the past ten years and more recently in Australia. In repeated surveys by Gallup, NOP, NORC, and the Survey Research Center at the University of California, people reporting these experiences show up as better educated, happier and better balanced mentally than those who don't report them. Furthermore, there seems to be an ethical spinoff. People talk of discovering directly through their experience that they are not alienated from the rest of reality. They say they feel more responsible for other people and for the environment.

Whatever else the data demonstrate, they do not prove that 'religious people are right'. Nevertheless, looked at dispassionately, we think the evidence reveals a culturally mediated prejudice. It's based on a conviction that religious ways of interpreting reality simply must be mistaken because they appear to conflict with or be irrelevant to cherished and successful scientific paradigms. It too easily discards the spiritual dimension of human experience as attributable to some kind of personal or social pathology and it creates a taboo a bit like the one there used to be about sex.

There are certainly religious ways of being crazy or eccentric. We could quote examples. But if spiritual experience, on the whole, is not obviously reducible to error or sickness, and if it is shown to have positive functions for individual and society, then the paradigm needs changing and the taboo should be abandoned.

(*A note on the Alister Hardy Research Centre follows.*)

The Alister Hardy Research Centre

The Alister Hardy Research Centre was founded as the Religious Experience Research Unit at Manchester College, Oxford, in 1969 by Sir Alister Hardy, FRS, after his retirement from the Chair of Zoology at Oxford University. The purpose of the Centre is to make a disciplined study of the frequency of report of firsthand religious or transcendent experience in contemporary members of the human species and to investigate the nature and function of such experience.

There was, and continues to be, a widespread popular belief that these experiences are seldom found in contemporary society. People who do report such experience are often dismissed as poorly educated, coming from socially deprived parts of the community, unhappy, somewhat mentally unbalanced, self–preoccupied; or perhaps members of offbeat religious sects. It was because of a doubt about the widespread dismissal of this dimension of human experience that the Centre was set up.

WHAT THE CENTRE HAS DONE

Since its foundation, the Centre has taken two major steps:

1. It has built up a unique body of research data consisting of more than five thousand case histories of individuals who have had some form of such experience.

2. The Centre has also conducted large scale surveys of reports of experience in Britain and United States. The very high positive response rates found by AHRC researchers have also been recorded in parallel studies conducted by independent research organisations in the United States and in Australia (e.g. the National Opinion Research Center at the University of Chicago, the Survey Research Center at the University of California, the Princeton Religion Research Center, and Gallup International). AHRC has also completed a number of in–depth studies in Britain. In all these latter studies, the positive response rate has been over 60 per cent.

The Centre has no official view on the nature of these experiences. However, it retains an openness to the possibility that the crisis through which Western culture (and hence the world affected by it) is now passing may in part be the result of an intellectually restricted perspective which appeared at the time of the European Enlightenment, especially during the eighteenth century. The Centre would claim that modern analyses of the rootlessness, meaninglessness and violence increasingly endemic to society may be limited by this dominant (and materially successful) thought pattern. In particular, it could be dismissing or failing to comprehend the religious or transcendent dimension of human experience.

Changing perspectives of a classroom

Traditional classroom design, accommodating row upon row of desks, often leaves little room for movement and confines teachers and pupils to static and sedentary learning.

One secondary teacher, Ginny Straugheir, changed her own and her pupils' perspectives on learning when she rearranged her classroom furniture. The tables lined the outside walls, with the chairs facing outwards for written work and inwards, making a horseshoe or circle, for discussion. The appearance of the room provoked such a variety of reactions and interest that explanation and comment was necessary. The responses and the changes she and the pupils observed in their behaviour over the following six months were recorded. This report of their findings considers two questions: what values does the classroom environment communicate, and what effects do changes in this environment have on pupils and on teachers?

Six months on

Although it seemed obvious to me that the room differed from other classrooms in the layout of desks, I was interested to learn whether that was the sole distinguishing factor in the eyes of the pupils using the room regularly. A questionnaire completed by approximately four hundred first to seventh–form students asked for their impressions together with a comparison with normal classrooms. In response to the first question, 'Our classroom does not look like a normal classroom because . . .', five other aspects were singled out for comment. A number of pupils no longer regard the desk arrangement as unusual, indeed after only six months some third-year students have forgotten what the room was like during their previous two years!

They drew attention to:

1. the CARPET, which is now much more obvious and provides a more homely environment;

2. the POSTERS and displays of work make the room 'bright, and friendly and colourful';

3. the NOTICE BOARD to which they can contribute their own material. When I pointed out that all our rooms have notice boards they were surprised (!) but countered 'they're not used' or 'they're boring';

4. the HEATING system guaranteed to produce a hot-house temperature in a school where low temperatures and draughts are the norm. The warmth contributes to the relaxing and homely atmosphere;

5. the SPACE created by moving the desks to the walls appears to be the vital factor for many children. It allows:

a) greater participation in activities during the lesson and increases the methods available;

b) an uninterrupted view of the blackboard, video,

screen, etc. A frequent complaint about rows of desks is, 'If someone bigger than me sits in front of me I can't see anything';

c) easy and constant vision of their peers so that body language now becomes a valuable tool in discussion and self-discipline;

d) an illusion of room to move. Although they actually have the same desk area they feel less crowded. Rows are seen as cramped, inhibiting and impersonal;

e) a tidier environment. This appeals to their aesthetic senses with quite a large number saying, 'It looks nice';

f) an improvement in clarity of hearing. 'The teacher can stand in the middle and everyone can hear.'

Asked to comment on the practicality of conventional desk arrangements, the pupils' replies reminded me of Thomas Gradgrind's school in *Hard Times* where children are described as 'the inclined plane of little vessels then and there arranged in order, ready to have imperial gallons of facts poured into them until they were full to the brim'. The classroom is like a factory production line — drab, impersonal and unfeeling. It provides the teacher with the opportunity for an ego–trip, 'so the teacher can make boring speeches'.

Both ends towards the middle

At first several fifth–form girls were suspicious of the new–style seating and were allowed to put their desks into rows each lesson. After several weeks they ceased to do this and became fervent supporters of the new system. In a long and detailed response, Lisa Corbett wrote, 'Desks are usually in rows to stop distraction. It doesn't help. People just get up and talk to others or they hurt their necks turning round. I know I've hurt my neck lots of times turning around! You can't hear people talking sometimes. I don't know why but you can hear much more clearly when you're spread out. *We don't want our desks in rows.*'

The majority of comments frequently centred on the improved atmosphere created by the present arrangement. This makes pupils more relaxed and aids their concentration. In turn this is credited as the main reason for a more positive attitude towards the subject. Typical comments from second years (who have not taken part in any of the experiential learning) include, 'You don't feel so uptight and you get a homely atmosphere', and 'my attitude to the work is a lot better since the layout of the classroom has changed. I quite like RE.'

In keeping with the more friendly atmosphere I have deliberately relaxed the restrictions on classroom behaviour. They are allowed to talk quietly while working, move around the room to seek advice, change their position, etc. without seeking permission, and even doodle (if it helps me to concentrate why not them?). CSE pupils discovered they can work more comfortably and efficiently when note-taking during discussion if they sit *on* the desks. This gives them greater control of files resting on their knees and removes the problem of dropping papers, etc. Not a particularly cooperative group in the past, they are now producing a high standard of work, whilst their behaviour and attitude have improved considerably.

In trying to reproduce the working conditions of an efficient and friendly office I have discovered that unacceptable behaviour rarely occurs. I no longer need to moan incessantly about the need to sit up straight, nor do I have to remind pupils to 'stop swinging on your chair' since nobody ever does that now, and the command 'put your pens down and pay attention' is a thing of the past. Not only does this give me more time to teach but I have had to punish only one person in six months.

Circle time

The use of the circle for discussion means that self–discipline is now essential if pupils are to obtain the approval of their peers. Everyone is visible to everybody else so attention–seekers do not feel isolated. There is equality within the circle and most use the opportunity to speak and contribute voluntarily. Discussion is no longer dominated by the few, giving greater interest and incentive to the rest of the class.

The flexibility of the room enables easy and rapid movement of desks to create islands for group work, segregated examination conditions, sitting on the other side of the desk when using the blackboard, circles of varying size for discussion, auditorium for video and film viewing. In the course of a lesson a class may utilise a number of different seating plans. Not knowing what is going to happen next, pupils appreciate this element of surprise. They are physically as well as mentally involved and find that the changes are conducive to learning since they combat boredom. 'You don't have to put up with the same scene all the time.'

When working with their backs turned away from the centre of the room they no longer feel under observation. The teacher is not visible to them and consequently they feel invisible to the teacher and in some cases tempted to talk. In discussion I asked them to consider the room from my point of view. This led to a number of expressions of surprise when they suddenly realised that I am now more aware of their activities than previously. My vision is no longer impeded by the presence of desks and other bodies.

They have acquired a sense of privacy when writing and I have noticed an increased tendency to cover up their work when they think I'm reading it over their shoulders. I'm able to walk around the room unnoticed and can see everyone's work, often without their knowledge of my presence. Improved opportunities for privacy have produced the recognition of the need for self–reliance. Copying no longer seems to be a practical possibility so there is greater incentive to prepare work in advance and to think before speaking.

During discussion I often move outside the circle so that I can be seen by few and heard by none. This can produce a less inhibiting environment allowing them to get on with the discussion themselves. It has been acknowledged as helpful to those who consider themselves to be shy.

Face the wall and concentrate

Since seating is not static, pupils feel confident to select or change their position to suit their prevailing needs. 'If the sun's in your eyes you can move.' A very tall boy is more comfortable since 'the desks are not in the way and you can stretch if you want. We can move around and feel free.'

'If you are facing the wall when you are trying to think about something it seems to come easier to you.'

Turning to face the wall is universally acclaimed as an important aid to concentration. Typical comments are: 'There's nothing to distract me.' 'I think better when I can't see anybody else.' 'I can concentrate more with no one turning around. People in front and behind can't put me off.' 'It's more private. You can block other people out when you are working.' 'It's easier to ignore the others with your back to them.' 'People can't see what you are writing so they won't take your ideas. It's my ideas I'm putting down and I do not want anyone else's ideas. Nobody can interfere in what you think.' 'You have to work on your own.' 'When you get a test you can't look at everybody else.' 'I've had to think for myself instead of consulting others.' 'You can't look around or day-dream.' 'You can look at the posters or out of the window and think about what you are writing.' 'There is less noise.' 'I can get on with my work without being disturbed.'

The greatest number of comments were provoked by the request for reactions to the use of the circle in discussion. Although this is used in other subjects by a number of teachers the pupils seem to regard our lessons as most effective.

'Being able to see everybody else is good because we can find out what they think of our suggestions and our reactions. Knowing the others can see me when I am talking is good because other people's reactions are important to me so I know whether I am talking sense or not. Then I like to turn away so I can write my own private suggestions without being disturbed.' (Christine Bankhead, third year).

'This has helped us with our work because we don't have to face the teacher. It's better because it is like we're talking to the class, not getting a lecture off the teacher. We are more at ease.'

'I can show my feelings and feel free. When I am in RE I feel I am just talking to all my friends.'

'I have learned to understand other people and not just think of myself.'

'You get more involved in the lesson.'

Facing everyone else within the circle inevitably produced mixed reactions. Many have recognised and tried to come to terms with their shyness and insecurity. Although they dislike this arrangement they recognise its value and quite a few see their confidence and self-respect increasing. Nobody wanted to return to conventional rows. Plus points were the chance to see, as well as hear, other people's views. Body language was often mentioned. They no longer feel isolated and gain encouragement from their peers. Discipline has improved since all are in the spotlight, although a negative aspect is seen in the tendency to talk more. Embarrassment is a major drawback but worthwhile in conjunction with the benefits.

Second-year pupils appeared to be more conscious of their embarrassment. They said, 'I get easily embarrassed when I talk in front of large numbers . . . You know what they are saying about you if you say something silly . . . It's good because it is horrible when nobody is listening to you when you are talking to them. Now you know you are talking to everyone and not just to yourself. If they can't see me they will soon lose interest when I am talking. Everyone pays more attention when we talk'.

There is unanimous agreement that the room is creating a practical and enjoyable working environment for all ages and abilities. When asked to assess whether the room encourages them to work harder or to relax more, the vast majority (well over 80 per cent) claim they are working harder. Of those prepared to admit they are not working so hard, a considerable number seem to equate only written exercises as work. The room now permits a greater use of non-writing activities so that a number of pupils have described lessons as fun, exciting, interesting and definitely not like work. Of course some individuals will inevitably take advantage some, if not all, of the time. Where this has become apparent, a quiet word, suggesting they cooperate or else they will be separated from the rest of class during lessons has so far produced the desired response.

The temptation to talk was most often cited as the reason why some pupils see themselves as less industrious when comparing the workrate with that in other lessons. 'I work less because the teacher can't see you as good and you can talk to your friends . . . People talk to you when you sit next to two people.' Other reasons for not working as hard were, 'I am very easily distracted as I look round all the time', 'The atmosphere makes you feel lazy', 'You are not pushed into doing things you don't want to', and finally 'We don't do any work'. This last comment came from a first–year boy who spent weeks giving up lunchtimes to finish off a model he was making of a Viking ship!

I found exactly the same reasons being given as encouragement to work harder. 'I work harder because all my friends are beside me . . . because you can talk . . . you can sit next to all your friends, not just one . . . and you don't have to shout at the other end of the classroom . . . If you turn your back on them they will realise you don't want to be disturbed.' What distracts one person is a positive aid to concentration for others, 'It's good. You can look straight out of the window. The view helps me to concentrate . . . I know what's going on all the time so I can work better.' It appears to be the atmosphere and lack of pressure which are most effective. 'It has a better atmosphere.' 'It is brighter and friendlier.' 'It is very cosy . . . a lot more homely . . . exciting.' 'You feel relaxed. Comfortable. You don't feel as though you have to work all the time so I want to work hard.' 'You feel you are important. You do what *you* feel is right and if you are wrong you are not told off. You feel free to tell your feelings and disagree with others.' 'You feel happy as you are not blocked in. You do not think you are in a prison. You are free to walk around.' 'It makes me feel more interested.' 'It helps me to enjoy my RE lesson so I work harder.' 'The arrangement of the desks gives the impression that this classroom is for solid hard work.' 'I think the way the desks is arranged is good because you can face away from everybody and have privacy or you can face them and have openness. I work less because I spend most of my time discussing things . . . I don't feel so lonely.'

You can see the people you hate

Suspicion and mistrust of their classmates appears to inhibit quite a large number of pupils regardless of their age or ability. Now, 'You can see the people you hate.' 'You can see who is talking about you.' 'You don't get sniggering.' 'You can see if people are laughing at you or talking about you.' 'There's more space to spread around the room so it's possible to avoid those you don't like.' I was fascinated to learn one boy's view. 'It's brilliant. You can't talk about anybody behind their back.' It seems he has been forced to moderate his antisocial activities and actually appreciates this change in his own behaviour. He admits, 'I like to be the centre of attention' and likes being visible to everyone in discussion. He does not need to misbehave to attract that desirable attention and this is also appreciated by him. Leaning forward or turning round to make snide comments to those in front or behind is no longer possible and so a common distraction has been removed.

The presence of friends is more often described as an aid to learning rather than a distraction. 'I know that other people are around so it is easier to get sorted out. My own work is not very good but the work I do in groups is good.' This affects behaviour and effect, 'You try better when you know other people can see you.' 'I am conscious of the others, but if they could not see me I would feel as if I was being ignored.'

Perhaps a third–year, Christine Bankhead, says it all, 'I work harder in this classroom because it is much more interesting than any other lesson. You can relax but also work while you are talking. This lesson makes you work harder because you aren't forced to work and you can say what you like. It's far more fun. I feel I can join in more . . . I think I have progressed a lot since the classroom has been changed because I feel more confident to talk. At first I had no confidence but then it began to build up and now I just come out with my feelings straightaway. Excellent. Instead of one person being the centre of attention all of us are able to believe and work out what other people think and feel. Everyone can join in and admit to our true feelings. The freedom is ours where in other lessons we are under supervision.'

Finally, a touching plea from a second–year girl, 'Please don't change it back. It would change the room's atmosphere and I like it as it is. I am getting to understand more about the lesson.' As in the Japanese art of gift–wrapping where the packaging can be of greater value than the present it contains, so my classroom has become a 'furoshiki'. It is an attractive container which enhances the contents in such a way that it has become an intrinsic part of the gift of religious education.

Ginny Straugheir

(This report was first published as 'Sit up straight and pay attention' in *Values*, September 1986.)

The seashore of endless worlds

RE in a multicultural society: tensions and approaches

Society and spirituality, politics and prayer, work and worship, deeds and devotions, conflict and convent, multitude and monastery, action and ashram, struggle and silence. How are these poles and tensions experienced, pictured and articulated in the religious traditions of humankind? What do they have to say to the contemporary tension between anti–racism (a task of politics) and inter–faith dialogue (a task of the heart)? What messages are there from these historic tensions for the modest — but serious, vital and potentially exciting — task of organising and planning RE in secondary schools? These are the questions of this paper by Robin Richardson which was first presented to the DES Short Course 'Religious Education and the Secondary School Curriculum' at Westhill College, Birmingham, in July 1987; a slightly different version was published in the British Journal of Religious Education, *Summer 1988.*

Part one: A folktale and interpretations — the five teachers of RE

An urgent call came to the Great Lama of the North from the Lama of the South, asking for a wise and holy teacher to initiate novices into the nature and purposes of life. To everyone's astonishment, the Great Lama sent five teachers instead of one. To those who enquired, he replied cryptically, 'We shall be lucky if one of them gets to the Lama of the South.'

The group had been on the road some days when a messenger came running up to them and said, 'There is a terrible famine in our village, the rains and crops have failed, beasts and people are starving, many have already died. Abide with us, we pray, care for us, teach us knowledge of health, science and nature.'

'I would not be a Buddhist', said one of the teachers sent by the Lama, 'if I did not stop here, and provide knowledge for these suffering people.' The other four continued their journey.

A few days later the four came to a city. Some of the people on the streets said to them, 'This place is corrupt; the system of this city is oppressive, capricious, uncaring, cruel. This is a racist and sexist society. Stay with us here, we pray you, to help us resist and replace the rulers of this city and to govern ourselves in justice and in peace.'

'I would not be a Buddhist', said one of the teachers sent by the Lama, 'if I did not stop here, and join in argument, politics and government'. The other three continued travelling.

A few days later the three came to a small settlement where there were many children playing in vigorous peace. There were dances and games, embraces and laughter; there was ripening fruit on the trees, there were solid houses and homes. 'Settle with us, we pray you', said the people, 'set up home, have children, join us here in building the future.'

'I would not be a Buddhist', said one of the teachers sent by the Lama, 'if I did not make my dwelling here, and live in love with kin and neighbours.' The other two went on.

A few days later the two came to a town where there was much discord and suspicion amongst members of different religious groups. 'Help us, we pray you, to understand and to tolerate each other's festivals, customs and traditions', said someone, 'so that each person here is grounded firmly in their own community but also is tolerant and respectful of the practices of others.'

'I would not be a Buddhist', said one of the teachers sent by the Lama, 'if I did not stay here, and teach the people about religious beliefs and practices, and did not help foster tolerance.' The other one went on.

Eventually the fifth teacher reached the Lama of the South, and began the work of initiating novices into the nature and purposes of life.[1]

Interpretations

How many is 'one', that is the first question — all you need, or one too many, or not nearly enough? 'We shall be lucky', said the Lama of the North, if one of the teachers gets to the Lama of the South.' Did he mean 'as many as one', or 'no more than one'? If we glimpse what the Lama meant by one, we shall glimpse also what the story itself may mean. The basic question is this: what genre does the story belong to, what is the tradition in which it is embedded? Is it a 'Pilgrim Avoids Temptations' story or a 'God is Everywhere' story? Wrestling with this question, we shall come to wrestle also with the story's questions about anti–racism and inter–faith dialogue, and about religious education.

At first sight, this is a pilgrimage–with–temptations story.

Question: how do you get to heaven?

Answer: with difficulty — there are so many allurements, blandishments, deflections along the way; so many soft options, false promises, wrong turnings. It is good that even one of the pilgrims, in this tradition, gets to journey's end. Each of the others is deceived and deflected. They all sing 'here we go' at the start, but alas only one stays the course to declare 'here I am' at the end. Spiritual/religious education is different from, and is in some sense closer to, the divine heart than humanitarian good works, anti–racist political action, the maintenance of close personal relations and warm community life, or the promotion of religious knowledge and tolerance. This is one cluster of inter–related meanings which can be unlocked from the story.

Alternatively, the story is about God incognito. All of the first four pilgrims, according to this interpretation, get it right — or righter, anyway, than the fifth, whose eyes are too fixated on the horizon to see needs close at hand, in the here and now. The idea that the divine is encountered in people, and in political work and interaction with people, not in holy God–slots removed and protected from the secular world, is of course a recurring emphasis in all religious tradition. 'I count no sacrifice too great', said Mahatma Gandhi 'for the sake of seeing God face to face.' But he added, 'The whole of my activity, whether social, political, humanitarian or ethical, is directed to that end.'[2] 'The road to holiness', said Dag Hammarskjold, 'runs through the world of action.' All religious traditions contain stories of pilgrimages in which the pilgrim meets God face-to-face (though in the first instance incognito) in human need on the journey itself. To travel attentively, lovingly, politically, is more important than to arrive. Particularly since prayer can deflect from politics, and can therefore act against true religion.

That religious belief and practice can obscure and indeed block and subvert the divine is emphasised time and again over the centuries by prophet and guru, roshi and sage, rabbi and mullah, sister and monk. One such teacher once ordered a new garment. Fine cloth was brought, and the village tailor was commissioned. The garment would be ready, promised the tailor, if this was the will of God, by the end of the week. Many days later and after much pressure from the teacher's disciples, the tailor sent a message, 'Sorry about the slight delay. But the garment will definitely, if this is the will of God, be ready tomorrow.' But the next day there was another message, 'Try again tomorrow, and the garment, if it is the will of God, will be ready.' When the disciples brought this message the religious teacher said, 'Ask the tailor how long it will take if he leaves God out of it!'[3] One main way religion blocks the divine is by gumming up the secular world as well.

So, two genres, two clusters of meanings and interpretations — and two kinds of programme for religious education. Either way, the story can be seen as a kind of recapitulation of the history of religious education in Britain over the last thirty years or so. In the late 1950s the five pilgrims set out, in order to teach effectively the goal of their journey — the Bible and Christianity. But they were waylaid and they turned aside. Teenage religion (Loukes[4]) and childhood religion (Goldman[5]) required that they should teach instead about humanitarian good works. Then, when this did not seem to be adequate, they turned to teaching about political action against injustice (such as Christian Aid and other aid agencies; development education). Thirdly, when this too seemed unfulfilling, they were into personal development and personal relationships (the influence, for example, of Active Tutorial Work[6] and the pastoral curriculum). Fourthly, when this also was felt to be unsatisfactory and insufficient, they turned to phenomenology and the promotion of tolerance and pluralism (Lancaster, Shap, the Agreed Syllabuses of the 1980s, the Swann Report).

Who and what is the fifth pilgrim so far as RE is concerned? In the one broad interpretation of the story, he or she is irrelevant and forgettable. For it is the first four pilgrims and, in particular, the one concerned with religious pluralism, who most reliably help us to construct a policy, syllabus and programme for religious education. In the other broad interpretation (which sees the first four pilgrims as seduced by snares and delusions), the fifth pilgrim represents some sort of possibility, of aspiration or goal, for the future. Let us consider this interpretation more closely. What could the story be offering us for the 1990s? What may it be suggesting about spirituality, about inter–faith dialogue and about possibilities in religious education?

Five messages

There are five main points worth particular emphasis.

1. By being systematically ambiguous, in that it can be embedded in two different genres of religious narrative, the story is *not*, in commending the fifth pilgrim, knocking the other four. On the contrary, it is asserting that the prayer life of the fifth must be informed and saturated by, and symbiotically related to, the concerns of the first four. The hopeful confidence of the first four pilgrims is akin to the hopeful confidence of the fifth. Faith that all manner of things shall be well is both political and spiritual, and each kind of faith, political and spiritual, nourishes and depends on the other. However, four prayers in five should perhaps be about various kinds of politics. Insofar as the fifth pilgrim represents a teacher in RE in the 1990s, the story is saying that the teacher will need, and depend on, colleagues teaching other subjects. A school simply cannot teach RE, the story is saying, unless it also teaches about politics and society, oppression and racism, personality and relationships, art and science. There is an important sense in which these other subjects come first; they have higher priority in the short–term. Anti–racism must precede inter–faith dialogue.

2. The story is nevertheless saying that RE is different from all other subjects, and different also from the conceptualisations of the Lancaster projects, the Shap working party, the Agreed Syllabuses of the 1980s, the Swann Report. It depends on other subjects and on other conceptualisations, but is not reducible to them; this is the story's essential challenging suggestion.

3. By situating itself in one particular religious tradition, that of Buddhism, the story is acknowledging and indeed emphasising that RE must include (even though it is not reducible to) the study and experience of specific traditions. To study a specific tradition is to study, most characteristically of all, the relationship between prayer and politics. What is spirituality and spiritual direction, within the Buddhist (or the Islamic, Jewish, Sikh, Hindu, Rastafarian, or Christian) tradition? What is the interconnectedness of spirituality and everyday community life? In what ways does spiritual experience challenge, and in what ways does it collude with, forms of oppression and exploitation, including racism and sexism? These are the basic questions for religious studies. Teaching about festivals, customs, public worship and symbols is irrelevant if it is not directed to answering these questions.

4. The story provides an image at one point of the good society, one in which there is peace and justice and in which these are not ends in themselves but the preconditions for love and for personal fulfilment. At other points this is contrasted with images of suffering, intolerance and oppression. These latter images recall that religious beliefs and practices are often associated with ignorance and intolerance, and structures of injustice. For example, the main Christian churches in Britain are very white in their membership and governance, and opposition to racism and racialism is strikingly absent from the vast majority of their agendas, synods, pulpits and bookstalls. Interfaith dialogue and openness are greatly hampered and obstructed by such whiteness and by such inertia.

Similarly, church education in general and religious education in particular, often communicate messages of white superiority. Thus, for example, it can happen that certain Church Schools in inner suburban areas are in effect (though not of course in conscious intention), white and discriminatory enclaves against their local black communities. Neither dioceses nor local authorities seem to be strenuously resisting this tendency. The vast majority of teaching materials currently readily available for teaching about world religions are written by white people with a Christian background, and even materials produced in the 1980s continue to present negative, dismissive or muddled views of faiths other than Christianity. It still happens that school assemblies expect children from devout Muslim, Sikh or Hindu homes to sing or mouth Christian devotional hymns, and to say 'Amen' to Christian devotional prayers. Barely a week seems to go by without a report in the mass media implying that to teach about world faiths in schools is unpatriotic and anti–British, and possibly part of a sinister, atheistic, communistic conspiracy to sap the moral vigour of the nation. Professional RE educators and teachers shake their heads and smile sadly at such media coverage, but seldom attempt to argue back where they might actually — and vulnerably — be heard.

To summarise, Britain is, in all sorts of respects, a racist, oppressive society. Neither the Christian churches in general, nor the RE teaching community in particular, are as prominent, visible and articulate as they should be in questioning, analysing and opposing racial injustice. Religious education and spiritual direction in the 1990s need, in their respective ways, to respond to and wrestle with these political facts.

5. The story suggests some connections and relationships between anti–racism and inter–faith dialogue. For example, anti–racism is not an end in itself but must be directed towards, amongst other things, enabling inter–faith dialogue. A major motivation for engaging in anti–racist action may be spiritual experience, particularly experience moulded and interpreted by encounters and dialogues between different traditions. Involvement in anti–racism may lead, at personal levels, to burnout, paralysis and despair if it is not accompanied, enriched and sustained by — in a wide sense — spiritual experience and spiritual nourishment.

But what, actually, is 'spiritual direction'? This is a major question underlying the story of the five teachers. What exactly was that fifth teacher of religious education going to *do* having arrived with the Lama of the South?

Part two: Spiritual direction

The question is vast, and finally unanswerable. It can at least be formulated, however, with some further stories from around the world about prophet and guru, roshi and sage, rabbi and mullah, sister and monk. For example, there is the story about the time God sought advice from such a person:

'I want', said God, 'to play a game of hide–and–seek with humankind. I've asked my angels where the best place would be to hide. Some say in the depths of the ocean, others on the top of the highest mountain, others again on the far side of the moon or on a distant star. What do you suggest?' The spiritual director said, 'Hide in the human heart, that's the last place they will think of.'[7]

Or there's the story of the spiritual director and the headteacher.

'As the fish perishes on dry land,' said the former, 'so you perish when you get entangled in your school. The fish must return to the water, and you must return to solitude.'

'What?' replied the headteacher, aghast. 'Must I give up my school and go into a religious community?'

'No.' was the answer. 'Hold on to your school and go into your heart.'[8]

To adapt Pascal: the heart has its politics, which politicians do not know.

Or there's that famous story, to be found in many different traditions and cultures, of the three sisters.

When they were grown up they decided each to seek God in her own way. The first said, 'I'm going off to look after the sick, the streets are full of them. I will bring them healing and care.' The second said, 'Everywhere I see people in dispute and conflict with one another. I will go out to reconcile them, I will bring them peace.' The third said, 'I am staying here.' After two years, the first two sisters came back. The first said, 'It's hopeless,

there are simply too many sick people, I can't cope.' The second said much the same: 'It's impossible, I'm torn to shreds.' They sat in burnt-out despair, looking at each other. Then the third sister filled a bowl with muddy water from a nearby pool. 'Look into that,' she said. They looked but saw nothing, only muddy water. 'Let it stand,' she said, 'Let it be.' After a while they looked again. The water was clear now, and they saw their own reflections in it, as clearly as in a mirror. The third sister told them, 'When the water is stirred up it is muddy. It is clear only when it is still. It is the same with yourselves. Only when you are still can you see your true self. Only then can you know who you are, where you are coming from, and what you ought to do. Only then can you have hope and faith in the future, and in the worthwhileness of political endeavour, and in your own giftedness, grace and creativity. Only then can you plunge into politics.'

Prayer, emphasise spiritual teachers, is not about being holy or being good, it's about knowing and being yourself. Contrast with this the view of prayer held by Rex in Evelyn Waugh's *Brideshead Revisited*.[9] Father Mowbray has been appointed to instruct Rex in the Roman Catholic faith, so that Rex can marry Julia Marchmain.

'"He's the most difficult convert I have ever met," says Father Mowbray. "I can't get anywhere near him. He doesn't seem to have the least intellectual curiosity or natural piety. The first day I wanted to find out what sort of religious life he had had till now, so I asked him what he meant by prayer. He said: I don't mean anything. *You* tell *me*. I tried to, in a few words, and he said: Right. So much for prayer. What's the next thing?"'

There is no next thing, reply spiritual directors, prayer is as endless as life, prayer is endless exploration; prayer, like politics, is an endless wrestling between hope and despair, an endless struggle to know both oneself and others to be gifted, to be graced.

Self–knowledge, continue spiritual directors, necessarily involves attending to the material and political world around you. Countless stories and sayings recall and emphasise this mutuality. One of the most famous is to do with three stages of spiritual development: the first stage is when trees are seen as trees and mountains are seen as mountains; the second is when one looks more deeply into things — then trees are no longer trees and mountains are no longer mountains; the third, the stage of enlightenment and hopeful confidence, is when 'trees become trees again and mountains, mountains'. Spirituality involves seeing the world as it is, unaffected and uncoloured by one's own projections, hopes, resentments, desires, self-pity, one's own buffetings and wounds from involvement in politics.

In all religious traditions, the struggle to attain enlightenment — to see and know oneself as one is, and politics and history and other people as they are — is excruciatingly painful and strenuous, for the enemies to be loved — white racists, for example — are resident within one's own heart. In all religious traditions, further prayer is believed to have a real impact — mysterious but not magical — on the real, the objective, political world. It is not just, as one guru put it, that it is easier to protect your feet with slippers than to carpet the whole of the earth.[10] Not just that prayer alters the self, by acting upon forces and enemies within; but, according to all the faith traditions of the world, that it somehow changes or influences external political reality as well. However, how exactly spirituality works in this respect is unknowable — we may have corrigible models and hypotheses about it, but never certainty.

The spiritual life, the life of wrestling towards enlightenment, and hopeful confidence in self and world, involves words, images, ikons, actions, chants, stories, koans, parables, music, candles, physical exercise, breathing and posture, mantras and mandalas, creeds and doctrines, silence. There are many techniques, many actions taught by the spiritual director. These are both essential and totally unimportant. 'What action shall I perform to attain God?,' asked the disciple. 'If you wish to attain God,' replied the spiritual teacher, 'there are two things you must know. The first is that all efforts to attain him are of no avail.'

'And the second?'

'You must act as if you did not know the first.'[11] Spirituality is a kind of game: 'on the seashore of endless worlds is the great meeting of children.' Politics, too, is this sort of graceful game.

Part three: some possible implications for religious education

It is high time we came away from these recollections of paradox and mysticism, came away from these monasteries of Tibet, and from these deserts and solitudes of other traditions of prayer. It is time we considered school classrooms today, and the initial and inservice training of teachers of RE. What in practice do we need to be doing? Or rather, what possibilities do we need to be exploring, if we are intrigued or inspired by the notion that RE teaching may have something to learn and adapt from traditions of spiritual direction, and that it should be principally to do with developing children's spirituality? There are several points worth noting.

The possible implications include the following:

1. Teaching techniques of real relaxation ('it takes a lot of doing to do nothing'), including attention to breathing, posture and mantras.
2. Teaching visualising and fantasising techniques, and the technique of inward dialogue both with people one knows and with the characters in one's dreams and daydreams.
3. Teaching all sorts of ways of exploring and living with parables, riddles, koans, spiritual folktales and wisdom tales.
4. Teaching attention to objects very close at hand — candle flames, pottery, ikons of many kinds, flowers, all the equivalents of Mother Julian's famous hazelnut.
5. Attending in all teaching to, and respecting, the unique giftedness and life stories of the children and learners, and their distinct learning styles, and having faith in them. The RE teacher, most of all, is the one who should see 'the adult in the child, the eagle in the egg, the butterfly in the caterpillar, the saint in the selfish human being'. 'But don't try to teach a pig to sing', said a guru, 'it's a waste of your time, and it irritates the pig'.[12]
6. Linking teaching others to one's own inner spiritual journey and in this respect, learning to know and accept the child within oneself: 'except ye become as little children' . . . 'on the seashore of endless worlds is the great meeting of children'.

Such activities must have links with, and to an extent depend on, studies of how religion and racism frequently intertwine; of how there are frequently religious motivations behind anti–racist action; and of how involvement in anti–racism can lead to burnout and despair unless it is rooted, in a wide sense, in spirituality and inter–faith dialogue.

These extremely brief notes begin to sketch what RE could look like, in classrooms and in teacher training (both initial and inservice), when the model of RE teacher as spiritual director is explored in practice. What are the main objections to this model, and how may the objections be answered, both in theory and in political and pedagogical practice?

One objection will come from the mass media. To reply to this requires political skill and courage, good public relations, and the intellectual confidence to maintain that the techniques and teachings of spiritual direction can be described and defended within the framework of much modern and secular science and medicine; they are not merely peculiar, at odds with widely legitimated knowledge and commonsense.

Another objection will be that normal school structures and assessment procedures are inimical to a concern for spirituality. ('How do you evaluate your pupils' spiritual development?' — 'Oh, out of 15, usually.') This objection should simply renew our determination to change radically customary school structures and procedures.

A third set of objections may of course come from the faith communities themselves — is not spiritual direction *their* rightful responsibility, not that of county schools? This is certainly an extremely important objection, and cannot be dealt with cavalierly. It would therefore be better dealt with in dialogue and reflection about real practice, rather than in a speculative think-piece such as this, in one-sided words on a printed page.

In real dialogue and reflection, it could be useful to have in mind that famous and beautiful song of Rabindranath Tagore[13] about children on the seashore:

> They build their houses with sand
> and they play with empty shells.
>
> With withered leaves they weave their boats
> and smiling float them on the vast deep.
>
> Children have their play
> on the seashore of endless worlds.

Tagore goes on to contrast the children on the shore with fisherpeople, sailors, explorers, merchants, out there beyond the horizon, and he notes their innocent unawareness of danger, and death by drowning. Nevertheless he finds in them an image of all humankind. Their playing and meeting is like that of adult religion and culture in the face of mortality. He finds the sea infinitely gentle as well as infinitely dangerous: 'death dealing waves sing meaningless ballads to the children, even like a mother while rocking her baby's cradle'. Let us go out into our classrooms and schools, Tagore is declaring, and into initial and inservice teacher training, and into conferences and dialogues between schools and faith communities. Let us go with hopeful confidence in ourselves and each other; in the insights and enlightenments of our respective spiritual traditions; in our children; in the futures which we are share.

> On the seashore of endless worlds
> children meet;
>
> Tempest roams in the pathless sky,
> ships get wrecked in the trackless water,
> death is abroad, and children play;
>
> On the seashore of endless worlds
> is the great meeting of children.
>
> *Robin Richardson*

References

1. Adapted from a story in *The Song of the Bird* by Anthony de Mello, Image Books, New York, 1984.
2. Quoted in *The Wounded Stag* by William Johnston, Collins Fontana, 1985.
3. This story is from *One Minute Wisdom* by Anthony de Mello, Gujarat Sahitya Prakash (India) 1985.
4. Harold Loukes, *Teenage Religion*, SCM Press, 1961.
5. Ronald Goldman, *Religious Thinking from Childhood to Adolescence*, Routledge and Kegan, 1964.
6. *Active Tutorial Work*, Basil Blackwell, 1970.
7. from *One Minute Wisdom*.
8. *ibid.*
9. Evelyn Waugh, *Brideshead Revisited*, Penguin Books.
10. from *One Minute Wisdom*.
11. *ibid.*
12. *ibid.*
13. From *Gitanjali* by Rabindranath Tagore, Macmillan of India, 1913.

Guided imagery and religious education

This article by Kathy Raban is intended as an exploration and invitation to those who are unfamiliar with the methods or rationale of guided imagery.

What is guided imagery?

"Imagine a waterfall of white light just a bit above your head and feel it flowing into the top of your head and then through every bit of your body — feel it pouring into your face and neck — feel it going into your arms and chest and heart, feel it pouring down through your stomach and legs and feet until every bit of you becomes part of the waterfall of white light. Now imagine this light inside your head and feel it coming into you so much that you are changing into the waterfall. I wonder how that feels to be the waterfall . . ."

This is an example of an exercise in guided imagery, a technique I use regularly for all areas of the curriculum in the primary school. Guided imagery or scripted fantasy (for the purposes of this discussion I will use the two terms interchangeably) is a directed method of tapping the creative, therapeutic and spiritual potentialities of the imagination.

Evidence suggests that the imaginative aspect of ourselves is located in a specific area of the brain.[1] Some researchers suggest that the processes of the brain are divided between the right and left hemispheres, each having its own particular function. The left brain, which is thought to control the right of the body, is responsible for the rational processes of thought, particularly logic, reasoning, language and numerical activities. The right brain, controlling the left–hand side of the body, encompasses the creative functions of metaphorical, intuitive and imaginative thought. It is the producer of sensory impressions. For instance, after suffering a stroke in one side of the brain some patients encounter a consequent lop–sided loss of function, for example, a patient was able to sort apples and oranges manually, but unable to name them.[2]

The point I am making is two–fold. First, that guided imagery utilises the resources of the right brain and secondly, education is traditionally centred in the functioning of the left brain. One implication of this is that our present educational emphasis is not developing the full potential of our children since it ignores the contribution of half the resources of the brain. Various studies have demonstrated that children learn more effectively when the right brain is engaged in the learning process: 'Technical terms introduced during a fantasy journey were remembered better than when they were introduced in the course of normal instructions'.[3]

Guided imagery is one way of fostering the creative potentialities of the right brain. This creativity lies in the interface between the conscious and unconscious layers of ourselves where impulses, intuitions, insights, which lie beyond the rational mind, are revealed to us in the form of symbols and images. These are multi–dimensional in nature and succinctly convey more layers of meaning than the linear process of rational thought. Singer[4] refers to this as the 'crystal-lising' potential of imagery and quotes the example of a woman who produced a vivid image of Siamese twins, an old and a young man joined together. This image was a dramatic representation of her feelings about her husband and son who had grown so close that she felt in danger of being excluded. It would have needed many words to convey the same depth of meaning.

This shadowy area lying between the known and the unknown aspects of ourselves is burgeoning with possibilities of creativity in all aspects of human activity. Mozart regularly 'saw' his compositions in completed form and needing only to be annotated. Much of our great literature and fine art also takes its inspiration from this area of human experience. Einstein conceived his theories in visual form and language came much later. S. M. Ulam, a mathematician and physicist, describes his experience thus: 'Very soon I discovered that as one gets a feeling for no more than a dozen other radiation and nuclear constants, one can imagine the subatomic world almost tangibly and manipulate the picture dimensionally and qualitatively before calculating the more precise relationships'.[5]

So the imagination, far from being a regressive

faculty of human nature, actually nurtures the seeds of the highest levels of creativity. In education, we cannot afford to ignore an area of our reality which can contribute so richly to our personal selves and to our society.

Imaging and spirituality

The creative aspect of the imagination is obviously important for education, but there are other gains in fostering the imaging aspect of ourselves. The point I want to make is that it is not illegitimate to regard guided imagery as a door to knowledge of the spiritual side of our natures. Jung refers to imaging as the 'transcendent function'[6] and as such it is a valuable and viable tool for religious education.

Guided imagery as a means to open the door on our spiritual natures has a long and honoured tradition amongst the major world religions. For instance, the ancient Buddhist writing 'The Tibetan Book of the Dead' is a text to be read to a dying man. It guides him through the terrors of death and rebirth and prescribes various forms of guided meditations.[7] Contemporary spiritual writers still use the same techniques for Christian uses of guided imagery; de Mello's[8] techniques are based upon the Ignatian tradition of spiritual exercise. Most cultures throughout history have employed fantasy as the traditional place where human beings transcend themselves and communicate with what they understand to be the ultimate.

Problems which might arise in using guided imagery as a method for religious education

It is tempting to be caught up in enthusiasm for guided imagery as a method of teaching religious education as it seems to have the possibility of touching upon one of the deep cores of what it means to be religious. However, as educators there is a need to be alert to the dangers of guided imagery as well as to its values. Opening a door which might give access to the spiritual side of one's nature is not the same as having a religious experience itself and it is important that we do not make such claims, or even imply them.

There is another possible danger in the use of guided imagery for religious education, that of indoctrination, either gross or subtle. Because it can be a powerful emotional tool, it is easy to influence the experiencer with a point of view. It is important to emphasise that the purpose here is educational and not evangelical. Some of the danger can be overcome by regarding guided imagery as a scientific tool to enable children to explore an area of experience in a disinterested but involved manner; in the same way that modern anthropologists study different cultures by becoming 'participant observers'. Another misuse of guided imagery is the subtle possibility of indoctrination through the unrealised assumptions of the person conducting the fantasy. I can illustrate this from my own experience. I conducted a fantasy for a group of religious education teachers, entitled 'The Light and the Dark Side of Ourselves'. Although many found it meaningful, some were angry with my underlying belief that knowledge of the dark side and integration with the light was a beneficial procedure. In holding a particular Christian view, they felt that the dark side was bad and that I was wrong in trying to integrate it with the light. Without their challenge, I would not have been aware of how deeply my own assumptions had constructed the fantasy that I devised. From this I conclude that it is important that those who use guided imagery be aware of their own 'metaphors' and scrupulous in the integrity with which they approach this kind of work especially in religious education.

Practical considerations

Starting points for guided imagery

When approaching religious education in the primary classroom, I use guided imagery to enliven and breathe spirit into my existing syllabus. Multi–cultural in outlook, this syllabus relies heavily upon an 'experiential' approach to RE. The stories, parables, symbolic and metaphorical languages, rituals, etc., of the major world religions are wonderfully rich sources of potential material. I regard guided imagery as one of my more important tools; for instance, I might take some of the stories of the major religious traditions and tell them with the children as participants. How would they view the Christmas story if they took the role of a shepherd visiting the stable and, through guided imagery, were able to use their powers of imagination and sensory perception?

My initial teaching develops skills which are not

overtly religious (in the sense of expressing the beliefs and practices of the major world religions), but are prerequisites to the sensitive work of guided imagery. The skills which help children feel free to enter and use their inner world in a manner which can be acceptable for them as a group activity include:

1. listening
2. relaxing
3. being still and quiet
4. perceiving with the senses
5. focusing concentration
6. being open and accepting
7. being positive about self and others.

The importance of the teacher's role

Working with primary children, the teacher's own attitudes and involvement are paramount. Young children tend to relate to the teacher for support, rather than to their peers, so that the teacher's role in modelling trust, openness and acceptance is vital. If this is taken seriously, it changes the teacher's role from 'the authority with all the answers' to a participant with personal experience to share. It entails a measure of personal honesty and I have found that children respond positively to this, resulting in increased respect on both sides. For instance, a six–year–old whose parents had recently separated, when 'looking inside' himself said, 'There's fighting inside me'. I shared with him the feeling of my own children upon my divorce; their anger with me. Although I felt rather unsure, it was valuable for Paul and assisted him to come to terms with his own experience.

Initial fantasy work

When the classroom climate feels ready it is best to have a few practice runs. Humour is an excellent non–threatening place to begin. This is a delightful introductory fantasy to limber up the imaginative facility.[9]

> Picture a room in the house,
> choose an object in the room,
> examine it from different angles,
> put it in different parts of the room,
> change its colour,
> make it make a noise,
> put it in the garden,
> sit a cat on it,
> stand mother on it,
> put it back in its rightful place.

Assuming that you have suitable facilities, you need to decide whether the children sit, lie or have a choice. Usually it is helpful if the children close their eyes but, as this can be difficult for some, I would echo Oaklander[10] who says at the beginning of a session that: 'You can peep if you want to'. It is important to create an atmosphere where whatever the children contribute is acceptable, where there are no rights or wrongs.

Some children can be anxious when asked to focus on their inner experience and I would always allow them to opt out and pursue another activity elsewhere or, if they wish to remain, keep them close by myself. Disruption has never been a problem. I believe this is because the children are given permission to indulge in something which is actual and meaningful to them.

Conducting a guided fantasy

When the children are settled in a comfortable position, I begin the guided fantasy with a relaxation exercise, and then talk the children through the story of the fantasy. It is helpful to maintain a gentle soothing tone of voice (especially if there is an interruption) because it does help to create a sense of quietness and relaxation. As the story unfolds, stress is laid on experiencing feelings within the fantasy and feelings about its key images. Attention is drawn to details, especially sense details, e.g. how does it feel (touch), smell, what colour is it? Further identification can be suggested by asking the children to become the different elements of the fantasy and to explore their feelings about them.

When the story of the fantasy is finished, it is important to bring the children back to the here–and–now in a gentle fashion. There are several ways of doing this which are similar to the initial relaxation exercises. Asking the children to focus on here and now body sensations, noises outside the room, to visualise their position in the room, the proximity of others, are all appropriate ways of 'coming back', plus a little physical activity such as stretching.

At this point I usually lead straight into some kind of creative activity, without giving a chance to 'debrief' the experience. If the children share their experience at this stage, there is a great temptation for them to echo what has been said by the first speaker and to move away from the uniqueness of their own experience. I presume that is because I have given a positive response to whatever has been offered initially, so the general assumption is that it is the 'right' answer. Subsequent responses then become variations of the first. This is overcome if the children draw or write immediately because they then have something which is concretely their own creation. It also gives the teacher an opportunity to talk to an individual and to discuss ideas which might not be appropriate for the whole group.

In helping children draw out the meaning of their images, I work in the manner suggested by Perls in Gestalt therapy[11]. I ask the children which part of the drawing they would like to talk about and ask them to describe it to me. Then I reflect back to them what they have said and ask if they feel it is saying anything about themselves. It is important to maintain the attitude that whatever is shared is acceptable even when the images identified with may be unpleasant or violent. They sometimes starkly reveal the 'shadow' side of the child. When we worked on dreams, Sally, a shy six–year–old, saw a milk bottle being pecked by birds. She chose to describe the bottle and said it felt very painful to be pecked at and related it to feelings of being laughed at by other children in the class. Obviously this conversation was important between the two of us, but not appropriate for sharing with the class as a whole.

Sometimes the images, like Sally's, can relate to painful or difficult personal areas. This begs the question as to whether the classroom is an appropriate place for such issues. Bettelheim[12] makes a strong case for the inclusion of the darker side of a child's experience. He points out that by the third to fourth year, children have developed many preoccupying fears such as death of a parent. The use of guided imagery provides an indirect, yet effective way for externalising inner anxieties and to find 'ordering' images by which the children can begin to shape their lives. I would also add that there appears to be a correlation between what the children reveal and what the teacher is able to receive.

Using guided fantasy — safety rules

1. Go through the experience yourself first. If you have any doubts or find it difficult, you may choose not to use the structure.

2. If you feel confident about using the structure, you can create a safe environment by:
   a) assuring them that they should go only as far as they feel comfortable.
   b) giving permission for opting out, and encouraging children to take responsibility for their choice.
An atmosphere of acceptance can be created where opting out is not seen as failure.

3. After the exercise, you may wish to make individual contact so that you can respond to any problems which might arise. It is helpful for this

contact to be made using a method which is at one remove from the immediate experience, for example by discussing a drawing, a piece of writing or a poem which has come out of the experience.

4. Approach experiential work gently and progressively. Start from what is more generally acceptable to share. Children need to build up confidence in gradual stages.

5. If you want your religious education teaching to touch on the profound issues to which religions address themselves, then entering 'dangerous' areas is inevitable. To what extent you wish to tackle this is ultimately a personal decision.

A final time of sharing

It remains to have a time of sharing together of the results and experiences of the fantasy. Most of the children are eager for this and happy to talk about personal details. It is essential to give them permission to withhold information and to respect their decision; also to ensure that they are not put in a situation where they could be embarrassed about their reticence.

One of the main difficulties about a group discussion is time. It is not possible to give every child the opportunity to talk. This can be partly overcome by letting the children share what they wish with a friend before gathering together in the main group. The work produced can be displayed or made into a class book.

As part of this final time, I set the guided imagery within the religious context that I drew it from. For instance, with the seed growing secretly, I explain that it came from one of the many stories that Jesus told to explain what he thought it was like to believe in God. I regard guided imagery as 'sowing seeds' or pointing directions to spiritual experiences which might not happen, or might take many years to mature. James Fowler[13] sums up our responsibility thus:

'The stage most typical of the child of three to seven, is marked by a relative fluidity of thought patterns. The child is continually encountering novelties for which no stable operations of knowing have been formed. The imaginative processes underlying fantasy are unrestrained and uninhibited by logical thought. In league with forms of knowing dominated by perception, imagination in this stage is extremely productive of long–lasting images and feelings (positive and negative) that later more stable and self–reflective valuing and thinking will have to order and sort out. This is the stage of first self–awareness and, therefore, spiritual awareness.'

Spiritual development defies objective evaluation, particularly on a short term basis. It is enough to open the door and to explicitly value the kind of experience that this particular door reveals.

Kathryn F. Raban

(This is an edited version of an article originally published in the *British Journal of Religious Education*, Vol. 10(1) Autumn, 1987.)

References

1. Blakeslee, T. R., *The Right Brain*, Macmillan 1980. See also Litvac S. B., *Use your Head*, Prentice Hall, 1982.

2. Singer, J., and Pope, K., *The Power of Human Imagination*, Plenum Press, 1978.

3. Johnson, Virginia, 'Fun, Fantasy and Feelings', in *Science and Children*, Vol. 15, Part 4, 1978, pp. 21–2.

4. Singer, *op. cit.*

5. Singer, *op. cit.*

6. Fordham, Frieda, *An Introduction to Jung's Psychology*, Penguin Books, 1953.

7. Singer, *op. cit.*

8. De Mello, Anthony, *Sadhana: a Way to God*, Anand Press, Gamdi–Anand, 1978.

9. Offord, Michael, 'Developing and guiding fantasy in schools', (M.Ed. Dissertation) University of Nottingham, 1979.

10. Oaklander, Violet, *Windows to our Children*, Real People Press, Utah, 1978.

11. Perls, Hefferline & Goodman, *Gestalt Therapy*, Penguin Books, 1951.

12. Bettelheim, Bruno, *Uses of Enchantment*, Penguin Books, 1978

13. Fowler, James W, *Stages of Faith*, Harper & Row, San Francisco, 1981.

Other reading

Crampton, Martha, 'The Use of Mental Imagery in Psychosynthesis', *Journal of Humanistic Psychology*, Fall, 1969.

Hall, Eric, *The Structure of Fantasy*, (Ph.D. Thesis) Nottingham University, 1979.

Hay, David, *Exploring Inner Space*, Mowbrays, 1987

Otto, Rudolf, *The Idea of the Holy*, Oxford University Press, 1950.

Rozman, Deborah, *Meditating with Children*, University of the Trees Press, 1975.

The Gifted Child Quarterly, Vol. XXIII, No. 1, Spring 1979.

Using story in secondary RE

There is no problem about the morality of scapegoat. That some are condemned to suffer as the price of the well–being of others is clearly immoral. The difficulty is that most of us tolerate it for much of the time. In the chapter, Rebellion, in his *Brothers Karamazov*, Dostoyevsky brings us to face the issue as Ivan recounts to Alyosha some frightful but not uncommon examples of cruelty to children. It is a very powerful piece of writing, but the content, style and meta-physics are too much for most pupils.

There is, however, a short story by Ursula LeGuin, 'Those who walk away from Ormelas',[1] on the subject of scapegoat which does work well with fourth and fifth years (if edited slightly). The inhabitants of Ormelas live lives of freedom and pleasure for the price of just one wretched life, a child again. Most of the inhabitants after an initial revulsion at the reality which underpins their good fortune, come to ration-alise it and accept the way the world is. But there are those who cannot, and instead choose to leave, turning their backs on the comfort and culture to look for another way. The issues are clearly presented and the location of Ormelas is obviously not far from home. The story works because the writing is compel-ling, catching the attention of even the most deter-mined non–participant. The lot of the snivelling innocent in its cold darkness is immediately seen by every pupil to be an affront to their sense of justice. But there is more to it. The rationalisations are familiar: to give up all the comfort and pleasure of Ormelas for the sake of one wretched life would not be an intelligent act, expecially as the child by now is irreparably degraded and would gain little from the world beyond its miserable cell.

The argument is familiar in the form of the 'Life–boat ethic': in a time of scarce resources some (the weakest) must be thrown in the water so that the stronger can survive.

The argument is a familiar one, but beyond this the story points us to other levels of moral discourse. Those who walk away from Ormelas at the end of the story and refuse to accept the cruel paradox, walk towards a place the author cannot describe, and might not exist. We are left with questions about the moral nature of the universe. Is their search for another world, one free from compromise and bad faith, naive, and, perhaps even undermining of the limited freedom and happiness that is now enjoyed? Can there be a world without suffering? In Dostoyevsky's story in the *Brothers Karamazov* this is a question about the nature and existence of God. If God can create only a world in which final happiness is possible at the cost of the innocent sufferings of children, then he must be morally inferior to the people he is said to create and so cannot be worshipped.

Three strands in values education

The Ormelas story makes possible an awareness and sympathy for the situation of another person: the child and those who know of it. It encourages the exam-ination of the consequences of a particular act: the balancing of gain and loss in the event of the child being set free. It also prompts questions about the way the world is, or should be: whether there is beyond Ormelas a world where the paradox of the suffering of the innocent does not apply. In an article on moral values[2], Mike Cross reminds us that these three strands: an awareness of the realities and possibilities of the world; a consideration of the consequences of an act; a real understanding of the particular situation of another, are central to the business of values education. I want to illustrate that narrative, the telling of a tale, can make an important contribution to growth in all three of these areas. In this sense good stories are always moral.

On the reality and possibilities of the world

Revisiting reality: Tolkien and fairy stories

According to Descartes, 'The seeds of knowledge are within us like fire struck from flint; philosophers deduce them by reason but poets strike them forth by imagination and they shine more clearly'. The storyteller produces a similar brightness. We know and deplore that in war men kill, and in civil war men kill their brothers. But when in Liam O'Flaherty's short story, set in the Irish civil war,[3] the sniper turns over the body of his victim and looks into his brother's face, the knowledge is given an emotional charge which conveys with a disturbing clarity the real cost and nature of war.

It is the ability of a story to convey vividly, and with power, a particular incident or topic which makes it an essential element in values education. Tolkien[4] called this quality 'art', the ability by which a writer or story teller gave to his or her imaginative creation 'the inner consistency of reality'. Yet to convey, in a convincing way, the reality of the world, the story did not have to be realistic. In fact for Tolkien, a fantasy story or fairy tale, because of the fantastic nature of its imagery, could convey even more than a strictly realistic one. Stories which combined art and fantasy could induce in the reader what Tolkien called a state of 'secondary belief', a kind of suspended disbelief, which enabled the reader to enter into the story fully, and while knowing it to be fantasy, take from it insights into the reality of his or her own world.

These insights Tolkien called 'Recovery', 'Escape' and 'Consolation'. In Recovery, one gained a fresh insight into things grown stale through familiarity and routine, and so one could sense again the queerness and significance of everyday things. The insights of Recovery lead to Escape, from the oppression of received common knowledge and so the ability to challenge what would otherwise appear inevitable. There is after all an alternative. The power to sustain the challenge of Escape is derived from Consolation, the final promise of a happy ending, which for Tolkien, is the true form and highest function of fairy tales.

It is not that fairy stories deny the existence of sorrow and failure, but they do deny universal and final defeat, and so make an optimistic claim about human experience and the way things are. For Tolkien, to grow up with fairy stories (not that he thought they were necessarily children's stories) was to grow up with a particular understanding of the realities and possibilities of life. Fairy stories give a critical but ultimately hopeful strand among the web of received ideas and experiences from which a person would judge what was desirable and possible.

Facing reality: Bettelheim and stories as therapy

In his *Uses of Enchantment*, Bruno Bettelheim[5] sees fairy story as combining a therapeutic function with

that of providing a map of the basic contours of human life. In both cases the process is largely subconscious. In this view, fairy stories enable a child to resolve the tensions and difficulties experienced as part of growth, without ever bringing them wholly into consciousness. Whereas it is possible to confront and come to terms with the problems in its changing relationships in the oblique mode of story, the child does not have the resources to cope with these traumas if they were to be made explicit in its own experience.

Here it is not the case of a story presenting in a vivid and compelling way, a fact of life we might otherwise overlook, but rather handling with great subtlety, elements of experience which are so urgent and potent that it is only through the disguising medium of story that they can be coped with at all. So the story of 'Jack and the Beanstalk' provides a means for the successful negotiation of the anxieties associated with the physical and relational changes involved in the transitions from boyhood to manhood ('Little Red Riding Hood' provides the female equivalent).

The story is said to enact on the conscious plane, what the child experiences in the subconscious. It is the story itself the child needs, not an interpretation. The story can help with difficult transitions. An interpretation which connected the characters in the tale with members of Jack's family: giant = father; Jack's mother and giant's wife = mother; beanstalk = unmentionable piece of anatomy would only create confusion and further anxiety.

I include 'Jack' and Bettelheim's interpretation not because his Freudian inspired reading is necessarily right, but as an illustration of the possible complexities of the traditional story and as a suggestion as to why the stories persist. Jack is first found in medieval English, while the oldest version of Cinderella appears to come from sixth–century China.

It is also a reminder that the manifest, surface meaning of a story may not be all there is, and so the child's demand to hear yet again a story which it can practically recite by heart, may indicate the presence of a need to which we have no direct access.

Endless interpretations

The patron of interpretation is the god Hermes, the messenger who mediates between the living and the dead. He is the patron of all those who go between: travellers; merchants; heralds; thieves and psycho-analysts. He is the trickster who affirms the superiority of the latent over the manifest and is associated with oracular utterances whose initial meaning seems trivial, the real worth being revealed only after delay and unforeseen circumstances.[6]

It is this uncertainty, personified in Hermes, that points to the riches of a good story. According to Ted Hughes[7] 'they not only attract and light up everything relevant in our own experience, they are also in continual private meditation, as it were, on their own implications. They are little factories of under-standing. New revelations of meaning open out of their images and patterns continually stirred into reach by our own growth and changing circumstances.'

On this view, stories have a unique contribution to make to the first of the three strands of values education: the awareness of the nature and possibili-ties of the world and so to the conviction of what is worthwhile.

Understanding others and considering consequences

Stories take us into the lives of their characters and, through them, we face dilemmas, weigh up alterna-tives and feel the consequences of an ill–considered or noble act. Which one should I choose? A good rule of thumb is to select stories which work for you. You know that these have Tolkien's 'inner sense of reality' and so are convincing and able to draw listeners into their fascinating webs. Interestingly, the storyteller in West African tradition is Ananse, the spider who spins from its own substance the web of its world, a sticky web which holds fast anything which brushes against it.

The story must also have the right style and language for the audience. Many traditional stories are remarkably versatile in this respect, able to intrigue and hold groups spanning three generations. Some myths, however, are too long and detailed and a good modern rewrite should be used.[8] Remember too that the piece must not be too powerful. Passages on the Holocaust from William Styron's *Sophie's Choice*, or D. M. Thomas's *White Hotel*, may well convey the possibilities of human nature and the depths to which it can sink, as well as the consequences of racism. But for most pupils they are too deeply disturbing.

There are available, a number of annotated lists of stories and suggestions for their use.[9] Bearing in mind the three strands cited above, I would like to offer five of my favourites.

1. *A Wizard of Earthsea*, by Ursula Le Guin
I have already mentioned this author in connection with her short story, 'Those who walk away from Ormelas'. As well as writing excellent science fiction — her *Left Hand of Darkness* and *The Dispossessed* would be marvellous with able fifth and sixth formers for exploring gender roles and the nature of political economy — she has written a fantasy trilogy called 'Earthsea'. All three are excellent, but the first, *A Wizard of Earthsea*, is the most accessible.

The young wizard unleashes unwittingly a 'shadow' beast from the other world, which pursues and terri-fies him until he learns he must turn to face his fear. Turned hunter, he finally catches up with the shadow and names it with his own name. The concept of a shadow self which we regret and try to conceal, but which needs to be faced and named, is difficult to address. Yet the story did enable the issue to emerge, and gave rise to some serious reflection on the kind of people we are and showed in a new light, Dr. Jekyll, Mr. Hyde and the Incredible Hulk.

2. *Warrior Scarlet*, by Rosemary Sutcliffe
Warrior Scarlet is the cloak awarded to the young males of a Bronze Age tribe, who pass through their rite of passage by slaying a wolf. When the time comes for the hero, a boy with a withered arm, he is savaged by the wolf but not killed, and so he has no identity. He has slipped between the either/or of warrior or corpse and becomes an outcast. We then witness his transition from disappointment and failure as these are first accepted, then transformed as he begins to discover the wholly unexpected dignity of another kind of life and the part he can play in it.

Before the arrival of the Europeans, young Native Americans would be sent off alone in the wilderness, to return only when they had found a name and a song: an identity and a history. For us, in a culture which has no clear means of marking the transition from child to adulthood, much of the search for an identity and a role for the future takes place in the years of secondary schooling. The story of the Warrior Scarlet can be a means of raising some of the issues on the road to maturity.

3. *The Dream Time*, by Henry Treece
Crookleg, a maimed Stone-Age boy, stands for art, imagination and ideals, in fact dreams, in a world of cruel tradition and shortsighted self–interest. His tribe's fear of his art and his rejection of their violence leads him to set off with Blackbird, a girl survivor from a raided village. They make for the fish folk who take their food from the sea instead of raiding, but there meet Shark, the chieftain, who, brandishing his whalebone axe, is as vicious as any they sought to leave behind. The boy's frustration and disgust at his

own impotence as Shark carries off Blackbird, changes to a resigned but hopeless courage when later, he must stand up to the chieftain's greed and cruelty.

When Shark is killed and his people massacred, Crookleg is so sickened, he feels he can never work at his art again, even though the killing seemed unavoidable. At the end of the book, he vows never to carry a spear–stick again, convinced that it is not spear–sticks but dreams which will save a man, provided he has the courage to hold them 'when the wolves glare into his eyes'.

The book offers a reflection on the nature of ideals and the courage to sustain alternatives, particularly with respect to the nature of violence and how aggression might be resisted. The violence which destroys the violent Shark, though nauseating to the boy, saves him and his tribe (although they later perish as a result of their own aggression). Any solution in the story to questions of pacifism and just wars, is not wholly clear. But through the story the nature of these questions in reality can become clearer.

4. *I Own a Racecourse*, by Patricia Wrightson
Among the games played by a group of Sydney boys is one in which they 'own' and so swap and sell to each other any large building or corporation in the city. But Andy is slightly retarded and though fascinated by the game, unable to participate until a tramp sells him the racecourse for three dollars. Gradually, his friends realise that Andy really believes that he is the new owner, a conviction supported by the racecourse staff, who take to calling him boss.

With his mates we are confronted with the dilemma of whether Andy should be shaken out of his fantasy into a sadder reality, or left in a happy dream world, which puts him further from everyday reality. In the humour and protectiveness the gang shows its back- ward member, we not only have the opportunity to consider the nature and appropriate response to mental handicap, but also the meaning of ownership and whether it rests on anything more substantial than the rights, respect and responsibilities Andy thinks he enjoys.

5. *The Clashing Rocks*, by Ian Serrailler
This rewrite of Jason and the Golden Fleece, like all good quest stories, replicates something of the struc- ture of our own life journey. It exhibits clearly W. H. Auden's six characteristics of the quest: hero; journey; testings; helpers; hinderers; goal. These can be sought and identified in other quest stories, films or TV series and also applied to our own stories. This can throw light on the nature of the testings we undergo, and give insight into the complexity of relationships when it is realised, as with Jason in the story, that our

helpers and hinderers are often the same people. And what of our treasure or goal in life? What is it that we would sacrifice all else for, but the attainment of which would not leave our journey without a goal?

The five books I mention are all different in kind. *Earthsea* is a fantasy; *Warrior Scarlet* an historical novel; *The Dream Time* hovers between the two; *I Own a Racecourse* has a contemporary urban setting; and *The Clashing Rocks* is a myth. All are fascinating, having characters of a depth and complexity con- vincingly to raise questions as to what is worthwhile. They set before us the consequences of acts which might be our own. They also provide a taste of ex- periences we will certainly encounter in others, if not ourselves.

In these books many of the main characters are maimed and all are male. As we and our pupils are also incomplete, suffering from some, usually concealed, handicap or misfortune, these heroes are more easily identified with.

This selection, in which all the main characters are male, even though three of the five writers are female, is still not untypical. This state of affairs too, raises a number of questions about a real understanding of the situation of others, about the consequences of unexamined attitudes and about the way the world is or could be.

John Hammond
(This article originally appeared in '*The Brown Paper*', Spring 1983 [forerunner of '*Values*'].)

References

1. The Wind's Twelve Quarters, Vol 1.

2. Classroom Practice and School Planning 1982.

3. Marland, M. (ed.), 'The Sniper' in *Loves, Hopes and Fears*,

4. Tolkien, J. R. R., *Tree and Leaf*.

5. Bettelheim, Bruno, *Uses of Enchantment*, Penguin Books, 1978.

6. Kermode, Frank, The Genesis of Secrecy.

7. See, Children's Literature, in *Education*, No. 1.

8. *Ibid*.

9. E.g. Shap Teachers' Handbook, C.R.E.
   'The Brown Paper', (forerunner of 'Values') Ed. M. Cross, Spring 1983
   Bedfordshire County Council: 15 Stories for Primary R.E. 40 Stories for Secondary R.E.

List of helpful books

For a general overview of the persistence of religion and religious experience, see,

David Hay *Exploring Inner Space* (2nd Edn.), Mowbrays, 1987.

On the view that religious experience is the heart of religion, the following are recommended,

Ninian Smart *The Religious Experience of Mankind* Fontana, 1971.

Mircea Eliade *From Primitives to Zen* Collins, 1967.

William Johnston *Silent Music* Fontana, 1974.

Evelyn Underhill *Mysticism* Methuen, 1911 (Reissued by E. P. Dutton, 1961).

On the religious experience of childhood, see,

Edward Robinson *The Original Vision* New York: Seabury Press, 1983.

On the empirical study of religious experience the classic work, first published in 1902, is still the best,

William James *The Varieties of Religious Experience* Penguin American Library, 1982.

Also worth consulting are,

J. M. Cohen & J-F. Phipps *The Common Experience* Element Books, 1979.

Alister Hardy *The Divine Flame*, Collins, 1966, *The Spiritual Nature of Man*, Clarendon Press, 1979.

David Hay *Exploring Inner Space*, Op. cit.

There are now very many books on the practice of humanistic education. Several contain exercises easily adaptable for the exploration of religion, including the following:

Donna Brandes & Howard Phillips *Gamester's Handbook*, Hutchinson, 1979.

Jack Canfield & Harold C. Wells *100 Ways to Enhance Self-Concept in the Classroom*, Prentice-Hall Inc., 1976.

Gloria A. Castillo *Left Handed Teaching: Lessons in Affective Education*, Holt, Rinehart & Winston, 1978.

Eva D. Fugitt *He Hit Me Back First*, Jalmar Press, 1983.

Gay Hendricks & Russell Wills *The Centering Book: Awareness Activities for Children, Parents and Teachers*, Prentice-Hall Inc., 1975.

Gay Hendricks & James Fadiman (Eds.) *Transpersonal Education: A Curriculum for Feeling and Being*, Prentice-Hall Inc., 1976.

Gay Hendricks & Thomas B. Roberts *The Second Centering Book*, Prentice-Hall Inc., 1977.

Ilse Klipper *My Magic Garden: A Meditation Guide for Children*, Pathways Press, 1980.

Violet Oaklander *Windows to our Children* Real People Press, 1981.

John O. Stevens *Awareness: Exploring, Experimenting, Experiencing*, Real People Press, 1971.

David Wolsk *An Experience Centred Curriculum — Exercises in Perception, Communication and Action* Unesco, 1975.

Handbooks to spiritual or religious practice are of course legion. Many are written from a perspective that is not easily adaptable to the school classroom. The following are a few examples of contemporary approaches to spiritual practice that may be helpful to the teacher:

P. & B. P. Albright *Mind, Body and Spirit — The Journey towards Health and Wholeness* Thule Press, 1981.

Roberto Assagioli *Psychosynthesis* Penguin Books, 1976.

Ram Dass *Journey of Awakening: a Meditator's Guide Book*, Bantam Books, 1978.

Ann Faraday *The Dream Game* Harper & Row, 1976.

Piero Ferrucci *What We May Be: Techniques for Psychological and Spiritual Growth*, J. P. Tarcher, 1982.

Anthony de Mello *Sadhana, A Way to God: Christian Exercises in Eastern Form*, Institute of Jesuit Sources, St. Louis, 1978.

Paul Reps (ed.) *Zen Flesh Zen Bones* Penguin Books, 1971.

Biographical notes

John Hammond read Religious Studies at Lancaster University and taught RE and PSE in high schools in London and Lancashire. He now teaches Religious Studies at St. Martin's College, Lancaster, and works with students training to be secondary RE specialists.

David Hay lectures in the Education Department of Nottingham University. In 1975 he founded the Religious Experience and Education Project which he now directs. In 1985 he became director of the Alister Hardy Research Centre at Manchester College, Oxford. The AHRC is concerned with the scientific study of the frequency of report, nature and function of religious experience in the human species.
Further information about the Centre can be obtained by writing (Freepost) to: The Director, Alister Hardy Research Centre, Manchester College, Oxford, OX1 3TD.

Josephine Moxon is a primary RE specialist and deputy head at Preston County Primary School in North Humberside. She has been involved in the planning of the Chichester Primary RE project and in-service training for local teachers in RE. She spent a year training primary teachers in the RE department at North Riding College, Scarborough.

Brian Netto taught in comprehensive schools for five years, including a period as head of RE in a Nottinghamshire school. He joined the team of teachers which began piloting the project materials in 1985. He was an advisory teacher in Religious Education for the London Borough of Brent, where he ran courses on the spiritual dimension of education with primary, secondary and special school teachers. He is now Inspector for Humanities in Islington, London.

Kathy Raban taught in Leicestershire primary schools for ten years and became involved with REEP whilst teaching, taking a particular interest in guided fantasy. She also trained as a therapist and is still practising as a dance therapist. She lectured in primary RE at St Martin's College, Lancaster.

Ginny Straugheir was head of RE in a large comprehensive school in Durham for ten years. After piloting experiential activities with 11–18 year olds, she was seconded to REEP. Working on this book revived interest in her former occupation of journalism and she is now education reporter for *The Northern Echo*, a regional morning newspaper.

Chris Williams is a Senior Lecturer and INSET tutor for Personal and Social Development at St. Martin's College, Lancaster. He has been a national trainer with the Active Tutorial Work Development Project. He is now a member of the Institute for the Management of Learning at St. Martin's and a consultant for a training agency specialising in staff development in education.

> **And the end of all our exploring**
> **Will be to arrive where we started**
> **And to know the place for the first**
> **time.**
>
> (T. S. Eliot)

> **We find that in spite of the willingness to explore, we still have the basic bewilderment within us and we have to work with that. This involves accepting the basic bewilderment as it is.**
>
> (Chogyam Trungpa, Rinpoche)

Acknowledgements

We are grateful for the assistance and support of all the teachers who sent in comments and examples of pupils' work produced during the course of their religious education lessons. Without their help this book could not have been produced.

JANET ENGLISH	Avenue Comprehensive School, Durham
ALAN MCKENZIE	Becket Comprehensive School, Nottingham
ROGER STEVENS	Bilborough College, Nottingham
VIVIEN PETERS	Bramcote Hills Comprehensive School, Nottingham
CHARLES REILLY	Christ the King Comprehensive School, Nottingham
SUSAN HUGHES	Frome College, Somerset
ALAN WEBSTER	Glaisdale Comprehensive School, Nottingham
RUTH HARRIS	Harry Carlton Comprehensive School, Nottingham
HAZEL BULLOCK	Middleton St George Primary, Durham
KATHY RABAN	Newcroft Primary School, Leicester
GINNY STRAUGHEIR	Pelton Roseberry Comprehensive School, Durham
JONATHON YARNELL	Quarrydale Comprehensive School, Nottingham
DAVID BEVAN	Roundhill Primary School, Nottingham
ELAINE SOWERBY	Seaham Comprehensive School, Durham
LINDA CHAPMAN	Skerne Park Junior School, Durham
KAY STEEL	Spennymoor Comprehensive School, Durham
JOSEPHINE MOXON	Sproatley Endowed Primary School, North Humberside
SR MARGARET MARY RYAN	St Edmund Campion Primary School, Nottingham
BRENDA CRADDOCK	Tanfield Comprehensive School, Durham
DAWN WHITTAKER	Tanfield Lea Junior School, Durham
MAUREEN HARRISON	Teesdale Comprehensive School, Durham
PHILIP DOUGHTY	Wilsthorpe School, Derbyshire
TOM LIMB	Woodborough Primary School, Nottingham
JOAN FORMOSA	Usworth Comprehensive School, Sunderland

We would also like to give special thanks to:

TED HUDDLESTON	St Luke's College, Exeter
MAUREEN POTTER	RE Adviser, Durham County Council
ROBIN RICHARDSON	Brent Education Department

for their contribution to Parts III and IV.

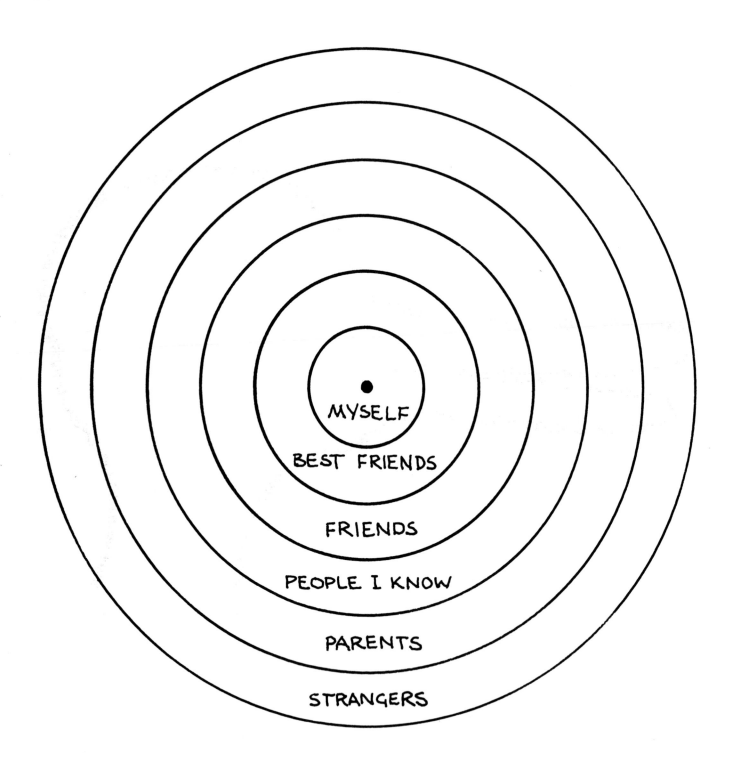

MYSELF

BEST FRIENDS

FRIENDS

PEOPLE I KNOW

PARENTS

STRANGERS